HANNAH MARY TABBS AND THE
DISEMBODIED TORSO

HANNAH MARY TABBS AND
THE DISEMBODIED TORSO

A Tale of Race, Sex, and Violence in America

Kali Nicole Gross

OXFORD
UNIVERSITY PRESS

OXFORD
UNIVERSITY PRESS

Oxford University Press is a department of the University of Oxford. It furthers
the University's objective of excellence in research, scholarship, and education
by publishing worldwide. Oxford is a registered trade mark of Oxford University
Press in the UK and certain other countries.

Published in the United States of America by Oxford University Press
198 Madison Avenue, New York, NY 10016, United States of America

Library of Congress Cataloging-in-Publication Data
Gross, Kali N., 1972– author.
Hannah Mary Tabbs and the disembodied torso : a tale of race, sex, and violence
in America / Kali Nicole Gross.
pages   cm
Includes bibliographical references and index.
ISBN 978-0-19-024121-6 (hardcover : alk. paper) 978-0-19-086001-1 (paperback)
1. Tabbs, Hannah Mary.   2. Murder—Pennsylvania—Philadelphia—Case studies.
3. Family violence—Pennsylvania—Philadelphia—Case studies.
4. African Americans—Pennsylvania—Philadelphia—Social conditions—19th century.
5. African American women—Pennsylvania—Philadelphia—Social conditions—19th century.
6. Racially mixed people—Pennsylvania—Philadelphia—Social conditions—19th century.
7. United States—Race relations—History—19th century.   I. Title.
HV6534.P5G76   2016
364.152'3092—dc23   2015032082

For Sylvia E. Neal

1917–2010

I love you. I miss you. I'm glad my daughter got to meet you.

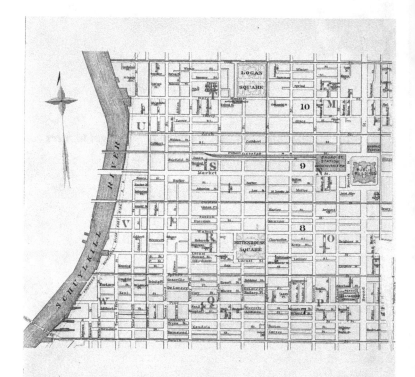

Frontispiece. Map: Outline & Index Map of 5th 6th 7th 8th 9th & 10th Wards. From *Atlas of the City of Philadelphia.* Courtesy of the Historical Society of Pennsylvania (Call #O.728 v.1).

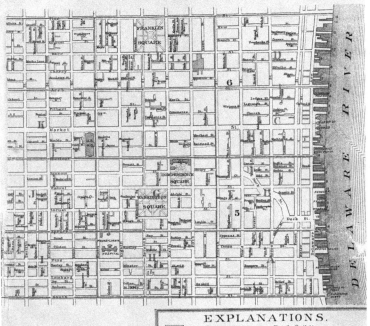

FRANKLIN
SQUARE

INDEPENDENCE
SQUARE

WASHINGTON
SQUARE

PENNSYLVANIA
HOSPITAL

Market

Dock St.

6

5

DELAWARE RIVER

EXPLANATIONS.

	Represents	Brick Building
	"	Frame Building
	"	Stone or Iron front
	"	Stable or Shed
	"	Fire Hydrant
	"	Improved two way Fire 'n
	"	Water Main
	"	Sewer
	"	Block dimensions & Street widths
	"	Lot dimensions
	"	House numbers
(B)	"	Adjoining Plate

Lot dimensions are in feet and inches
Block dimensions are in feet and hundredths of a foot
Plates are all drawn at the Scale of 80 ft. to an inch

NOTE Red letters are Plate Letters and
red lines are boundaries of the same

CONTENTS

HANNAH MARY TABBS AND THE
DISEMBODIED TORSO

Prologue

Instead, her manner of self-presentation draws attention to the fact that both these narratives and her autobiographical persona are disorderly.

—Rhonda Frederick, "Creole Performance"

When I stumbled across the story of a murder and dismemberment that occurred in Philadelphia in 1887, complete with a love triangle and press coverage across the country, I knew that it wasn't your average African American historical tale.[1] Like hundreds of turn-of-the-century readers before me, I scoured newspapers to follow day-to-day accounts of the victim's demise. All of the figures involved enthralled me, but especially the black woman at the heart of the story, Hannah Mary Tabbs. The case captivated me as a scholar of black women and criminal justice, but I was also mesmerized by the entire ordeal because it was a different kind of story about a black woman and her relationships with not just black men but also with her world—a world in which she navigated the difficulties of moving between the black and white communities. Much about my discussion of the crime will be deliberately vague from this point on, as I want readers to experience the story as I first did, letting it unfold step by step in the following chapters.[2] However, I do want to highlight the reasons I find Tabbs so compelling.

Rather than simply bowing to the social mores of her time, ideals such as chastity and morality, Hannah Mary Tabbs lived by a different set of values. Her life and daily interactions evidenced someone who appeared to adhere to mainstream notions of respectability but instead employed deceit, cunning, and cold-blooded ruthlessness to control those around her, both in her home and in her neighborhood. Her ability to slip seamlessly between displaying deference to wealthy and middle-class whites whose houses she cleaned while violently coercing other African Americans in her own fraught effort to be self-determining amazed me. Tabbs's maneuvers seemed to expose the inherent disorder within restrictive categories such as race, gender, and geography. In many ways, her role in the gruesome murder afforded a multidimensional historical rendering of a black woman and the complexities of her life that defied the customary narratives of suffering, resistance, and, ultimately, redemption.[3]

These narratives, which dominate much of African American history, are rooted in structural and institutional biases. Historical research methodologies largely mute the experiences of African American women—particularly those of poor and everyday black women. Enslavement and its legacy severely stunted their ability to access the written word, silencing many voices, save the most elite and learned with enough education and resources to create and save documents such as personal papers, letters, and memoirs. Barring this, most records about everyday black women exist only because they mark a moment when a black woman's life intersected, or collided in some way, with white people. Typically in positions of authority, whites— such as slave owners, employers, doctors, journalists, lawmakers, teachers, and prison administrators—have unwittingly left behind many of the sources that scholars rely on to reconstruct information about the black past. Historians have done some incredible work in finding ways to tell black women's stories; often they have done so by writing against one-sided historical records that would otherwise map these women only in the barest sense.[4]

Still, through these materials we have come to know black women as laborers—unfree or impoverished domestics and field hands. We know them as victims—of rape, sexual exploitation, and other forms of violence. We encounter these women as problems—subjects that shame the race or are used to pathologize it. We understand them as displaced—those denied civil rights, protection, access, and justice. We glorify them as freedom fighters—resisting enslavers and corrupt authority figures. We do our best to animate them—as clubwomen, as mothers and wives, as sexual beings, as queer, as entrepreneurs, as artists, as sanctified, as activists, and as teachers and legislators.[5]

Indeed, historians of African American women's experiences have done much with very little. Yet even as I have laughed, cried, and cheered aloud while learning about black women's tribulations and triumphs, I have also found myself yearning for histories that permit black women to be fully visible, fully legible, fully human, and thus vulnerable, damaged, and flawed. Most of our stories—my own research included—are often one-dimensional portraits. We piece together fragments of lives and events—good, bad, and traumatic— but rarely do we stumble across figures or sources that sustain richer accounts. Few records reflect the historical difficulties that bisected black women's lives at the same time they reveal in nuanced ways how black women managed to survive between heroism and heartache. We have precious few examples of black women who lived as people with depression and joy, with desire and love, as well as contempt and rage. We do not have many stories of individual women who lived for themselves and did not put the race or their children or families first. And we certainly do not have tales about African American women who were very good at being very bad. Enter Hannah Mary Tabbs.

Though Tabbs is appealing not just because she is a kind of anti-hero. Equally compelling is the fact that while the circumstances of white supremacy and antiblack violence encapsulated Tabbs's life, the case and all of its macabre elements do not depict her or other African Americans as existing solely in opposition to or engaging with white people. Rather this crime opens a window onto violence within the black community and shows how that violence is deeply rooted in the pervasive racism of the criminal justice system.[6]

The 1887 murder, then, serves as an evocative meditation on both the vicissitudes and rewards of violence as deployed by Hannah Mary Tabbs, because Tabbs, as the Philadelphia investigation would reveal, used physical aggression and intimidation in ways that afforded her power and agency in black enclave communities. Simultaneously, Hannah Mary's prolific record of violence, as fearsome as it appears, also seems to have been an artifice of her profound vulnerability. Black women such as Tabbs were at tremendous risk for violence and sexual assault because the legal system so often failed to protect them. Being formidable in her home and neighborhood—reprehensible though her actions may have been—nonetheless had a practical function. Further, her record of brutality, existing largely in the absence of detailed information about her early life, may well constitute evidence of her otherwise-unknowable past: in the sense that she had to have had prior experiences of violence to learn how to wield it so deftly.[7] With this in mind I consider Hannah Mary Tabbs's life and her more troubling behaviors.

Even so, despite this analytical approach and rigorous, historical investigation, there is much about Hannah Mary Tabbs and her crimes that will ultimately remain a mystery.

Chapter One

Handle with Care

Most people who have seen the body agree that it is that of a negro of rather light color, but there are others who assert that it is that of a Portuguese or an Italian, and a theory that obtained a great deal of credence was that it was the trunk of a Chinaman or Japanese.

—*Evening Bulletin*, February 18, 1887

On Thursday morning, February 17, 1887, Silas Hibbs trudged to work along Bristol Turnpike in Eddington, a small village in Bensalem Township in Bucks County, which borders Philadelphia County, in Pennsylvania. Eddington consisted of large farms, a handful of local businesses, and roughly two hundred residents. Silas, a local white carpenter in his early sixties, was a married man and father. In addition to supporting his wife, thirty-two-year-old Clara, and their eight-year-old daughter, Anna, he housed two boarders—an elderly man and a young local carpenter named Charles Adams. A native of Pennsylvania, Silas knew the terrain along this route well and noticed almost immediately the peculiar object resting on the bank next to William B. Mann's ice pond. With his curiosity piqued, Silas crossed the bridge over the pond to get a better look.[1] As he advanced, he noticed odd red lettering on the label of the object's heavy brown paper wrapping:

HANDLE

WITH CARE[2]

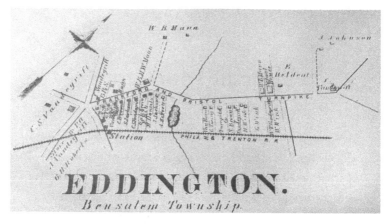

Figure 1.1. Map: Eddington. From *Combined Atlases of Bucks County, Pennsylvania, 1876–1891: Indexed.* Courtesy of the Historical Society of Pennsylvania (Call #MSS O.61).

Scrambling down the bank, he opened the seemingly fragile bundle, only to be shocked by its contents. Silas Hibbs had stumbled upon the headless, limbless torso of a man.[3] "Blood flowed from the openings" and the flesh was soft, suggesting the victim had been dead only a short time. The winter season had likely staved off the odor of decomposition, but it did little to blight the visual horror of the mutilated trunk's sagging entrails.[4] The package's contents would soon horrify most of Eddington's residents, but it also titillated them. Townspeople and city dwellers alike awaited revelations about the origins of the trunk, and the investigation that they so closely followed would shed light on the private lives of otherwise-obscure historical figures and would profoundly test the skills of two coroners and two teams of investigators. Ultimately, the disembodied torso would lay at the murky intersection of violence, policing, science, and the vagaries of race in America.

* * *

Whereas Philadelphia employed a uniform, centralized police force comprising patrolmen, detectives, and a web of magistrates, district attorneys, and judges, the administration of justice in towns such as Eddington relied on a local sheriff or police chief, a few constables, a coroner, and a state's attorney.[5] This system allowed citizens to play a more robust role in policing, as Bucks County neared a frontier type of justice. As early as 1820, local residents had created organizations dedicated to curtailing horse theft and other crimes against property.[6] When a series of robberies plagued Bensalem in the 1890s, the *Intelligencer* implored the public to assemble "a vigilance committee... to run [the thieves] down and effect their arrest." The piece concluded that "Judge Yerkes will do the rest."[7] This approach to policing is certainly reflected in the events following Silas Hibbs's unsettling discovery.

Almost immediately after Silas raised the alarm, Eddington's citizens answered the call and summoned neighboring authorities. Coroner William S. Silbert, a thirty-three-year-old Bristol resident and saloonkeeper, was first on the scene, along with fifty-three-year-old Evan J. Groom, the coroner's physician. Locals clustered and whispered among themselves, speculating about the identity of the victim and the circumstances surrounding the repulsive package. Some hypothesized that the torso had been ill-discarded medical waste.[8] This initially seemed plausible given that Philadelphia served as a hub for medical research and training. Indeed, the city boasted Jefferson Medical College and the medical school of the University of Pennsylvania, and it housed the nation's first medical college for women.[9]

However, Silbert and Dr. Groom dismissed the theory based on the amateurish nature of the cuts to the torso. Although the head had been severed with a degree of precision at the fourth vertebra, one arm had been removed above the joint, through the shoulder. The other arm had been sawed off at the joint. The torso had been cut off above the pelvis, roughly "four inches above the hip bone," leaving distended bowels protruding from the abdomen. Based on the striations of the wounds, the cutting instrument appeared to have been a fine-tooth saw similar to the kind butchers used. Moreover, the wounds were fresh. Groom concluded that the dismemberment had most likely taken place sometime during the evening of Wednesday, February 16.[10]

A search of the crime scene yielded other clues. Investigators fished a shawl strap from the pond. From the appearance of its nickel buckles, they surmised that it had not been soaking for very long. A faded piece of calico, probably from a dress or wrapper, was discovered on the bridge across the creek. Bloodstains on the material suggested that the body had been wrapped in it before it was hurled onto the bank, most likely from the bridge. Authorities believed that the torso had been thrown because of the deep indentation in the earth at its landing spot.[11] John Murray, another local, told the coroner that he remembered kicking the shawl strap out of his way as he crossed the bridge late Wednesday night, sometime before 1 a.m.[12] Murray's observations would help investigators home in on the time of death and the time that the body was discarded.

As Coroner Silbert took charge of the torso and finished gathering the witnesses' statements, primarily those of Silas Hibbs and John Murray, he carefully collected the bloody garments found in the pond and along the bridge. Constable Frederick Jackson, a forty-five-year-old resident of Bristol, spent much of his time that day in hip-high rubber boots, dragging the pond with a scoop net and an iron rake. After two hours in the rain, reportedly "in the presence of District Attorney Hugh B. Eastburn, Coroner Silbert, Chief of Police Saxton and nearly all of the two hundred inhabitants of Eddington," his efforts failed to produce additional body parts. Constable Jackson and Silas had hoped to drain the pond partially and resume the search the following day, but ongoing rains swelled the creek and derailed their plans.[13] On Friday morning Silbert returned to the crime scene hoping to recover more evidence.

Although heavy rain would keep most idle spectators at bay, District Attorney Eastburn, in his early forties, braved the nearly impassable road conditions to assist the coroner and observe the investigation. Eastburn must have known that this case would likely become a scandal. Either in an attempt to get ahead of news reports or in an effort to take the reins of the investigation, he issued the following statement to reporters: "We will make a strenuous effort to discover the perpetrators of the crime, if it has been a crime and if they can be found we will find them."[14] Perhaps this tack seemed wise given the early stages of the inquiry, but his tentativeness regarding the torso's circumstances did little to soothe public fears. Further, the halting nature of the statement appeared to be less an effort to avoid reaching hasty conclusions and more a sign of his unwillingness to tackle the challenges that such a case might pose.

Eastburn's position—as the state's attorney and in his refusal to rush to judgment—made him a kind of lightning rod for the public's frustration with the handling of the case. Articles published subsequent to his comments and after investigators determined with certainty that a crime had been committed called for a more vigorous response from the authorities. As the *Intelligencer*'s opinion piece charged, "The remains have been found in Bucks County, and it becomes the duty of the officials here to use all diligence and faithfulness in the discovery of the guilty party or parties." Calling for county commissioners to raise a substantial reward for any leads in the case, the piece suggested that the investigation should take priority at the upcoming commissioners' board meeting on February 28. As representatives of the public, local officials needed to "give assurance that a crime like this cannot escape attention and that everything possible will be done to protect the citizens." A succeeding article supported Eastburn by noting that "the district attorney has grave responsibilities, but other officials do as well." A small follow-up piece even attempted to come to Eastburn's aid by stating that he had "girded up his loins and is grappling vigorously with the crime."[15] Despite this affirmation, Eastburn was unable to escape being entangled in the quagmire. He would have to balance the pitfalls of local politics with obstacles in the investigation, amid widespread media attention.

As journalists descended upon the otherwise-quiet town, a number of townspeople assumed informal investigative roles in the ensuing drama. The local store, run by J. V. Vandergrift, served as the place for area residents to meet and discuss the facts of the case and even speculate on possible victims and perpetrators—every detail seems to have found its way into press accounts. Discovery of the torso rattled the residents' sensibilities, and their speculations afford a glimpse of the community's underside. African American servants and other transient workers figured prominently in their theories. Local whites told officials of a black man in Byberry, a nearby settlement, who had been missing; they suggested that he might be the victim. Others speculated that the torso belonged to Henry Killum, a young mulatto, whom I. P. Morris, the hotelkeeper, had hired as a driver. The boy had left about a month earlier. Given the size and relative racial homogeneity of the close-knit town, those blacks who entered into or labored in the community proved extremely visible and ultimately vulnerable.[16]

Before long, speculation about a black man being the victim shifted to fears that an African American may have been the perpetrator. The primary witness, Silas Hibbs, commented on two unfamiliar black men he observed on the road the following morning. He told reporters, "Two suspicious looking colored men passed along the pike right here in front of my house at 7 o'clock this morning. They had a wagon with a green canvas cover and sides and one of the sides was torn off. They kept looking behind them, and when they got to the bridge they drove very slowly and looked over the stone wall." The possibility that the two men were as curious about the crime scene as the rest of Eddington's residents seems to have escaped Silas as he continued, "I was going to stop them, but I changed my mind. I'm sorry now. I can't get it out of my head that they knew something about that body."[17]

Outsiders were not the only ones vulnerable to accusation. The torso created an opportunity for residents to cast doubt on neighbors whom they had long mistrusted or against whom they harbored grudges. Vandergrift hypothesized that the victim had been murdered for money, most likely by a man of unsavory character. He claimed to have knowledge of just such a man who lived in Hulmeville, a small village nearby. Frank Allen, a Bucks County resident who held "an important position in the wholesale clothing department of Wanamaker's store" told reporters of dangers he encountered on the night in question. As Allen, his brother, and a friend walked home from the train station Wednesday evening, he claimed that three men jumped a nearby fence and ordered him to "halt" and surrender his wallet. Allen had responded, "If you did get it you would not get much. Before you get that though, you may catch the contents of something else." This response, reportedly delivered in a most stern tone, was enough to send the three would-be assailants back over the fence. Allen, his brother, and the friend thought the incident must have been a prank—at least they did before the "mangled remnant of humanity" was discovered. Although hardly conclusive, Allen and his party as well as the suspicious men, it was noted, had all come through the field from the direction of William B. Mann's now-infamous ice pond.[18] As the *Evening Bulletin* put it, "Suspicions are rife in Eddington to-day, and the people thereabout are full of many such stories."[19]

Yet as theories about possible motives and victims surfaced, two key pieces of evidence were missing: the victim's head and racial identity. The coroner's physician worked swiftly to discover the latter. All who saw the torso had a different theory about its race—based both on the hue and the "rounded shape" of the shoulders. A number of spectators believed the victim to be Chinese: "The back showed that the man had very high shoulders. There is a natural hollow at the base of the neck, between the shoulders, as large as a man's hand and the humped shoulders make the cavity look deeper. The back looked more like the anatomy of a Chinaman than that of any other race."[20] Others argued that it had to be the torso of an Italian or a Portuguese. On Friday Dr. Groom examined the trunk, which lay in a "rough box at Rue's undertaking establishment," for clues about the victim's race. Not only did he conclude that the torso was evidence of a homicide but he also asserted that it belonged to "a negro"—someone between the ages of twenty-five and thirty who weighed 125 to 130 pounds, with "one-fourth white blood." Based on "a close examination of the skin," he claimed that it contained evidence of "pigments that are found only in the skin of the African."[21] Groom's racial metrics gestured toward the larger social issues surrounding the case and the era.

Anxieties about race and racial social hierarchy profoundly shaped the post-Reconstruction period. Whites feared the racial transgressions that the abolition of slavery and newly conferred black citizenship might encourage. Whereas slavery and indentured servitude had kept blacks geographically confined and under the control of local whites, the Thirteenth Amendment, and subsequent amendments guaranteeing blacks citizenship and access to due process of law, diminished white oversight. This legislation gave all blacks freedom and an unprecedented measure of spatial mobility, but certain light-skinned blacks could also potentially pass as white among the general population.[22] Or so many feared. Moreover, increasing numbers of European immigrants also raised questions about whiteness; Irish, Italians, and Poles all represented ethnic others that proved almost equally as troubling as blacks to native-born whites.[23] Quantifying whiteness, and further cementing its purported superiority, then, renewed scientific interest in discerning the biological origins of race.

Skin pigmentation figured centrally in those discourses, and Dr. Groom's examination of the torso reflects his own foray into race science. To be sure, speculation about the origins of blackness had long run the gamut—everything from blackness being contained in the blood to being a product of the liver. But all theories held to one guiding principle: the existence of unequivocal racial distinction. Few have expressed it more precisely than Thomas Jefferson in his 1783 treatise, *Notes on the State of Virginia*. Jefferson asserted, "Whether the black of the negro resides in the reticular membranes between the skin and the scarf-skin itself; whether it proceeds from the color of the blood, the color of the bile or from that of some other secretion, the difference is fixed in nature."[25] However, even as proponents advanced this notion, the presence of *white* blacks fundamentally undermined it. From those blacks who suffered from skin diseases such as vitiligo and albinism to African Americans whose mixed blood allowed them to pass for white, their existence troubled notions of fixed racial differences.[26]

Yet blacks with vitiligo or albinism tended to be easily dismissed by mainstream whites. Even with white skin, their features and hair texture typically rendered them quickly identifiable as "Negro."[27] Moreover, many of them ended up in vaudeville shows, becoming spectacles that could be ridiculed and thereby rendered less intimidating. However, "miscegenated" blacks proved infinitely more troubling.[28] Mixed people embodied taboo racial and sexual transgressions that represented unnerving challenges to the purity of whiteness. That blacks and whites could successfully breed at all countered racist propaganda that depicted blacks as a less evolved species. The term "mulatto" rooted in the Spanish word for mule (the sterile progeny of a horse and a donkey), reinforces those racist ideas and helped spawn scientific discourses that marked mulattoes as particularly degenerate.[29] The prospect of race mixing both sparked and renewed provisions against intermarriage in states such as Nevada, Oregon, Idaho, and Arizona during the Civil War, while states like Georgia and Maryland updated preexisting laws in 1866 and 1867, respectively. States such as Alabama, Florida, Kentucky, and North Carolina enacted laws in the postwar years.[30] The spate of laws underscored growing fears about miscegenated blacks.

Blacks who could pass also troubled whites because their presence stirred fears that the reverse might also be possible. If blacks could essentially be white, might it not be possible for whites to become black? An 1880 news article claimed to have proof of just such a horror. Titled "A Black White: A Beautiful Baby Made to Look like a Negro," the *Philadelphia Times* piece suggested that an otherwise-healthy white baby's fine brown hair "grew stiff and jet black." It further charged that his "eyes grew darker, so that the line between the pupils and the iris could not be distinguished." In spite of medical treatment the boy's condition worsened until "he became as black as a full blooded negro."[31] Depicting blackness as a potentially contagious disease revealed the height of white social paranoia as well as the role that science and medical research could play in stoking those fears. At the same time, racial science had the potential to become a more effective regulatory institution than enslavement because it could assert and, ideally, prove biological differences between the races. This scholarship could further attest to the superiority of whiteness under the guise of scientific neutrality.[32] It had the potential to provide much-desired clarity in a moment of otherwise-fuzzy notions of race and ethnicity.

Given his approach to determining the victim's race, Dr. Groom apparently subscribed to the belief that the origins of skin color difference could be found in the "epithelial cells." This would have been one of the three prominent schools of thought; the others theorized that the origins lay in connective tissues or that it stemmed from both connective tissues and the epidermis.[33] Moreover, his confident declaration about the race of the torso seemed geared toward reassuring the public that racial differences could be discerned and that science was capable of doing so. In service of that goal, he had conducted microscopic studies of the torso's flesh. Groom's observation of black "pigment granules" most likely represents a combination of the contemporary scientific discourse and his firsthand observations of the skin of black cadavers in medical school. Black corpses were often used for medical and scientific research, since cutting up these bodies was less jarring to the public than the wholesale mutilation of white corpses; many still believed that anatomical science fundamentally defiled the dead.[34] Early autopsy manuals would have aided Groom as well, since their descriptions of the corpses' pallor likely helped him distinguish between early decay and the actual hue of the cadaver's skin.[35] Yet despite the potential benefits that such knowledge could offer, an uneasy relationship existed between medical science and policing. Rather than trusting physicians and anatomists, investigators tended to rely on what they could see and, in this case, what they saw confused them.[36]

Although Dr. Groom appeared certain about his findings, Coroner Silbert, the district attorney, and the police chief still had their doubts. As part of their investigation, Silbert recruited local blacks to help in the identification process. Specifically, he brought two black women into the undertaker's chamber and compared their skin to that of the torso. The investigators also asked the women about whether they thought the corpse belonged to a black man. One of the women explained, "White folks look so much like colored folks nowadays, hard to tell the difference."[37] Indeed, these were confusing times.

These responses, those of the police and the citizens summoned to assist, foreshadow and parallel shifts that would occur in racial science. Most researchers moved away from studying skin in their efforts to definitively determine race; they would instead look inside black bodies for more solid cues. The more invasive techniques that would be cultivated, such as delving deeply to peel back layers of flesh and bone, were undertaken so that they might ultimately "regain control over the black bodies that were slipping from their intellectual and literal grasp."[38] Likewise, rather than giving up their search or trusting Dr. Groom's findings outright, the authorities, together with the residents of Bucks County, redoubled their investigative efforts,

The quadroon's comparison.

Figure 1.2. "The quadroon's comparison." From "Coon Chops," *National Police Gazette*, March 5, 1887.

perhaps spurred on, in part, by their anxieties about the racial ambiguity of the human trunk.]

As Silbert prepared for the coroner's inquest on Saturday, which would be held in Silas Hibbs's home, his chances of solving the case seemed nearly impossible. Although he had recovered significant clues, the evidence proved little. Even Dr. Groom's finding that the man did not die a natural death, while confirming what many suspected, ultimately did not bring investigators any closer to figuring out the victim's identity, much less the identity of his assailant. In light of these grim prospects, Samuel Rue of Mill Street, a carpenter and the local undertaker, buried the remains in Potter's Field on Saturday morning. Interment was a rather simple affair: "A plain, pine wood box, a deep hole, three feet by two, and all was over."[39] It was a quiet burial for what would quickly become one of Philadelphia's most sensational murder victims.

On Saturday afternoon, Constable Jackson interviewed Pennsylvania Railroad conductor Frank G. Swain about a strange passenger he encountered Wednesday on the 6:27 p.m. train from Philadelphia. Swain, a thirty-three-year-old Bristol resident who had worked his way up from baggage master to conductor on the Pennsylvania line, remembered a tall and dark-skinned "colored woman," wearing a brown knitted cap—a toboggan—with a dark shawl and a dark dress. The woman had a southern accent and had boarded the train at the Broad Street Station in central Philadelphia. She had an excursion ticket for a round trip from Philadelphia to Cornwells Heights. She carried two bundles, a large one and a small one.[40] In his recollection, the larger appeared to be wrapped in a combination of paper and calico and bound by a shawl strap. Both packages fit the description of the paper and cloth recovered at the pond and on the creek bridge. The woman left a lasting impression on Swain because almost as soon as she reached her seat, she opened the train window—somewhat curious behavior given that it was the middle of winter. After punching her ticket for Cornwells Heights, he noted the raised window and asked, "Madam do you feel sick?"[41]

Apparently realizing that his inquiry was related to the window, she responded, "Oh, yes, sir. I've been in the hospital." But when the train reached Cornwells Heights, the woman did not exit. Instead, she continued on to the Eddington station. She said, "I'm going to Mr. Brock's; that's halfway between Cornwells and Eddington. Mary Coursey lives near there, too." Because she paid ten cents in excess on the new fare, as per the practice of the day, Swain gave her a rebate check, which she could present to the station ticket agent to redeem.[42] But this exchange is not the only thing that made the encounter memorable.

When the train arrived at Eddington at 7:32 p.m., roughly an hour later, Swain offered to assist the woman with her bags. Rather than accepting Swain's offer, the woman strenuously objected, hurriedly responding, "Oh, no, no. I can carry them."[43] Based on the subsequent events in Eddington and the passenger's strange behavior, the train conductor expressed little doubt in his interview with the constable that "she had with her the remains of the murdered man."[44] The story Swain recounted led Constable Jackson to follow up with the station agent on duty on the night in question.

The curious woman Conductor Swain described also left a lasting impression on Mrs. Josie Knight, the Eddington station agent. Knight told Constable Jackson that the odd woman's hand trembled as she sought to redeem the excess ticket. The woman quickly took the money and disappeared into the night.[45] But she left quite a trail for the constable to follow.

The woman next appeared at the home of Dr. George Stroup. Mrs. Stroup told authorities that the woman said she was looking for George Brock's estate but had lost her way as the sky "was as black as pitch" with not a star shining.[46] The woman mentioned that she was going to see George Redding, a mulatto servant who worked there, and Mrs. Mary Coursey, a black widow who lived on Bristol Turnpike.[47] Mrs. Stroup gave the woman directions and told her that she would have one of her servants escort her with a lantern. The woman explained that she had left some bundles at the front gate and needed to go retrieve them first. The servant, Thomas Matthews, met the woman with the lantern and walked her toward the Brock farm, but he claimed that the woman went in the opposite direction, past the Vandergrift store, toward the pond.[48] She walked at such a brisk pace that he soon lost track of her and returned home. As Constable Jackson searched for a black woman who perhaps had lived or worked in the area, Philadelphia detectives had begun to grapple with the likelihood that the crime had been committed in their backyard.

The racial questions surrounding the torso not only pointed to social tensions but also complicated the police investigation. [Blacks and whites in the post-Reconstruction period—including in the urban North—lived vastly separate lives. Even where blacks and whites could be found living on the same block in cities such as Philadelphia, it was not uncommon for them not to know one another's names.[4] Identifying the race of either the victim or the assailant in a crime would help authorities determine which neighborhoods and taverns to canvass and what witnesses to question. Not knowing the race of the torso meant that the police did not know which world to investigate. With the promising lead about the mysterious black woman and her apparent connection to blacks in Eddington, the police effectively narrowed their search and moved closer to believing Dr. Groom's claim that the torso was that of someone with black blood.

With these fresh clues, Constable Jackson went to see George Redding, the mulatto servant that the mysterious woman claimed she was going to see. Apparently, terrified at the thought of being implicated in such a ghastly crime, Redding nervously answered Jackson's questions and denied encountering the black woman. His employer, George Brock, a white farmer who owned a country estate worth upward of $40,000, also told the authorities that he did not currently have any black women in his employ.[50] Brock's property was surrounded by an iron fence and manned by a small cadre of servants—a housekeeper and a number of farm laborers. One of his servants, a white housekeeper, Mrs. Brown, mentioned that she thought she saw the shadowy figure of a tall woman wearing a shawl standing near the icehouse on the estate Wednesday evening. Alerted by barking dogs sometime around 9:00 p.m., Mrs. Brown went to the window and saw a figure that seemed startled by the ray of light that was cast when she pulled back the curtains. The figure hastily took off toward the road. Since it was so dark Mrs. Brown could not be certain of the race of the woman, and she—perhaps a bit startled herself— elected not to investigate further.[51]

Still, Brock had employed black women in the past, and one servant in particular quickly became a person of interest for the press, local Bucks County authorities, and Philadelphia chief of detectives Francis Kelly, with whom Hugh Eastburn had met shortly after the torso's discovery.[52] On February 20, 1887, the *Times* reported that a black woman known in Eddington as both Mary Tab and Mary Sheppard had worked on the Brock estate the previous year. Apparently brought up from the South to work as a domestic, the woman came with her young niece, a mulatto girl named Annie Richardson, who went missing sometime in May 1886. Brock had been generous enough to offer a $100 reward for any information pertaining to her whereabouts. Unfortunately, the girl was never found, and the woman she accompanied ended up leaving the estate to reside somewhere in Philadelphia. Constable Jackson was especially interested in finding either Annie or Mary, because this Mary Tab or Mary Sheppard was "the only colored woman in this city who knew George Redding."[53]

A black female suspect also pointed to the likelihood that the victim was indeed a black man, since even in the late nineteenth century, the majority of black crime, like white crime, was intraracial. That the woman and the victim were essentially outsiders to the Eddington community also brought a sense of relief. White citizens remained extremely interested in the investigation, but now they could do so without the fear that they themselves might be in some kind of mortal danger. At the same time, the few local blacks found themselves subject to an even more peculiar kind of scrutiny.

Mary Tab or Tabbs, as would later be discovered, had returned to Eddington during the investigation. She made a number of inquiries about the case and moved largely unnoticed among the residents, at least until her interview with reporters from the *Evening Bulletin* was published on February 21, 1887. It seems that while Constable Jackson went on the hunt for the suspect and additional witnesses, the black woman he sought had been listening in on a discussion about the crime at the Vandergrift store.[54] Under the subtitle "One of the

Anxious," the story detailed how Mrs. Tabbs had, after seeing her name and that of her niece in the paper, decided to take the train to Eddington to get answers. Described as a black woman in her mid-thirties, Tabbs was neatly if plainly dressed, wearing a simple black dress with a long black overcoat. She confirmed her former employment at the Brock estate as well as her departure from the farm in September, some months after her young niece disappeared. Claiming to have come looking for Constable Jackson, Tabbs encountered a reporter in the local store as she waited for the 3:25 p.m. train back to Philadelphia. Before her departure, she gave a rather lengthy statement that implicated the servant George Redding and two other men in the disappearance of her niece:

I do not know what connection there is between this murder and the disappearance or whereabouts of my niece, but something seems to tell me that there is something between them. My niece was always a good girl, and I never could understand why she went away, and why she did not let me know where she was. There was one thing about her disappearance and that is that on the night she left me George Redding did not come in to supper. He was always very prompt before and I never knew him to miss a meal, but this night he did not come to supper and I thought it was very strange. When Annie did not come home in the evening I began to worry a great deal, and Redding said to me "Annie's getting to be a big girl now and you must allow her some freedom." From that day to this I have not heard from her. Somewhere about last of January a young man, whose name is George Wilson, and whom I had often seen about the neighborhood, came to my house and asked me if I had heard anything from Annie. I told him that I had not heard a word. He said, "I know where she is. She is in Jenkintown." I said, "George if you can bring me that girl, or tell me how I can find her, I will give you two dollars." This was in the early part of the week. He said he would see about it and come and let me know what he would do. On Thursday he came to my home with Waite Gaines. I did not know before that he knew Gaines, but they seemed to be quite friendly. When Gaines was not observing he told me that Annie needed clothes and money for her fare, and if I would give him money for fare and a suit of clothes he would bring her to me on the following Sunday. I gave him forty cents for fare, a suit of clothes and a hat, and he went away saying that he would bring Annie sure on Sunday. When he was gone Gaines asked me if Wilson was going with Annie now and seemed to be very jealous. I told him that I knew nothing about that, but all I wanted was my niece.

Sunday came, and it brought with it neither Wilson or my niece. I heard nothing from Wilson, and by accident saw him in a cigar store. I asked him where Annie was. He appeared very much confused, and told me that she was not well, and could not come. I told him that if he did not bring Annie to me or give me back the money and clothes I had given him I would have him arrested. On the Sunday following this he came to my house and rang the door-bell for sometime when I was out. A girl who lives next door told me about this and told me that he had stuck something under the door before he went away. Upon examining I found a letter addressed to Waite Gaines and supposed to have been written by Annie but it was in Gaines's own handwriting, I know. The letter said that the writer was tired of life and that she was going away some place where they would not try to find her. This is the last I have heard of Annie, Waite Gaines, or George Wilson. Gaines has been away from the house where he boards for the last few days, but Saturday he wrote there saying that he would be back to-day. I am convinced that this affair at Eddington is somehow mixed up with Annie's disappearance.[55]

As the investigation would soon demonstrate, the disembodied torso was linked to the odd disappearance of Annie Richardson, although not in the way Hannah Mary Tabbs suggested.

The article in the *Evening Bulletin* concluded with a final section titled "The Mysterious Woman." The paragraph noted that several townspeople recalled seeing a black woman leave Eddington station Wednesday on the 9:48 p.m. train. The descriptions suggested that it was in fact the same black woman that Conductor Swain and several others had encountered earlier that evening, although when she departed she had no bundles. According to the article, there was "not a particle of doubt that this woman" carried the body to the pond and left it there.[56] It was an interesting choice of words for a piece that reveals, perhaps more than anything, just how much doubt there was to be had. The reporter and a number of purported witnesses sat face-to-face with the very woman they were searching for and, apparently, were none the wiser.

That the woman on the train returned to Eddington essentially undetected does not simply highlight the problematic aspects of eyewitness accounts but also points to the ways that race renders African Americans highly visible to whites yet strangely featureless, somehow indistinguishable under that indiscriminate surveillance. Hannah Mary Tabbs worked in the town, among a handful of other blacks, for more than a year. Her missing niece was also the subject of a police search. And yet, upon Tabbs's return—that Wednesday evening as well as in the days after—none of the townsfolk recognized her. Mrs. Knight, the ticket agent who told authorities about the mysterious woman's trembling hands, sold that very same woman a ticket the following Monday without incident and without recognition. Mrs. Knight would be as stunned as the rest of Eddington's residents when newspapers would declare Tabbs captured under the bold headline "The Woman Found."[57]

Chapter Two

The Woman Found

Chief Kelly also thinks that the body was that of Waite Gaines, the young colored man who used to live at bachelor George Brock's, at Cornwells, and he also thinks that the woman under arrest has something to do with butchering the body.

—*The Times*, February 22, 1887

It was a brisk, cloudy day when Francis Kelly received word that the remains found in Eddington might be evidence of a crime that occurred in Philadelphia.[1] At the detectives' headquarters in Central Station, located at Fifth and Chestnut Streets, Chief Kelly labored in his private office—a compact room adorned with decorative wallpaper and dark wood furniture. His desk was adjacent to a carved armoire displaying a broad array of tools and skeleton keys—possibly including confiscated keepsakes he had amassed over his two decades in law enforcement. Forty years old, Kelly had an average build with closely cropped dark hair that had just begun to gray at the temples. He sported a pronounced mustache, fashionable for his day, and his piercing eyes bespoke a hard resolve.[2]

As chief of detectives, Kelly relied on a select group of lawmen who worked aggressively to arrest suspects and capture criminals. Their investigative methods reflected Kelly's personal policing philosophy and the Philadelphia Police Department's tradition of community control and public order. It also signaled a broader shift toward

Figure 2.1. "Chief Kelly in His Private Office," *The Philadelphia Police.* Courtesy of the Historical Society of Pennsylvania (Call #UPA/Ph HV 8148.P5 S67 1887).

preventive policing.[3] Although larger than police forces operating in other major cities such as Chicago—1,200 officers in contrast to Chicago's 362—Philadelphia's police nonetheless struggled to adequately protect the public. The entire operation comprised a chief, four captains, one detective unit, twenty-eight lieutenants, sixty-one sergeants, sixty-three telegraph operators, ten patrol sergeants, ten drivers, four pilots and engineers, and five van drivers, plus patrolmen. In 1860, the department's ratio of patrolmen to the population was roughly one officer to every 870 citizens, but that ratio would drop to approximately one policeman to every 705 residents by 1880.[4]

City officials worked to remake the force's public image against a legacy of corruption and political cronyism.[5] After winning the mayoral race of 1884, in his inaugural address Republican William B. Smith promised to create a police force that would "protect life and property, and secure the fearless execution of the laws." Under his administration, promotions would be "the reward of faithful service," where no requirement would be extracted "except that of honesty and fidelity." Results became paramount in the re-energized departments and, in the case of the dismembered torso, Chief Kelly and his men aimed to get them.[6]

Even so, the police force's investigative skills alone did not precipitate criminal arrests in the case. The interaction between local blacks and police marked a rare, critical moment. Just as law enforcement officials strengthened their investigative apparatuses (especially to better police the growing numbers of blacks and ethnic European immigrants), black Philadelphians expanded social support networks to serve the swelling community's needs and to push back as blacks were blamed for rising urban crime rates. Under those circumstances, an aggressive and suspicious police force typically met a wary, equally suspicious black community that knew about the brutality visited on black suspects during police interrogations. Yet the exchanges between the two groups around the torso case would be fruitful, albeit in deeply fraught ways, as blacks in custody encountered a range of the Philadelphia police officers' coercive practices.[7]

From his earliest days in office, Mayor Smith made fortifying the police department one of his primary objectives. In addition to installing a formal application process for patrolmen and adding a police surgeon and solicitor, Smith worked to reestablish the office of the chief of detectives with Kelly at the helm. The position had long been mired in controversy because, in its first incarnation, the chief of detectives was not required to report to the chief of police, resulting in skirmishes between the two. In reinstating the position, however, Smith placed the chief of detectives under the direction of the police chief, which clarified the department's administrative hierarchy.[8]

Smith's decision to appoint Kelly to the job is understandable given his prolific law enforcement career. He had served as a Philadelphia patrolman when he was twenty-five, was later recruited by the Secret Service to help bust organized criminal rackets and illegal distilleries, and he had helped nab a gang of counterfeiters who papered the City of Brotherly Love with phony bank notes. William "Gopher Bill" Robinson led a fairly elaborate counterfeiting ring that involved players from Philadelphia to Baltimore. However, Kelly and his fellow officers would seize over $1,500 in phony bills along with crucibles, metals, acids, bank dies, and a cast iron machine used to mill coins. His work on the case prompted an offer from Mayor Smith to rejoin the Philadelphia force as a police lieutenant and acting chief of detectives, which Kelly accepted in 1884.[9]

Kelly employed a muscular brand of surveillance in investigations that made use of his version of shadowy, undercover operatives. Presumably contacts he had in the Secret Service, these men were said to have firsthand knowledge of nearly all of the "expert criminals" in the country. Kelly reputedly used their information to track, and in some cases detain, would-be criminals, but these informants never appeared on any official documents. Although the use of such men might be considered a violation of the Sixth Amendment, particularly the right to confront witnesses, the spirit behind the practice dovetailed nicely with the growing legislative support for the development and implementation of a systematic means to identify members of the "crime class," an impetus that would lead to the passage of the "Act for the Identification of Habitual Criminals," in 1899. In absence of that law, however, Kelly's secret "officers" likely relied on rogues' gallery books, the Bertillon System of Criminal Identification registers, which relied on intricate measurements of inmates' physical features, and their own knowledge of the most notorious as they watched railroad stations in an effort to intercept professional criminals coming into the city.[10]

Once spotted, the reputed criminals would be warned to leave the city immediately or face arrest if found cavorting with the local criminal element or seen acting in a suspicious manner. Most suspects heeded the warning, but those few holdouts were arrested and brought before a magistrate under a special "professional criminals act," which allowed them to be imprisoned or, as the local authorities phrased it, "sent below" for ninety days. Although the measures violated basic civil liberties, police enthusiasts attributed the absence of marauding criminal gangs to Chief Kelly's emphasis on crime prevention.[11]

That prevention had strong ethnic and racial implications too. Industrialization had spurred growth in Philadelphia, which had increased in population from approximately 848,000 in 1880 to roughly 1,047,000 by 1900. The black population in the city had nearly doubled, totaling close to 40,000 by 1890, and the number of Italian immigrants rose from 300 in 1870 to almost 20,000 by the turn of the twentieth century. Poles, Germans, and Russian Jews also came to the city, but Irish immigrants remained the largest foreign-born group, accounting for almost half of all foreign immigrants in 1880 and roughly one-third by 1900.[12] With an influx of immigrants from abroad, combined with the increased migration from newly freed blacks, justice in Philadelphia—which had long operated under a cloud of prejudice and corruption—took on even more pronounced racial contours.

Officers emphasized surveillance of certain groups, which would eventually be codified in turn-of-the-century patrolman's manuals that instructed them to detain "all persons from some place outside of the State and found loitering here without visible means of support."[13] Protocols also directed lieutenants "to suspend any officers who failed to make an arrest whenever a crime occurred on their beats." Further, Philadelphia police routinely detained black men on suspicion simply because they carried clothing or bags of goods in "strange neighborhoods" or in the case of one professional boxer, "because he was big, and black, and had a record."[14] Such practices would find the city's poor and its black residents—southern migrants especially—vulnerable to undue scrutiny, detention, and baseless charges.

At the same time, however, patrolmen tended to turn a blind eye to certain parlors and assignation houses in black areas—allowing the places to exist not only for black patrons but also for slumming whites who were attracted to the allegedly exotic and dangerous urban underworld.[15] In his ongoing effort to challenge the growing linkages between blackness and criminality, W. E. B. Du Bois noted that measuring crime tended to be hugely inefficient due to "the varying efficiency and diligence of the police, by discrimination in the administration of the law, and by unwarranted arrests."[16] Ultimately, the uneven application of law enforcement would contribute to an ongoing mistrust of the police by the black community. But as the names of local blacks appeared in news accounts in connection with the torso case, the two groups would be thrust together as Chief Kelly and his men searched for a black woman known as either "Mary Sheppard" or "Mary Tabs."[17]

The men assigned to this task had extensive track records in pursuing criminals, and none appeared hesitant to use strong-arm tactics in the apprehension of alleged or wanted fugitives. Peter Miller, the most senior officer at age forty-four, had arrested a number of the city's most infamous criminals. He had also busted the "notorious pickpockets from New York," Henry "Poodle Murphy" Robinson and Robinson's longtime associate, James "Pretty Jimmy" Watson, when the pair had begun plying their trade at Philadelphia's Broad Street station in 1885.[18] Miller's fellow detective Thomas Crawford, forty-one, also a longtime lawman, had made rank by breaking up the last vestiges of the urban street gangs—such as the Schuylkill Rangers—that ravaged the Schuylkill riverfront. Considering their reputation for committing daring crimes, Crawford's involvement in taking down John "Screwey" Nelson and John "Three-fingered Jack" Toner was no small feat.[19]

At age thirty-eight, Detective James Tate was one of the youngest men working the torso case. Tate started off as a patrolman but left to work for the Pinkerton Detective Agency before returning to the force as a special officer in 1882. Having joined Chief Kelly's unit in 1886, Tate had only been in Central Station a short time before he was assigned to the torso case.[20] Frank P. Geyer, the youngest member of the team, would later be well known for his part in the capture of Herman Mudgett (alias H. H. Holmes), America's first serial killer, in 1896.[21] Geyer joined the force as a patrolman in 1876 and was immediately assigned to duty during the Centennial Exposition—an international fair commemorating America's first century.[22] He then served as an officer in the Eighteenth Police District before being detailed as a special officer, charged with investigating murder cases, in 1886. Despite his relative youth, Geyer was among only a handful of investigators who had experience taking down a female killer. In 1885 he had arrested Annie Gaskin, a white woman eventually found guilty of murdering her ten-week-old infant with a butcher knife. Although Gaskin would be sentenced to an insane asylum rather than the penitentiary, her arrest and subsequent conviction probably taught Geyer that female offenders could be just as deadly as those of the opposite sex.[23]

The collective breadth of the detectives' experience would be brought to bear as they searched the African American community for the torso killer. They would not only be charged with gleaning information from reluctant constituents but would also be canvassing a community adjusting to the substantial influx of newly freed blacks migrating from the South to Philadelphia—the vast majority from Virginia and Maryland. Because of the city's Quaker origins and lengthy history as a hub of the abolitionist movement, blacks had high hopes for actualizing the rights of citizenship there. Their migration also reflected a desire to escape lynching, mob justice, and sheriffs moonlighting as Ku Klux Klansmen—characteristics that typified southern "justice." Their hopes for greater equality and freedom in the City of Brotherly Love were quickly dashed, however, as they found themselves barred from industrial jobs and confined to low-paying domestic service work. Housing discrimination and poverty consigned many African Americans to some of Philadelphia's worst slums in the Fourth, Fifth, Seventh, and Eighth Wards.[24]

In the Seventh Ward, a section that housed the largest concentration of African Americans in the city, southern migrants accounted for nearly 40 percent of the residents, with Virginians making up 20 percent and those from Maryland representing approximately 12 percent. Most of the residents were members of the working class, and lived off tight, dank alleyways. Housing consisted primarily of cramped back-to-back rear dwellings, where overcrowding and waste led to disease and fatal fires.[25] The more disreputable among them

spent their time drinking, gambling, and cavorting with local prosti-
tutes, activities that frequently occurred on notorious thoroughfares
such as Alaska Street, Minster, and Middle Alley.[26] Although well
known to police for illicit activities, Gil Ball's seedy, black-owned sa-
loon just south of Eighth Street on Lombard Street, nonetheless
afforded blacks a space to drink and be merry or to scuffle and fight
and to occasionally solicit more risqué forms of entertainment.[27]

In response to the bleak conditions, both southern migrant and
native-born northern blacks had formed tight-knit communities based
on familial and social networks. These networks helped blacks create
small businesses, secure employment, and establish mutual aid societies. Local churches such as the Mother Bethel African Methodist
Episcopal, one of the oldest black churches in the country, constructed in 1794, stood on the corner of Sixth and Lombard Streets,
and the Protestant Episcopal Church of the Crucifixion, located at
Eighth and Bainbridge Streets, organized relief efforts to meet the
community's needs.[28] These ties would ultimately help authorities
crack the torso case. Once Chief Kelly learned of Conductor Swain's
statement about the black female train passenger from Philadelphia,
he and his men wasted little time chasing down leads among the residents of the Seventh Ward.

Exactly when Philadelphia authorities identified Hannah Mary
Tabbs and the woman that Conductor Swain had encountered as
one and the same is difficult to pinpoint, because a profusion of
mounting evidence steered them in this direction. Since the "mysterious woman" told Swain that she had been hospitalized, Philadelphia
detectives canvassed local infirmaries. A woman fitting the description had been admitted to Pennsylvania Hospital under the name
Mary Tabbs. Hardly the kind of men to believe in coincidences, the
detectives immediately went to the residence listed on the patient's
forms—1642 Richard Street, located in the Seventh Ward—only to
find it empty.[29]

This setback proved temporary, as another crucial break in the case came that afternoon when Jane Cannon paid a visit to Chief Kelly. Cannon, a "mulatto"-complexioned woman who had moved to the city from Seaford, Delaware, had grave concerns about the fate of her missing brother, a young light-skinned man named Wakefield Gaines; "Waite" Gaines had been among the handful of blacks mentioned as having once worked at the Brock Estate in Eddington. As it turned out, both Jane Cannon and her brother were well acquainted with Hannah Mary Tabbs, who was, among other things, her brother's former coworker. As Kelly took Cannon's statement, Hannah Mary quickly moved from a person of interest to the primary suspect, particularly as Cannon's anxiety suggested that the missing Gaines might actually be the unfortunate owner of the disembodied trunk.[30]

According to Cannon's account, Hannah Mary had visited Cannon at her home at 1018 Lemon Street that morning. She had shown Cannon the newspaper article about the torso, the mysterious black woman, and mention of Tabbs's name, along with that of Wakefield Gaines and Tabbs's niece, Annie Richardson. Overwrought and agitated, Tabbs expressed to Cannon her fears that the torso might belong to Gaines. She told Cannon that she was going to Bristol to try to get some answers—both about Gaines, who had been missing since Tuesday, and her niece, who had not been seen in over a year. The visit, apparently designed to convey concern as well as a lack of knowledge regarding Gaines's whereabouts, managed to achieve the opposite. Cannon was immediately suspicious of Hannah Mary and her motives. Shortly after Tabbs's departure, Jane Cannon contacted the police.[31]

Although Hannah Mary Tabbs avoided being detained in Eddington, she would not escape Detectives Miller and Tate, who waited at Broad Street station thanks to Cannon's information. The two men promptly took Hannah Mary into custody when she exited the train at 4:16 p.m. They informed her that she was a person of interest in an ongoing investigation. While Tabbs protested that there must be some mistake, the two detectives put her into a cab headed for Central Station.[32]

Once Hannah Mary Tabbs was secured in the holding cell, Chief Kelly charged his men with the work of "hunting up colored people who, it was believed, could help to couple Hannah Mary Tabbs with the horrible crime."[33] By nightfall, more than a dozen black women and men, including John H. Tabbs, Hannah Mary's husband, had been rounded up and brought to the stationhouse for questioning.[34] The majority of the likely terrified residents denied having anything to do with Hannah Mary or knowledge of the alleged crime. However, John Tabbs's account of his wife's whereabouts proved both damaging and surprising. [While most African American women practiced the social conventions governing marriage—such as fidelity and respecting a husband's authority—behind closed doors, Hannah Mary Tabbs appeared to have breached those codes entirely, perhaps much to her spouse's chagrin.[35]

John H. Tabbs worked in the American Hotel as a carver. Described as "a great deal older" than his wife, he claimed to have little insight into her travails on Wednesday night, but his statement told otherwise. By his account, he returned to their home from work around 8 p.m. on the night in question; at that time he found that his wife had gone out so he lay down on the lounge and took a nap until about 9 p.m. He woke to find that Hannah Mary had yet to come home. He told detectives that she did not return until 11 p.m., at which time he asked, "Where have you been?" She ignored the question both times he posed it, instead asking, "Has anybody been here for me?" John did not answer her, nor did he learn her whereabouts. As a point of fact, he explained to Chief Kelly that it was "not unusual for his wife to be out late." That night, he went to bed and then on to work the next day.[36]

After seeing his wife's name in the paper on Saturday he asked her about her involvement in the reported events. She responded with surprise but beyond that appeared to brush the incident off. John "thought nothing more of it."[37] It seems that he was a man who had grown fairly accustomed to looking past his wife's indiscretions. The police however, were not so inclined. Of particular interest were John's comments about his wife getting home at 11 p.m. This information coincided nicely with the theory that whoever dumped the torso in Eddington left town on the 9:48 p.m. train headed toward Philadelphia, which arrived at Broad Street station at 10:35 p.m. It was completely possible for Hannah Mary to have been the passenger that Conductor Swain encountered on the earlier evening train. She would have had enough time to reach Eddington, discard the remains, and return to the station in time for the 9:48 p.m. train, which would have put her in the city at roughly half past ten. It could have taken another thirty minutes for her to get from Broad Street station to her home on Richard Street at 11 p.m. As if evidence was not already mounted, more incriminating facts would soon be revealed.[38]

Just as his shift was ending in Bristol at 7:30 p.m. on Monday, February 21, 1887, Conductor Swain was forced to head back into the city, this time at the behest of Chief Kelly, who had sent Detectives Miller, Tate, and Geyer to meet him. The trio made haste as they escorted the conductor to Central Station. Before long Swain stood face to face with Hannah Mary Tabbs. He stared at her for nearly a minute without uttering a word. The investigators asked her several questions, which she answered with a pronounced southern drawl, much like the one Swain had described. He left the room and informed Kelly that she was indeed the woman he encountered Wednesday night. The chief inquired about his certainty, and Swain answered, "That is the woman who rode on my train to Eddington last Wednesday night and carried a big bundle. I can't be mistaken." Chief Kelly nonetheless spent another hour going over Swain's statement to Constable Jackson and his identification of Hannah Mary Tabbs. Swain never wavered, and he asserted without equivocation that Tabbs was the woman in question. Finally satisfied, Chief Kelly released Swain at 10 p.m. When reporters approached him the following day in a coatroom on the third floor of Broad Street station, a flustered Swain refused to answer anything pertaining to the case stating, "I'm tired and sick of the whole business and will not say another word about it."[39]

Despite Monday's developments, Chief Kelly and his men still had their work cut out for them. The evidence pointed to the torso belonging to the missing Wakefield Gaines, but without the rest of the remains the investigators remained severely disadvantaged. Some police were dispatched to the Tabbs home to search for the head and limbs of the victim, but in the meantime, the detectives relied heavily on the coroner's description of the trunk—in particular, the notation of some kind of peculiarity about the shoulders. Described by his sister as twenty-two years of age, Gaines had a slight build with high, rounded shoulders—a feature that uniquely matched descriptions of the torso.[40] That Gaines was also light-skinned could account for the complexion that had so confounded the first set of investigators in Eddington. All of the details proved compelling—but would that be enough for prosecution?[41]

Although detectives had yet to secure the murder weapon, a motive had begun to take form as Chief Kelly reported that "Mrs. Tabbs and Wakefield Gaines had been on intimate terms for some months past."[42] Jane Cannon appeared to corroborate this claim by suggesting that Hannah Mary had designs of a more salacious nature on her brother, and Cannon stated that the two had had a heated confrontation roughly two weeks before his sudden disappearance—but could that alone account for such a violent murder? It was hard to say definitively, particularly since it seemed that the torso case might actually be mixed up with an older missing person's case: Hannah Mary Tabbs's niece Annie Richardson. Tabbs herself had produced the letter that she mentioned to the press in her impromptu interview in

Eddington—a letter that Tabbs believed Gaines had penned, advising her to stop searching for the girl. Dated February 7, 1887, it read:

> Dear friend, I hope you will forgive me for this as I have become weary of life. It seems to me I have nothing to live for except troble [*sic*] those that has cared for me has gone back on me and I feel that I am forsaken by every one who knew me it has been more than 6 weeks since I have done a stroke of work and I feal [*sic*] that I wont no more troble I dont wont you to think hard of me for theas [*sic*] few lines I want theas few lines to let you know that you need not write eney [*sic*] more to me for I am not at the same place and you need not try to find me out.[43]

Sent in a plain yellow envelope together with another piece of paper on which was written an address—94 River Street, Newark, New Jersey—the letter was curious because it lacked a postage stamp despite being addressed to a "Mr. Wakey Gaines, Seaford, Sussex County, Del., P.O. Box 46."[44]

Chief Kelly believed that Hannah Mary had returned to Eddington with the letter to throw off the authorities, and the letter and the girl's disappearance did, in fact, raise more questions. Further, Gaines's landlady—one of the many rounded up and hustled into the station to answer questions—also had a letter, supposedly from Gaines, telling her that he would be out of town caring for a sick friend. Gaines's sister told authorities that the handwriting did not belong to her brother and that he never signed anything "Waite Gaines." Though this note was obviously aimed at covering up the murder, Kelly and his men needed to discover its author and address the lingering questions raised by the one Hannah Mary received on February 7.[45]

An arguably more serious issue jeopardizing the case concerned the contradictory statements from Eddington's residents regarding the identity of the now-identified woman on board Swain's train. Josie Knight, the station agent in Eddington, told reporters on Tuesday morning, "I said I would recognize the woman who redeemed the excess ticket Wednesday night if I were to see her in the same way again and yesterday I saw this Mrs. Tabbs in exactly the same position and I am confident that she is not the woman."[46] According to Knight the woman was "quite black" and a "stranger." Neither Mrs. Stroup nor Thomas Matthews, her servant, saw the woman's face that night on account of the darkness. Another witness, James Preston, a local blacksmith who claims to have been at the station when the woman returned to travel back to Philadelphia, said that the woman he saw boarding the train into town that night did not look like Hannah Mary Tabbs.[47] It seemed that the residents who so eagerly undertook the task of solving the gruesome crime were determined to unravel it now that the investigation had largely moved to Philadelphia. Perhaps their response reflected disappointment at losing their place in the limelight, or maybe it resulted from an excessive sense of their role in the mediation of justice. The pride that locals took in being a part of the case is perhaps best conveyed by the sentiments of Heston Smith. A Cornwells Heights grocery store clerk who claimed to have been at the Eddington Station on Wednesday night, Smith declined to give a statement to reporters on the grounds that he occupied "too important a position in the case to assist anyone who was not 'duly authorized.' "[48]

Also threatening Kelly's investigation was that his office and the Eddington authorities seemed to be working at cross purposes. Reportedly, Constable Jackson was "very much chagrined that the arrest of Mrs. Tabbs was made by Chief Kelly's men." He believed the investigation was still in the early stages and that such a move was premature.[49] Given this belief, Coroner Silbert and Constable Jackson spent much of the day following Tabbs's arrest working a lead suggesting that someone had seen Gaines alive after Wednesday night.

Certainly such a clue would upend Kelly's investigation but also it might explain why Eddington witnesses had failed to identify Tabbs, let alone draw the connection that she was the "mysterious woman."

Despite unanswered questions and friction between the Philadelphia and Eddington authorities, Chief Kelly told reporters that he felt confident that he would have a confession within twenty-four hours. True to form, on February 23, 1887, "MURDER CONFESSED" appeared on the front page of the *Philadelphia Times*.[50] After a night in confinement during which she was denied contact with anyone except the detectives on the case, Hannah Mary Tabbs talked. Accounts after her night in custody described her as worn and haggard, somehow thinner looking, and reporters noted that her coat had been torn at the sleeve. The black eye she reportedly sported at the time of her apprehension now appeared more pronounced.[51] No account explains exactly what occurred in custody as white investigators interrogated Tabbs, but existing evidence suggests that, in the service of justice, Philadelphia authorities could be brutal. Physical violence had long been regarded as a "normal part of police work," and while officers risked public rebuke if they deigned to attack one of the "respectable classes," those considered to be "lower-class criminals" were fair game. Working-class whites and people of color in general could be especially vulnerable. Moreover, conditions inside Philadelphia jails were harrowing. One white female prisoner noted in her memoir that she ultimately submitted to the sexual advances of the night-keeper in a desperate effort to escape the rats in her cell.[52]

In other cases, investigators threatened both violation and violence to get suspects to talk. According to Elizabeth Banks, a black woman charged with the murder of a white man, masked detectives interrogated her, but while their faces were obscured, she could still see their eyes. In Banks's words, those eyes belonged to men who were "all looking her over." Given black women's history of rape and sexual assault—often at the hands of white men—let alone what kinds of trauma the image of white men in masks stirred, it should come as little surprise that Banks made a confession only to recant later under allegations of police intimidation.[53]

According to the police, Hannah Mary Tabbs's questioning moved from basic information about her life and how she ended up in Philadelphia to how she came to work at the Brock Estate and her connection to Jane Cannon and her brother, Wakefield Gaines. Hannah Mary said that she knew Gaines but adamantly denied having anything to do with his disappearance or any connection to the discovery made in Eddington. The detectives grilled Tabbs repeatedly about Gaines's and her own whereabouts the previous Wednesday. Just how long the questioning went on is unclear, but at some point Tabbs began crying. She sobbed answers, claiming no knowledge of Gaines's whereabouts, yet she could not give a straight account of where she was on the day in question. Chief Kelly kept her in custody that evening, locked in a cell adjoining his office—though at some point that night she was removed from the cell and "secretly taken to the Fifth District Police Station," at Fifteenth and Locust Streets.[54]

When Kelly looked in on Hannah Mary the next morning, she complained of a headache and had a handkerchief tied around her head. Sensing that she may have been crumbling, Kelly got her a "good breakfast" and asked her if she wanted to tell him anything. At that time, she declined to add anything further to the statements she had already made. Chief Kelly reportedly told her, "I will leave you to your own thoughts for the present. I may call again this afternoon. If you have anything to tell me you can send for me at any time." Chief Kelly left her and went to meet with his men. He sent Crawford to find George Wilson, the man Hannah Mary had mentioned in the news article and the name that she continued giving while she was in custody, to bring him in for questioning. Geyer traveled back to Bucks County to canvass Bristol and Eddington and to conduct follow-up interviews with potential witnesses. Miller and Tate would return to the Tabbs home to continue searching for clues and gathering evidence from neighbors.[55]

At 1 p.m. Crawford began to question Hannah Mary again. By then she was in an agitated state and just kept repeating, "Why don't you get Wilson? Maybe he knows something. Why don't you get Wilson?" Crawford had probably broken people before and felt confident that she was almost ready to crack. He telegraphed for the chief, who came with Clerk Moffitt to take her statement. Officers in the Fifth District stationhouse moved Hannah Mary to Lieutenant Usilton's office, where she sat facing the light. A white handkerchief partially covered one eye, which appeared "a good deal darker than her skin" and severely contused. When questioned about the black eye, she said that she had fallen and hurt herself. She may well have had bruising around her eye when she first arrived at the precinct, but the fact that the swelling was more pronounced suggests that she had been struck again, perhaps by one of the detectives. This might explain why they did not pursue this line of questioning further; instead, they waited for the woman to unburden herself.[56]

In a low voice, Hannah Mary recounted a terrible story, reportedly shivering and choking at points.[57] Her police statement was as follows:

> On Wednesday morning, February 16, between nine and ten o'clock, I was in the kitchen of my house at 1642 Richard Street. Wakefield Gaines came there to see me, and three or four minutes afterward George Wallace, also known as Wilson, came in. Gaines was sitting on a settee reading a paper, and I was eating my breakfast. Wallace knocked at the door and Gaines opened it for him. Wilson's first conversation was about the breaking up of some wagons. Gaines did not talk. Wilson after awhile arose and said he was coming back to see me on Sunday and was going to

bring my little girl from Jenkintown and would take her out riding. I asked him about what time on Sunday, and he said "exactly at 12 o'clock." Then Gaines said to me: "Is he going with her now?" I said, "I don't know and I don't care, as long as I see my little girl." Gaines jumped up and struck George Wilson. Wilson kind of ran backward, as though looking for something. Gaines followed him up and they clinched and fought all over the kitchen and fell up against the sewing machine.

George Wilson grabbed up a green chair standing there, struck Gaines on the head and knocked him up against the stair steps, and from there he slid down to the floor. He struck him several times more with the chair while he lay there. He never got up again, never spoke. I had been standing upon the steps and I came down and stepped over Wake Gaines's legs and said: "George Wilson, this is awful." He said: "Well, he shan't get the best of me. He struck me first." Then Wilson pulled the carpet from under the dead man and I washed it out and hung it out on the clothes line. There was some blood on it and some on the steps. Then George Wilson grabbed hold of the body, moved the coal scuttle off the cellar steps and pushed and pulled the body down in the cellar. He gave it a chuck and it stuck half way down and he pulled it the rest of the way. I went half way down the cellar steps after him and asked: "What are you going to do with it?" He said: "I am going to take off his clothes." And he took them off and tied them up. I saw him pull the shirt over Gaines's head and take his clothes off. I went down in the cellar and we stood and looked at the body.

Suddenly he asked me if the cellar window was open and he wanted something to put in front of it. He could not find anything. Then he said he would go out and eb [sic] back in a little while. He came back in twenty minutes. I waited in the door in the meantime. When he came back he had with him a butcher's cleaver, but I did not see it. I went up stairs and looked through the slats of the window to see if anyone was coming. He went down in the cellar. When he came up he said: "I have got him all fixed now." I went down in the cellar. The head was wrapped in paper; the body was leaning against the side of the cellar steps. The legs and arms I did not see. They were under the steps. He said: "I am going out with this head and will bring something back to wrap up this body, and if you can make away with that I want you to take it to Media and I will get away with the rest of it." I told him that I could not take that big body. He told me he had cut it off very short; that it wasn't heavy, and the way he would wrap it up I would have no trouble.

He said: "We can get it all out of here to-night if you just help me." Then he wrapped up the body and I told him I did not know the way to Media; only knew the way to Bucks county and would take it there.

It was 12 o'clock then and he went out of my door, carrying the head of the body with him. I stayed upstairs at the window until 5 o'clock or after when he came back, I was all dressed. He brought the body up from the cellar. I got an old skirt of Annie's off of the sewing machine and a shawl strap out of the closet up-stairs. The strap belonged to Gaines. It was too light for me to go out just yet, so he went down in the cellar and brought up a leg wrapped in an old bag with him and took it out. After he was gone I took the body and started to the depot and met him on Seventeenth street, below Spruce, as he was coming back. He said: "I can't get in the house," and I handed him my key. He said: "When will your husband be home?" and I said: "At half-past 8 o'clock." He said he would meet me at the depot.

I took the 6:37 train at Broad street and had a return ticket to Cornwells station. I did not get out at Cornwells, but went on to Eddington and paid the conductor the difference. I got out at

Eddington, went to the ticket office and got ten cents on my ticket, then started up the hill, stopped at a house and knocked at the door. A white lady came to the door and I asked her the way to Bridgeport. I left my two bundles at her gate, for besides the body I had a bundle containing Gaines's clothes. A colored man came out with a lantern and showed me the road. He asked me if I wanted to go to Mary Coursey's house. I told him no, that I was going the way by Eddington's post office. He started to walk with me, but I did not want him, so I walked on faster and stopped in somebody's yard until he went past.

He went on as if looking for me and then came back and blew out his light. I went on along the road to the bridge and set down my bundle of clothes; took the shawl strap and calico off and threw the body over into the water. I went on the side where I threw it and I saw that it did not sink as I expected. I threw the shawl strap over into the water and brought the piece of calico over the bridge and threw it down. Two men came along in a buggy at that time and they were talking about the road being muddy. I ran off the road close to some bushes until they passed.

I brought the bundle of clothes away, walked back the pike to Cornwells and got on the train leaving there after nine o'clock. I did not throw the clothes in the water, for fear Gaines's name was on them.

When I came out of Broad Street station Wilson was there to meet me. We walked on a piece and I told him I threw the bundle over, but it did not sink. He said it was because of the brown paper. I gave him the clothes and he left me at Market street, saying, "I will see you in the morning." He came at 8:30. I did not say much, for I did not sleep all night. He asked: "Is anything out?" I said: "I don't know what's out." He stayed five minutes. On Friday he came back and said it was in the paper and told me not to give him away; if I did it would be an awful thing and as bad for me as him.

I have not seen him since that time nor have I heard from him.

Sig.—Hannah Mary Tabbs

Taken in the presence of
  Francis R. Kelly
  J. B. Moffitt

Witness Thomas G. Crawford[58]

That chilling confession matched, rather precisely, the detectives' evidence. It also, rather conveniently, placed blame for both the murder and dismemberment squarely on George Wilson. Hannah Mary took pains to implicate him but she never explained why she did not go for help, particularly when Wilson left the house to purchase the butcher knife. Her statement also raised questions about her relationship with both men. How did she come to know Wilson? What John Tabbs knew or thought about her proximity to the two young men is also puzzling. Investigators may have had questions about the statement— indeed, Chief Kelly said that he believed she played a more direct role in the commission of the crime—but for the moment detectives concentrated their efforts on bringing George Wilson in for questioning and gathering corroborative evidence.[59]

Detective Crawford redoubled his efforts and by late afternoon he had learned that Wilson also lived in the Seventh Ward at 1241 Lombard Street with his aunt, Martha Wallace. Chief Kelly dispatched Detectives Miller and Tate to set up surveillance on the house. It was a blustery winter day, but the detectives maintained their posts. Their efforts were not in vain. They apprehended George Wilson as he returned home at 7 p.m. The eighteen-year-old was startled by detectives and denied that he had any knowledge of the crime save what he read in the papers. Throughout his initial interrogation, Wilson maintained his innocence. He claimed that Hannah Mary Tabbs was "down on" him because she thought he knew the whereabouts of her niece Annie Richardson.[60]

With Wilson in custody, the detectives busied themselves tying up the loose ends of the case. Despite the investigation's rocky start, the gruesome murder did indeed appear to be largely solved. Detective Geyer brought in the station agent Josie Knight, accompanied by her sister, Georgie Roberts. Although Knight had already faced Hannah Mary again since Wednesday night and had previously failed to recognize her, this time she made a positive identification. It seems the detectives had located more potential witnesses in Bucks County, as a number of those residents were brought in as well. For example, a Thomas Matthews was brought in to identify Tabbs, but he maintained that he could not be certain. Harold McCalla, the twelve-year-old son of George McCalla of Bucks County, was brought along, and Geyer stopped into Wannamaker's Department store to collect Jessie Van Zandt, who also lived in Eddington. Both McCalla and Van Zandt identified Hannah Mary Tabbs. With this additional corroboration, there was little doubt that the crime and those involved in its commission were from Philadelphia. This meant that the torso would have to be exhumed and transported to the city for the inquest and subsequent disposition of the case.[61]

With Hannah Mary's confession and their other primary suspect in custody, authorities wasted no time in bringing the two before a magistrate. The hearing room at Central Station on February 23 was packed with citizens eager to steal a glimpse of the principal actors responsible for the crime that had captivated the press and public for nearly a week. The space inside the rail was filled with reporters, policemen, and detectives. One reporter noted that the space outside the rail left the large number of listeners little "room to breathe."

According to an *Evening Bulletin* article, "The benches were unused except to stand upon, and the crowd pressed so that those near the rail were nearly crushed."[62] Officers escorted a number of prisoners in at ten minutes to the hour. Their arrival caused a stir. Many in the crowd jockeyed to get a look at the prisoners entering the dock. However, it was not until five minutes before 10 a.m. that Detective Tate ushered Hannah Mary Tabbs into the room.[63]

The crowd buzzed as the spectators gazed at the woman believed to be responsible for dumping the torso of the presumed victim, Wakefield Gaines. The *Times* noted that she had one front tooth missing and commented: "She is not a good looking colored woman." Further, Hannah Mary's condition had deteriorated greatly since she had given her interview to the *Evening Bulletin* in Eddington on Monday. Her clothes, the same ones she had been wearing since that day, were no longer fresh. The soft black dress, covered by a heavy black double-breasted overcoat of webbed material and matching black turban, was rumpled and torn. Her black eye, which had become the subject of much speculation, remained prominent. She looked harried, and reporters noticed that she had lost weight. Hannah Mary kept her eyes down. Several of the spectators knew her personally either from Richard Street or Schell Street, where Gaines resided. Some of the women burst into tears at the sight of her.[64]

Hannah Mary's present condition and demeanor ran counter to what some knew of her but it was all that the investigators would see. And while Kelly held to his suspicions about her role in the murder, he believed that Wilson was responsible for the dismemberment given their discovery that he had once worked at an abattoir. Few of them could believe that a woman, even a black woman, could commit such a brutal act. However, as the investigators followed up with witnesses from Richard Street, they would soon learn that Hannah Mary Tabbs was not as fragile as she appeared.[65]

Chapter Three

To Do Him Bodily Harm

The theory that Mrs. Tabbs is chiefly responsible for Gaines' death gains strength with every new development.

—*The Times*, February 24, 1887

With two suspects arraigned, Chief Kelly obtained what he and his detectives considered a positive identification of the victim—namely that Jane Cannon, Wakefield Gaines's sister, described physical peculiarities about her brother's shoulders that matched that of the torso in custody. Given the condition of the "body," it was really the best identification that authorities could hope for.[1] This information, together with Hannah Mary Tabbs's confession implicating George Wilson, a young man with butchering experience, initially led investigators to believe that the crime was solved. However, as detectives worked to fit the final pieces together, inconsistencies emerged. Interviews with family members, neighbors, and acquaintances would cast serious doubt on the notion that Wilson was the principal murderer. Instead, all eyes would again be focused on the woman found.

As a working-class black woman, Hannah Mary would typically remain a faceless figure left out of history, but her involvement in the torso case made her exploits in the City of Brotherly Love particularly visible and scrutinized. The more her actions came into focus, the more they conflicted with the authorities' prevailing theory about the case. Rather than making her appear as a fearful, hesitant accessory to a vicious murder, new information unearthed the more illicit elements underscoring the case and her role therein—elements that exposed rarely visible marital negotiations around sex, violence, and the limits of female agency.

There is little in Tabbs's life in Philadelphia that could account for the reports of her violent behavior that would surface during the investigation, let alone anything that could have predicted her involvement in the torso case. Rather, it seemed that her experiences before her residence in the city might hold the answers. However, Tabbs purposefully kept details about her history hidden. She gave authorities false information about her place of origin, stating that she was from Virginia when in fact she was from Maryland. Exactly why she would have lied is unclear, though she may have been trying to conceal a longer criminal history. Maryland criminal justice records list scores of black women in her age range with similar names having been arrested for everything from petty larceny to homicide but there is little that conclusively identifies Tabbs.[2] Even in her day-to-day existence in Philadelphia prior to the case, she employed a variety of aliases, going by either Mary or Hannah and using the last name Sheppard.[3] Despite her machinations, historical records indicate that she was born in Anne Arundel County, Maryland, in the 1850s and that her birth name was Hannah Ann Smith.[4]

Maryland, like Virginia, was a slave state, yet Maryland's geography placed it midway between slavery and freedom in the United States. The state embodied all of the tensions and contradictions that pulled the country into a bloody civil war. At the time of Tabbs's birth, Maryland served as home to roughly seventy-five thousand free blacks and held just over ninety thousand in captivity. Whereas the enslaved accounted for 54.7 percent of the state's black population, Maryland itself had the largest population of free blacks of any of the slaveholding states.[5]

Still, chattel slavery divided the region. Blacks represented roughly 16 percent of the population in northern Maryland, and of that group only 5 percent were enslaved. The northern counties were overwhelmingly white and relied almost solely on free labor. Counties on the Eastern Shore tended to be mixed in terms of labor and population; with roughly 40 percent of the population being black, enslaved blacks accounted for 20 percent. The southern part of the state was "a backward agricultural region devoted primarily to tobacco." Southern counties, including Anne Arundel, were 54 percent black, with 44 percent of that number enslaved.[6] The city of Annapolis served as the county seat and brought some economic diversity to Anne Arundel's tobacco plantations and many of the county's free blacks resided there as well. Likewise, whereas Baltimore was largely a free-laboring city, slaves were sometimes hired out to shops and families, and small numbers of enslaved men worked on the docks and in local shipping yards.[7]

Despite the geographical divides, the porous nature of the relationship between enslavement and freedom permitted a complicated yet intimate intermingling of the two. Among blacks, families living in close proximity with half of the members being owned by white farmers or children born to unions where one parent was free and the other enslaved were common. That shared reality intensified the hardships of chattel slavery and the yearning for all to be free, and so it is perhaps no coincidence that Maryland should have birthed two of the most revolutionary antislavery activists: Harriet Tubman, the prolific Underground Railroad conductor and Civil War nurse, scout, and spy who had been enslaved until her mid-twenties in Dorchester County; and Frederick Douglass, the renowned abolitionist, social reformer, and statesman who was born enslaved in Talbot on the Eastern Shore. Along with their abolitionist organizing, each shared harrowing accounts of their own suffering and the violent abuse of other enslaved women and men.[8]

Anne Arundel County housed a particularly notorious slave-owning family, known for physical cruelty and driving enslaved men and women hard at the same time that they gave them "food of a coarser grade and not much of it." Caroline Hammond, a formerly enslaved woman born in Ann Arundel County in 1844, referred to "the Revells of the county, a family whose reputation was known all over Maryland for their brutality with their slaves."[9] Hammond's mother was a cook, and she and Hammond lived in the main house. However, most enslaved blacks in the county sheltered in small cabins or huts with crude furnishings. They typically labored from sunrise to sunset and could not hire themselves out or leave the grounds without permission from planters, lest they suffer savage consequences.[10]

Punishment was at once brutal and mundane. Narrative after narrative tells of enslaved blacks having been beaten bloody with rawhides, anywhere from ten to ninety-nine lashes—the latter akin to a death sentence. But the lash was not the only form of violence to which enslaved men, women, and children were subjected. Punishments also had a psychological component as masters sought not only to discipline but also to break slaves in total submission. This seasoning started early for enslaved children, as Francis Fredic recalled being told by a slave owner in Fauquier County, Virginia, "Look you niggers! You have no souls, you are just like those cattle, when you die there is an end of you; there is nothing more for you to think about than living. White people only have souls."[11] Fredic, too, would describe scenes of extreme violence and humiliation as his own grandmother's back was stripped bare and flayed with a cowhide wielded by her own son as the master looked on shouting obscenities.[12] This tactic was a cruel one but typical of the contours of mastery.

As a part of their ability to dominate enslaved blacks, masters cultivated particular customs that maximized their sovereignty by ordering and structuring discipline at the same time that they aimed to appear separate from the lower aspects of it. The most practiced masters were supposed to have employed a system of rewards and chastisements as part of their management system. These planters used whippings, which would be carried out by overseers or other enslaved blacks, when otherwise recalcitrant slaves broke rules. Said masters did not strike with their own hands nor did they act "at random with passion or anger," but rather supervised the cruelty impassively.[13] This kind of mastery aligned with notions of southern statesmanship in that planters exercised a similar style of government that blended white supremacy, power, and commerce. The identity of masters and statesmen went hand in hand, operating as mutually constitutive identities, where those in power imagined themselves as pressed into service and forced to bear the burden of "servants."[14] In reality, southern statesmen, most of them slave owners, could be infamously violent— one of the basest examples being Preston Brooks, the South Carolina senator who nearly killed the antislavery Massachusetts's senator Charles Sumner on the Senate floor with a cane in 1865. Moreover, historical accounts are replete with portraits of despotic men who abused not only the enslaved but also their own families.[15]

Anne Arundel County planters may have been among the more notorious, but all slaves endured unspeakable cruelties. In addition to using beatings, starvation, and harsh confinement, planters made bloody whippings spectacles as a way to condition other slaves and to discourage disobedience. The more sadistic masters and overseers took pleasure from the torture they inflicted as women would be positioned and stripped to maximize punishments and the punishers' gaze. Enslaved women had few options other than submission or violent resistance to sexual assault, as no laws prohibited their victimization.[16] Enslaved men, too, could be victims of such sexual sadism. Harriet Jacobs, a formerly enslaved woman in North Carolina, recalled a slave, wearing only a shirt, who was chained to his master's bed. If he did not submit to the "freaks of despotism" demanded by the "cruel and disgusting wretch," he would be savagely flogged.[17]

Ultimately, great and small infractions met harsh discipline. Nancy Howard, a formerly enslaved woman born in Ann Arundel County and reared in Baltimore, where she labored in a kitchen, told of having her scalp split because she forgot a fork in one of the place settings. She also recalled that "I was frequently punished with raw hides,—was hit with tongs and poker and any thing." She described slavery as "one of the blackest, wickedest things."[18] She was not alone in this estimation.

Though freedom hardly proved to be salvation for Maryland blacks. Planters resented their presence and regarded free blacks as embodied threats to their way of life, so much so that the legislature's Committee on the Colored Population recommended in the late 1850s that all manumissions be ceased and that "Black people who were already free should be compulsorily hired out for terms of ten years." Black children, any born during their parents' terms, should become the property of "the owner of the mother's labor." Although these measures were not adopted, the reality of black freedom was tenuous under the best of circumstances, as free blacks were not citizens. To make certain that there was no confusion about that, the state's 1850–51 constitutional convention approved a provision that expressly excluded free blacks from the protections granted under the Bill of Rights. Free blacks' economic opportunities were limited too, as counties placed strict regulatory controls on their ability to obtain peddlers' licenses, sell merchandise, and operate boats. Authorities could also sentence free blacks to compulsory labor for up to a year for charges such as vagrancy. If black parents were too impoverished to care for their children, magistrates in orphans' court could bind them out as apprentices.[19]

Hannah Mary Tabbs, then known as Hannah A. Smith, grew up in this world. She had at least one brother, Augustus Smith, and at the time of her arrest in the torso case, both he and her stepfather were still living in Anne Arundel County.[20] Physical descriptions of Tabbs's body, namely the absence of extensive scarring or keloids, suggests that she was not the victim of the rawhide lash.[21] Accounts of Tabbs's complexion ranged from "light-skinned" to "mulatto" suggesting that perhaps she was the progeny of a master or overseer, though others have labeled her as "quite black" and "ugly."[22] Under the circumstances, it is difficult to know with certainty whether she spent her childhood enslaved or free. As an adult she enjoyed some acclaim for her cooking ability, suggesting that she may have been apprenticed out to learn the trade; either as a free black child or if she was enslaved, perhaps a planter had her trained in the hope of hiring her out later for the high fees that good cooks could command.[23] She could have grown up like Caroline Hammond, working alongside an enslaved mother who worked as the head cook for a wealthy planter. Or perhaps her experience was closer to that of Nancy Howard, brutalized on a daily basis as a servant in a white home in Baltimore or some other nearby city such as Annapolis. Maybe she was owned by one of the vicious Revells. The 1864 docket of the *Anne Arundel County Commissioner of Slave Statistics* listed a number of enslaved black girls in the age range with names such as Hannah, Ann, and Mary and with the surname Smith that also could have been Tabbs. One in particular stands out: Joseph Sheppard listed among his property a young woman named "Ann Smith." Given Tabbs's penchant for using the surname Sheppard, there may well have been a connection. Whatever her precise origin, young Hannah would have been well acquainted with white violence and the vicissitudes of white supremacy.[24]

The ravages of war would also mark her childhood. She would have been eleven or twelve years old at the start of the Civil War. Marylanders experienced violence at the war's outset as a fracas erupted between the state's citizens and Union soldiers from Massachusetts. The troops had been passing through the state on their way to guard the nation's capital in April 1861. The ruckus in Baltimore moved quickly from the hurling of paving stones and bricks to gunfire on Pratt Street. When it was over, sixteen lay dead with many more wounded. Annapolis was the first city to be occupied by Union troops, followed by Baltimore, soon after the "Pratt Street Riot." Rather than restoring order, however, occupation, the suspension of habeas corpus, and other practices such as warrantless arrests turned the state and Baltimore specifically into a fairly chaotic hub of sporadic mob clashes and urban violence. Large numbers of wealthier whites left the city to take up residence farther north or to dwell in rural farmhouses, leaving the less fortunate to confront the dangers.[25]

With angry citizens on either side of the issue and raucous soldiers roaming about, the risks for black women and girls were manifold, compounded especially by the ongoing threat to the sanctity of their womanhood. Soldiers on both sides of the war took black female bodies as a part of their spoils, though not without resistance and the frequent shedding of blood.[26] Bloodshed would become commonplace, as seven battles took place on Maryland soil. The bloodiest among them, the Battle of Antietam, resulted in an estimated 23,000 casualties in September 1862—the war's highest body count in a single day.[27] While the physical suffering of soldiers is more visible and readily cataloged, the victimization of the women— black women in particular—cannot be overstated. The wholesale rape and sexual exploitation of black women and girls proved so endemic that to speak of it was essentially "an old saying."[28] Moreover, while a good many women and children used the occupation to take flight from bondage, Maryland planters were dogged in their efforts to recapture them. Even after the state's loyalists managed to push through the 1864 constitution, which freed all those enslaved, recalcitrant planters continued to resist statewide emancipation. In one instance, a former planter from Anne Arundel County followed the newly freed nineteen-year-old Margaret Toogood to Baltimore where he accused the young girl of larceny. Using the pretense of returning her to Anne Arundel County to face the charges, he instead had a special chain and lock constructed and fitted around her neck to keep her as his prisoner. Not until Union Maj. Gen. Lew Wallace dispatched

Figure 3.1. "The Last Slave-Chain in Maryland," *Harpers' Popular Cyclopaedia of United States History.* Courtesy of the Historical Society of Pennsylvania (Call T.58 1892 v.2).

the cavalry was the young woman again freed. Still, she had worn the "horrible necklace seven weeks."[29] Toogood's vile abduction is but a glimpse of the vulnerability of black women seeking to exercise freedom.

Although precious little information has been found about young Hannah's life during this period, if her legacy of violence in Philadelphia may be taken to speak for this murky past, there can be little doubt that she witnessed, and likely experienced, the brutality of the era.[30] At the close of the Civil War in 1865, she would have been in her midteens—essentially on the precipice of womanhood. What exactly her impending womanhood would mean would take on new dimensions as newly freed black women and men fought to actualize their citizenship at the same time that newly imposed limitations jeopardized it. Indeed, freedom remained elusive despite the abolition of slavery and the surrender of the South. Pass and curfew restrictions ensnared large numbers of black men, women, and children, who found themselves either forced to work in rural areas on defunct plantations or detained in pens, often unbeknown to family and friends. Existing accounts also detail routine verbal abuse, physical assault, and torture. Black women found that their homes were just as likely to serve as sites of their violation as was the local jail, where black women were "thrown into the cells, robbed and ravished at the will of the guard," with women's frightful cries heard "almost every night."[31]

While speaking about their violation may have been "an old saying," the women nonetheless took pains to shield themselves from unwanted attention and sexual harassment. Like most women of the time, black women aimed to protect their reputations and conceal sexual liaisons, whether coerced or consensual, that took place outside of marriage.[32] Accounts place a single Hannah Ann Smith at approximately nineteen or twenty years of age in Maryland with a baby in tow. Annie Richardson, the missing young woman that Tabbs had identified as her niece, had grown up believing she was orphaned, that her parents, Tabbs's sister and brother-in-law, had died during Annie's infancy from yellow fever. Given that in the early 1870s and 1880s such outbreaks had left many children orphaned and eventually cared for by extended family, the account does not seem peculiar.[33] However, Annie is said to have doubted the veracity of this story because her own earliest recollections were of a young Hannah Ann, who she always just knew as her aunt, living with a man whose name was "Richardson," in Annapolis. She had suspected that Hannah Mary Tabbs was her biological mother, especially after she had learned that Richardson was her father.[34]

The rumor did not mention the man's race, though descriptions of Annie as a "beautiful mulatto" with long hair, "black as coal and scarcely a kink in it," suggest that Hannah Mary Tabbs had a child out of wedlock with either a light-skinned black or mulatto, or perhaps a white man.[35] Creating an alternative story of the girl's birth would provide a discreet cover that could satisfy mainstream social conventions while simultaneously sparing Annie the stigma of being the progeny of an illegitimate birth. Such a story might also conceal any exploitative or traumatic aspects of the child's conception. Ultimately, it could help both women navigate society without the stigma of sexual violation or impropriety. Whatever Annie's parentage, records show Hannah Ann, and presumably Annie, moving up the coast just a few years after Annie's birth.

In Baltimore, Hannah Ann Smith would eventually marry a black man, John H. Tabbs. Annie Richardson's narrative suggests that Hannah Ann reached Baltimore sometime after Annie's birth in approximately 1870. However, Baltimore city directories list a "Hannah Smith" living at "48 Park" as early as 1865. This is compelling because this name most closely matches the name on her marriage certificate, "Smith, Hannah A.," and Baltimore city directories list her future husband, John H. Tabbs, as living at "43 Park" in 1868, suggesting that they knew each other from the neighborhood. Birthdates and ages tended to be imprecise given the contours of enslavement, but John, listing his age as thirty-seven, and Hannah, stating hers as twenty-one, were married on June 4, 1873, at the "Bethel Church corner of Centre and Grand Alley."[36]

For a young woman from somewhat-dubious circumstances, the partnership was a smart move. John had enlisted during the Civil War and had been honorably discharged from the 5th Massachusetts Colored Cavalry in October 1865.[37] More than fifteen years older than his bride, John Tabbs was a hard-working porter who provided for his wife and Annie. The marriage afforded Hannah financial stability—at the time of the wedding she was not working—and a level of respectability. For John Tabbs, in addition to the allure of marrying a younger woman, the fact that she had a child may have been something he found desirable, as he was good to his niece, and she believed that he was fond of her.[38] While marriage furnished Hannah Mary with the outward appearance of propriety, in an interview with police, John Tabbs described her as "always crazy" as well as "very ignorant and foolish"—so much so that he even helped educate her by sending her to a school on Rayborg Street in Baltimore.[39]

Perhaps at that school Hannah Mary learned to curb, or at the very least, camouflage her coarse ways. Prison records indicate that she was able to read and write. She probably developed better manners as well, because she would eventually have little difficulty securing domestic employment in good businesses and homes. This may also be in part because she was a skilled cook.[40] Baltimore city directories in 1871 and 1872 list John Tabbs as a porter, which was a good job for blacks at the time. Most railway porters made beds, assembled curtains, served as chambermaids, and generally kept train cars tidy.[41]

However, after 1873 he seemed to bounce around between less lucrative jobs, which might explain his decision to move to Philadelphia. John Tabbs made the transition first in 1876, sending for his wife and Annie later that year.[42] It was an ideal time to relocate because the city was in the midst of a great expansion. The 1876 Centennial Exposition brought jobs and a boom to the local population, which grew from roughly 674,022 inhabitants in 1870 to upward of 817,000 by April 1, 1876.[43] The exposition alone was not responsible for the city's growth. Between 1870 and 1900 the entire state witnessed a massive increase in industrial productivity. Indeed, much of John D. Rockefeller's fortune stemmed from Pennsylvania's oil, while the state's iron lined Andrew Carnegie's pockets. Philadelphia's port was the second largest in the country, and its textile mills furnished more goods than any other in the United States.[44]

A great deal of the city's physical expansion was westward, aided by the completion of several new bridges that crossed the Schuylkill River—at Callowhill Street in 1874, at South Street in 1875, and at Girard Avenue in 1874. Ironically, the very bridges that created the conditions that led many new residents such as Hannah Mary Tabbs to Philadelphia, according to Tabbs's confession would serve as the dumping grounds for a variety of unsettling remains.[45]

Concentrated in the Seventh Ward, the African American community would be home to John and Hannah Mary Tabbs and Annie Richardson. John found steady work in domestic service, and when Hannah Mary first arrived in Philadelphia she cooked and washed for a tailor on Sixteenth Street for a number of years before working for George W. Haines, a real estate broker at 1020 Chestnut Street in Center City.[46] It is here that Hannah Mary, now in her early to mid-thirties, would first meet the twenty-year-old Wakefield Gaines, who worked as a coachman for the lawyer—before being fired in 1885 for drunkenness on the job.[47]

Just when the pair became "criminally intimate" isn't clear, but evidently Hannah Mary Tabbs acted the part of a faithful wife, though

WAITE GAINES.

Figure 3.2. "Waite Gaines." From "MURDER CONFESSED." In the *Philadelphia Times*, February 23, 1887.

she subverted those strictures by indulging her own, otherwise illicit desires.[48] Still, just how convincingly Tabbs concealed her more taboo behaviors is debatable because in the days following her arrest and subsequent confession naming George Wilson as Gaines's murderer, neighbors, potential witnesses, and those closest to her offered evidence against her. Each one described Hannah Mary Tabbs as a woman with a volatile temper, a startling propensity for brutality, and a frightening ability to enact her will whether it meant violating traditional social mores or, literally, the personhood of others.[49]

Hannah Mary wielded violence in a manner that allowed her to exercise a surprising amount of control and agency within the black community. If the testimony of her peers is to be believed, she did so with few limitations. While much of her brutality was domestic, she also attacked neighbors as well as strangers, young and old, male and female. Though prolific, her violence was not completely arbitrary or without reason. She did not invoke it against whites, indicating that she knew there would be serious consequences for such a breach, judicial and otherwise. Rather, she purposefully deployed it among others in her vicinity; other blacks who, like Tabbs, tended to be alienated from the legal system. Especially since justice during this period shifted from fee-based, citizen-initiated arrests and prosecutions—which had granted black people a measure of power in judicial proceedings—to the process where police made the arrests and prosecutors tried defendants. This shift amplified blacks' estrangement from the law; disaffection that may well have been intentional. Among charges of corruption in fee-based prosecutions, advocates for the change also invoked images of blacks and other social outcasts purportedly clogging the courts with frivolous complaints.[50]

Whereas echoes of mastery can be seen in Tabbs's behavior, against this urban context, it reflects preemptive as well as predatory forms of violence, revealing both a compulsion to dominate and the need to establish a kind of personal safety perimeter.[51] It may not have been as dangerous as the Deep South, where white men could horsewhip a black woman over a disagreement with one of the men's wives, as was the case in Columbus, Mississippi, on April 30, 1887, but African American women in Philadelphia nonetheless faced daily hostilities that could quickly spiral into more violent actions. Black women battled sexual harassment and sexual assault as domestics in white homes, and also they fended off routine insults and lewd gestures as they traversed the city. Many women carried small knives and remained ready to defend themselves.[52]

By engaging in a kind of signifying violence then, as it was no secret that Hannah Mary frequently and "violently insulted inoffensive persons," she might put neighborhood toughs and other loafers on notice: she was not to be messed with and if they did, she would not hesitate to lash back. Indeed, even John Tabbs told of his own encounters with Hannah Mary's wrath, explaining that about a year and half before she went to live at the Brock estate in Eddington, she had become "actually violent" with him and that she "often threatened to do him bodily harm."[53] This escalation coincides with the heating up of her relationship with Wakefield Gaines. Hannah Mary also terrorized the residents of Richard Street—all of whom "condemned Mrs. Tabbs unstintingly," noting that "she had a very violent temper, and that they were all very much afraid of her."[54]

Hannah Mary's vicious proclivities had become so notorious in her community that when Annie Richardson went missing in the early part of 1886, many local blacks believed that she had killed the girl. According to the rumors, neither Annie nor Wakefield was Hannah Mary Tabbs's first victim. An anonymous letter sent to the county jail when she was in custody promised to "put Mrs. Tabbs where she belongs for killing Wake." The author further charged that "she killed a man in Richmond, another in the Meadow, and also killed Annie, and if people only knew that they would not fool long with her." While authorities did not initially concern themselves with the crimes alleged to have occurred out of state, after learning more about Hannah Mary Tabbs, even Chief Kelly told reporters that based on the evidence and Annie's disappearance, he suspected that Hannah Mary had "murdered the girl."

However, Annie surfaced, very much alive, in early March 1887. She had been living with and working for a white family—Mr. and Mrs. Dennis V. L. Schenek—on a farm roughly four miles from Lambertville, in Hunterdon County, New Jersey.[56] Reporters gushed over Annie's beauty, one account noting that "the girl is very pretty. Her complexion is about the shade of a Cuban woman, her eyes bright and expressive, her features regular and pleasing, her teeth milk white, her hair long and wavy, and figure petite and trim."[57] Annie explained that Hannah Mary had started to treat her badly when she was eleven years old. The women she knew as her aunt claimed, "I was bad and had stolen things and then [she] had me put in the House of Refuge, where I stayed thirteen months." But when Hannah Mary went to work on the Brock estate she took Annie with her. The girl told reporters that "whenever I did anything to displease either Wake or my aunt, my aunt would beat me awfully, and finally, on the evening of the 25th of May I ran away. I walked down the road toward the city. I walked all night, stopping at times to cry, and got to the city the next afternoon."[58] Tabbs's aggression against Annie reached the boiling point when her affections for Gaines seemed to be threatened. As one witness explained, Hannah Mary had become extremely possessive of Gaines and grew quickly enraged and "jealous if he joked" with Annie. A second anonymous letter, sent by "Margaret," claimed to have witnessed Tabbs threatening to "put Annie out of the way, because she loved Wake and had intended to marry him as soon as old Tabbs was dead."[59]

Hannah Mary's violence intensified at specific moments that served to shield her personal pursuits with Wakefield Gaines—in this instance, activities that were of a more forbidden nature. She also intimidated her neighbors, which, in effect, led most of them to turn a blind eye when it became clear that she engaged in extramarital sex. They knew that Gaines frequently visited the house that Hannah Mary shared with her husband, a man who worked long hours. Save for the victim's sister though, all stopped short of making actual accusations about the adulterous implications, until after Hannah Mary's arrest, at least. Moreover, violence was not the only tool in Tabbs's repertoire. When Hannah Mary interacted with Gaines outside of her home and neighborhood she used deceit to maintain a veneer of propriety. Just as Gaines frequented her home, Tabbs also spent a lot of time at Gaines's residence, a rented room at 207 Schell Street in the city's Tenderloin section. In an effort to stave off suspicion about their liaisons, Hannah Mary introduced herself using the alias Mary Sheppard, and she told Gaines's landlady that he was a relative. Relying perhaps on a trusted cover, she referred to Gaines as her "nephew."[60]

On the face of it, Hannah Mary Tabbs came close to successfully presenting as a pillar of the community—dutiful wife, charitable aunt, and trusted employee. There is no indication that she left former jobs under any sort of dubious circumstances, and she had no prior arrest record in Philadelphia. To many she would appear to be working earnestly toward uplift and adhering to accepted notions of respectability.[61] Never mind that she carried on an adulterous relationship with a younger man.

Perhaps most astonishing about her sexual escapades is that it appears as if she and her husband had come to a fairly frank understanding about his physical limitations and her carnal needs. At some point in their relationship, John Tabbs revealed to his wife that during the war, "he was wounded in the groin and was ruptured there." Such an injury, compounded by their age difference, would likely have interfered with his ability to achieve or maintain an erection. That he was unable to perform sexually may explain why John seemed to tolerate Wakefield Gaines's presence in their lives, as investigators found Gaines's clothes in their home on Richard Street. Still, there appeared to be some ground rules. John Tabbs told authorities that he knew his wife and Gaines were "friends," but that he "had never seen Gaines." In an era marked by black women's concealment of all things sensual (actions undertaken to guard against assault), and with the general heightened emphasis on female chastity and sexual purity, that Hannah Mary Tabbs mediated some sort of extramarital sexual arrangement was extraordinary.[62]

That she moved stealthily, though, indicates that she was also sensitive to the disparaging discourses about black women and especially those about newly freed black women in Philadelphia. In his seminal treatise on black Philadelphians in the late nineteenth century, even W. E. B. Du Bois decried the fact that the "lax moral habits of the slave regime still show themselves in a large amount of cohabitation without marriage." He bemoaned the supposed "sexual looseness" of working-class blacks and insisted that it brought "adultery and prostitution in its train." Overly critical of poorer blacks, Du Bois's bleak assessment, like so much of the prevailing rhetoric, failed to acknowledge the incredibly difficult situations that newly freed blacks could find themselves in—crippling poverty, isolation, loneliness, and profound marital discord. Slavery and the war disrupted families, and sometimes one partner would remarry, assuming the other dead, only to discover that the original spouse was alive and had been searching to reunite.[63] Still, there is little doubt that Hannah Mary Tabbs committed adultery.

Further, Hannah Mary's affair with Gaines appears to have been an extremely intense one. She displayed a level of devotion to the young Gaines that bordered on obsession, and she tried to exert significant control over him. In addition to Gaines visiting her home and keeping his personal items there, Hannah Mary periodically paid his rent, cooked his food, and did his washing. Distance did not adversely impact the relationship as the two remained in contact and she followed him to the Brock estate in Eddington for work before returning again to Philadelphia at the end of 1886. In fact, because the Brocks had advertised for southern help in particular, Hannah Mary had lied, "saying she came direct from the South, [and] had only been in Philadelphia a short time."[64] Indeed, she went to some lengths to be with Gaines.

But volatility accompanied passion. As one neighbor reported, the two argued everyday "Sundays included."[65] Moreover, Annie commented that while she knew of Hannah Mary's deep affection for Gaines and believed that "he was wrongfully intimate with her," she doubted that his feelings were the same.[66] Further evidence points toward Gaines losing interest. The problems in the affair came to a head when Tabbs learned that Gaines was in a relationship with another woman. At the time of his demise, Gaines planned to wed Annie Johnson of North Thirteenth Street the following June.[67] Gaines's betrayal proved too much for Hannah Mary to bear. According to Jane Cannon, two weeks before his disappearance, Tabbs confronted Gaines with the woman in question. A heated confrontation ensued, sending the young woman fleeing while Tabbs slashed Gaines's face with a razor.[68] Gaines took refuge in his sister's house, rushing in with blood flowing from a "big cut across his cheek." As he ran, Tabbs called after him saying that she "would kill him yet."[69] Overcome at points with emotion when she recalled the incident, Cannon told the police that Tabbs had a powerful hold over her brother and that, like the residents of Richard Street, "he was afraid of her."[70] According to Jacob Elliott, who lived near Gaines's sister, Gaines told him that Tabbs destroyed letters he received from other girls and had prevented him from seeing them by threatening to "fix him so he couldn't."[71] Hannah Mary reportedly "dogged Gaines' footsteps" and waited for him for hours near his sister's home, going so far as to ask folks she knew in the area to let her know when he stopped by; behavior suggesting that she intended to make good on her promise to "get square" with Gaines for his betrayal.[72] Gaines certainly was not in the dark about the temper of his paramour, and based on evidence of their arguments he also was no passive victim. Still, Tabbs's rage after finding out about Gaines's marriage proposal to another woman must have shocked him.

However, Ms. Johnson—the young woman who was supposed to become Gaines's bride—would be in for a shock of her own: Wakefield Gaines was married already. His wife, an African American from Seaford, Delaware, would surface during the investigation into his death and prove to authorities that she and Gaines were married in 1882—a fact that Jane Cannon would later confirm. The two lived together in Philadelphia for two years before deciding to separate due to "connubial infelicity" and an inability to "live peacefully together." A year later Gaines and Tabbs would meet. Gaines may not have been the most sympathetic of victims, but this did not diminish the dreadfulness of his death, nor did it quell inquiries into the life of the woman at the center of the investigation.[73]

As the *Times* reported on February 24, 1887, the "theory that Mrs. Tabbs is chiefly responsible for Gaines' death gains strength with each new development." The account contained a damning portrait of Tabbs, describing her violent temper and the fact that she was always "ready for a quarrel."[74] Their article echoed the sentiments of her family members and the residents of Richard Street.[75] It also provided evidence from Gaines's landlady, stating that Gaines believed that Hannah Mary Tabbs had tried to poison him. According to her story, Gaines said that he was drinking a beer that Tabbs had given him. He noticed white powder at the bottom of the glass and stopped drinking it. When he returned home, he "looked ashen" and suffered severe stomach pains, becoming convinced that Tabbs put arsenic in his beer. This reportedly took place two days before his murder.[76]

As the authorities delved deeper into the case, each new clue suggested that Hannah Mary Tabbs was the prime suspect. This was especially so when the investigation led to seventeen-year-old Hattie Armstrong, who lived at 1635 Richard Street. Armstrong told police that on the day of the murder Hannah Mary had asked her to run an errand at 2 p.m. Hannah Mary told Hattie that she was desperate for money and had asked the girl to pawn a large bundle of clothes for her. Hannah Mary had hoped that Hattie would negotiate $2 for the items but the young woman returned from the pawnshop at 17th and Bainbridge Streets with $1.50. For her trouble, Hattie received 25 cents and, perhaps fortunately for the authorities, a good look around Hannah Mary's home. Hattie described a house that was in complete disarray. From the state of things, Hattie assumed that Hannah Mary was just undertaking a thorough cleaning of the place, though she noticed that furniture in the kitchen appeared "all topsy-turvy."[77] Based on this information, detectives visited the shop later that afternoon.

At the pawnshop, authorities recovered a number of items directly related to the case. The pawned bundle contained an overcoat, two sack coats, a pair of trousers, and a blue vest. Elizabeth Williams, Gaines's landlady, would later identify these items as articles of clothing that belonged to him. Williams would also tell detectives at Central Station that the coats and the blue trousers and vest are what Gaines wore the day he met his brutal end. The recovered bundle, however, offered even more ominous clues. It was wrapped in heavy brown paper, similar to what had concealed the torso. Like the paper marked "HANDLE WITH CARE," it, too, was stained with blood, along with the trousers and vest.[78] In addition to the discoveries of the clothes recovered from the pawnshop, the detectives uncovered blood evidence on the floorboards and the stairs leading to the cellar in Tabbs's house. The cellar floor was also covered with ash that matched the ash on the back of the torso left on the bank of William B. Mann's ice pond. The technician who gathered the ash reportedly "saw blood-stains in it."[79] The ash and the remains were collected for more conclusive studies. The leads were promising, in spite of the fact that the authorities had yet to secure the murder weapon.

Even though nearly all of the evidence cast Hannah Mary Tabbs as Gaines's murderer, she had crafted her mainstream image so well that the authorities still had difficulty believing that the woman they had in custody and the fiend behind the gruesome crime could be one and the same. Hannah Mary appeared frail and shed trembling tears in her cell. She had a strong employment history with some of the region's more well-to-do whites. In this sense, her method for navigating the urban landscape served her well because, although she clearly transgressed a multitude of strictures personally and within the black community, the persona she maintained in the white world—the world where power counts—gave the detectives pause. In their hesitation the detectives would construct an alternative theory of the crime that had little to do with evidence and more to do with the state's investment in maintaining the sanctity of whiteness and masculinity—boundaries that, by virtue of his very being, George Wilson, a mulatto who could pass for white, had unforgivably crossed.

Chapter Four

Wavy Hair and Nearly White Skin

His face is very light in color; so light, indeed that he would not be taken for a Negro at all.

—*Evening Bulletin*, February 23, 1887

Unlike the respectable office occupied by Chief Kelly, holding cells in Central Station and the Fifth District stationhouse, where Hannah Mary Tabbs and George Wilson would be confined, in cells 8 and 9, respectively, were grim at best. Described as "vile-smelling" holes by one former inmate, the accommodations had only a bench and an exposed toilet. The filthy and vermin-infested conditions may well have contributed to a rough night for both, as Tabbs reportedly spent "nearly all night" weeping, and Wilson suffered a seizure. That morning guards found him with "glazed and staring eyes and froth oozing from his mouth." After having been roused and medicated by the prison physician, Wilson, alongside Hannah Mary Tabbs, was whisked by the jailers to arraignment.[1]

En route to the hearing Wilson likely got a fuller measure of both the scope of his troubles and his sudden notoriety. Roughly a week after the crime occurred, the murder and dismemberment had taken Philadelphia and its surrounding counties—and neighboring states—by storm. What initially seemed like a gruesome case that would probably go unsolved had instead grown into an adulterous love triangle that was headline news.

Wilson, who was escorted by Sergeant Malin, quickly followed Tabbs into the dock. Wilson wore soiled work clothes consisting of a well-worn white shirt and a faded pair of pantaloons cinched by a strap buckle. He completed the ensemble with a tattered coat, and he had no hat. He proved to be of equal interest to the crowd, though it seems that it was both his involvement in the case as well as his physical appearance that intrigued the onlookers. Reporters partly fixated on his somewhat-dazed expression—a look most likely influenced by his purported illness and subsequent treatment. According to one account, "While in the dock he appeared like a man conscious of his innocence or like a guilty man who thought he had a good excuse for his crime."[2]

Sergeant Malin silenced the din that threatened to overtake the court. In a deep monotone voice, Malin announced, "Hats off and come to order!" Magistrate Smith broke off a hushed conversation as he rose and instructed both prisoners to stand. Addressing Wilson, Magistrate Smith began his questioning. After obtaining Wilson's name and current and previous addresses, he inquired about Wilson's age, which was eighteen, and his occupation—he did caning for a local upholsterer. Tabbs answered the same questions, noting that she had no children, had lived on Richard Street for eight years, and said she was thirty-two years of age. The magistrate then turned his attention to Chief Kelly. He addressed the magistrate, stating, "I would ask your Honor to hold the prisoners until Monday next for further hearing for the murder of Wakefield Gaines, on Wednesday last, in order that further witnesses may be produced." After a pregnant pause, Magistrate Smith broke the hush that had fallen over the courtroom by responding briskly, "I commit you both to the County Prison for a further hearing next Monday." He then directed the sergeant to remove the prisoners to their cells. Detective Tate took charge of Tabbs, while Malin took Wilson to be photographed for the rogues' gallery books.[3]

Figure 4.1. Hannah M. Tabbs and George H. Wilson, *Rogues' Gallery Books,*
1887. Courtesy of the Philadelphia City Archives.

Figure 4.1. Continued

[Aside from noting his odd expression, journalists analyzed and commented extensively on Wilson's hair, skin, and yes—that he had "regular features, wavy hair and nearly white skin."[4] Whereas being light-skinned could be valuable intraracially, as many so-called mulattoes had better access to education and greater earning potential, Wilson's uncanny proximity to whites seemed too close for comfort. The specter of interracial sex notwithstanding, academics and scientific researchers regarded mulattoes as deviant physiologically—weaker than superior whites and even full-blooded blacks—and more susceptible to diseases such as tuberculosis and syphilis.[5] Fears of infiltration and degeneracy aside, the implicit race mixing also represented a kind of holocaust to some whites because it upended notions of whiteness as distinct and supreme.[6]

In Wilson's case, his light color motivated an investigation into his ancestry and upbringing, ultimately calling greater attention to his time served in the city's House of Refuge for Colored Youth, an institution for delinquent minors. Between his mixed race, his past juvenile record, and his work at a local slaughterhouse, Wilson's legal predicament worsened, despite the fact that evidence mounted against Hannah Mary Tabbs.[7] Most damning to Wilson's case would be his interactions with the investigating authorities. His experiences in custody and at the courthouse exemplify the perils of running afoul of white supremacy and customary notions of race in the criminal justice system.

Two images of George Wilson emerged in the aftermath of his arrest. The first depicted a self-confessed tough who flaunted his whiteness and seemed to relish his newfound infamy, so much so that he actively assisted detectives in locating incriminating evidence. The second cast Wilson as a pitiable youth, easily misled and dim in his thinking after years of hard knocks and bad breaks. In some ways the notions paralleled mainstream attitudes held about mulattoes in general—regarding them as either immoral and degenerate on one hand or tragic and isolated on the other.[8] Of course the competing public images aligned closely with the storytellers' legal affiliation and, in the days immediately following Wilson's arrest, Chief Kelly and the boys at Central Station were the ones doing most of the talking.

By Wednesday afternoon, February 23, 1887, less than twenty-four hours after being arrested and arraigned, Wilson, according to the Philadelphia Police, had offered a partial confession. Chief Kelly informed reporters that he immediately went to the Fifth District stationhouse, at Wilson's behest, and upon his arrival, Wilson was brought to the lieutenant's office where he "volunteered to make a statement."[9] Wilson's statement managed to corroborate and challenge the one given by Tabbs. The following day, Chief Kelly told reporters that Wilson had again "unburdened himself," but that he would not release the full statement because "there is something that must be worked up before it is made public." Still, rather than leaving the public hanging, Chief Kelly offered the following: "He admits that he struck [Gaines] on the head with a chair."[10] Wilson's full statement would not be released until Friday, February 25:

I have known Mrs. Tabbs about two years. I was at her house, 1642 Richards street, on Wednesday, February 16. I got my breakfast and went into the shop and opened it up. About half-past eight or nine o'clock Mr. Mattheas came down. I told him I was going to Second and Callowhill streets to get some cane (used in caning chairs), but I did not go there. I went around to Seventeenth street and stood in front of the candy store for a while and then went to Mrs. Tabbs.

Mrs. Tabbs came to the door and let me in.

She said, "How is it you didn't fetch Annie to me on Sunday?"

I said: "I didn't go after her."

Wake Gaines was sitting on the settee. Wake said he knew I was lying; that I wasn't going to fetch her, and didn't know where she was anyhow. I said: "Well, you will see whether I don't fetch her pretty soon."

I started to go to the door; he made a hit at me with his fist.

I jumped on one side and he jumped up and hit me in the side and knocked me down; he jumped on top of me and we fought awhile and rolled over on the sewing machine. Mrs. Tabbs said: "Let him up, Wake; don't hit him while he is down on the floor."

He got up and I got up and then he hit me again. I picked up a chair by the back and with both hands hit him on the back of the head with it; he kind of staggered and went and sat down on the settee.

I ran out the front door and went around to Seventeenth street and did not come back till five minutes of twelve. As I came in Mrs. Tabbs handed me a package done up in paper and told me to go throw it in the river. If I pawned it or opened it she would kill me. I took it out and went up Twelfth to Market, out Market to Twenty-second, along Twenty-second to Callowhill street, and over the bridge. I took it over the railroad back of the place and made a hole in the ashes and put it in and put some loose ashes over the top of it. I then went back to the house again. She asked me what I did with the bundle. I wouldn't tell her. She then gave me another package containing the arms wrapped in light brown paper. I took that to the same place I did the other and came back to the house again and she gave me the legs done up in the same kind of paper. I took them to the same place and covered them up the same as the other. I went down to the slaughter house and stayed there awhile; then went over to Mrs. Tabbs house again. This was between seven and half-past. I knocked at the door and nobody came. I went up to the corner and talked to some boys and girls awhile. Then I went to

Seventeenth street, to Callowhill, and over the bridge to where I had hidden the things. I had a piece of twine in my pocket. I tied them all together and tore a little piece of paper off the legs to see what they were. I took the legs and then the arms and then the head and tied them around twice with a bit of twine. There was a piece of string hanging down, and I tied a brick and a half to it. Then I walked back on Callowhill street on the down-river side, past the canal boats that were under the bridge, took the bundle up in both hands and threw it out into the river, so that it would not strike the boats. It was about as large as a hind-quarter of beef. I heard it strike the water, I went down the railroad by the slaughter house and over Market Street Bridge and down to Seventeenth street, I stood around Seventeenth st. and then went down Pine street to Broad. I stood around there a while with some white fellows and then went home about eleven o'clock. I did not see Mrs. Tabbs again that night after I threw the things overboard. I didn't see Mrs. Tabbs again until I saw her in the police station February 23. As I was going over to tie things up I saw a clock in a tavern near the bridge and it was nearly half-past eight o'clock.

George Henry Wilson

The above statement was made in our presence and, after being reduced to writing, was read to George H. Wilson, who pronounced it correct.

Francis R. Kelly
John B. Moffitt
James Tate[11]

In the coming days, there would be much debate about what transpired while Wilson was in custody and whether undue pressure from authorities resulted in a confession that lacked veracity. In the immediate aftermath of his damaging "confession," however, police worked feverishly to conclude their investigation by producing evidence that corroborated their theory and timeline for the crime, and authorities and the media produced images of Wilson's mixed race that damaged his credibility.

With a statement placing him at the scene of the crime and claiming knowledge of the missing remains, Detectives Miller and Tate wasted no time in searching the named locations. The two reached the Callowhill Street Bridge by 3 p.m., with Wilson in tow. Reportedly Wilson told the detectives, "If I were at the bridge I would show you at once." Apparently, the detectives took him up on the offer and, according to accounts, he led them to an area roughly thirty feet from the bridge, where he claimed to have initially buried the head, arms, and legs of Wakefield Gaines.[12]

As the three men walked along the bridge, Wilson reportedly told authorities of the difficulties he faced in finding an "open place in the river south of the bridge" because there were two canal boats tied up there. Accounts described Wilson as exuding a measure of satisfaction when he pointed to a dark spot on the planks, spots made by "blood from the gory package."[13] He reportedly explained to the detectives, "I managed at last . . . to shove the bundle off so as to clear the boats and after a splash when it struck the water it sank out of sight, and I hurried back home." Although the boats he referenced had been moved, harbor police confirmed that there were in fact two canal boats docked in that location a week earlier. But other reports countered those appearing in the *Times* and the *Evening Bulletin*, as the *Public Ledger* reported that Wilson recanted, saying, "They may search the river until their hair turns gray before they will find [the remains]—so far as I know."[14]

Still, using his purported confession and subsequent information about the disposal of Gaines's remains, authorities quickly requisitioned the police tugboat, the *Samuel G. King*, to drag the river. Detective Crawford would prove especially important for this aspect of the investigation, not only because he was a seasoned member of the team but also because he had worked as a harbor police officer early in his career. The police began operations just after 4 p.m. and concluded sometime around 7 p.m. with a plan to resume the following morning. Throughout the search Wilson reportedly watched the movements with more intensity than anyone else, and one paper noted that he had gone so far as to give "directions to assist the men."[15]

Amid lingering skepticism that any remains would be recovered, Chief Kelly worked to temper the public's expectations. He gave a lengthy explanation: "We may not be able to recover the head, arms and legs, which undoubtedly are in the river... for several days, and possibly never. There was an extraordinary rainstorm on Friday night, followed by a great freshet, and it probably moved the bundle from where it sank. Another thing, Wilson in his haste may not have fastened the three packages and bricks together tightly, and if this was the case and they came apart they would drift more easily with the

Figure 4.2. "Schuylkill River Police Boat, *Samuel G. King*," *The Philadelphia Police*. Courtesy of the Historical Society of Pennsylvania (Call #UPA/Ph HV 8148.P5 S67 1887).

rapid current during the freshet." Kelly went on to add, "But we will leave nothing undone to find them if they are within reach."[16] However, police investigators had to contend with more than the rainstorm. The search was also impeded by a rocky, jagged riverbed that dogged recovery efforts. At the same time, both the press and local residents scrutinized police efforts.

During the first day of the search, *Evening Bulletin* reporters managed to question Wilson about reports that he had attempted suicide while in custody earlier that day, to which he responded, "I am not ready to die yet." Seizing on the opportunity to speak with a murder suspect during an ongoing investigation, reporters showed Tabbs's confession to the young man. Apparently it was the first time he was fully made aware of it. According to the account, Wilson replied, "Yes, most of that is true, but some things said there are not right." When questioned specifically about the erroneous information, Wilson reportedly explained, "Well, it was this way: Gaines and me was fighting, and when it was over he turned to leave me, and then I brought the chair down on the back of his head with a whack. That broke his skull and he fell down. I did not hit him after that, and I didn't cut the body up as she [Mrs. Tabbs] says." This statement certainly provided fodder for the public, accuracy notwithstanding, but the spectacle of the police tugboat dragging the river proved equally engaging.[17]

In spite of the crowds and less-than-ideal crime scene conditions, the *Samuel G. King*, which had been moored at the southeastern side of the eastern end of Callowhill Bridge, resumed searching for a second day. A flotilla of canal boats just to the south of the bridge hindered search efforts, but searchers still managed to dredge about one hundred square yards, which brought up remnants of calico that had supposedly contained the remains. It was likely that the remains themselves, if in fact dumped there, may have drifted beneath the flotilla that blocked tug efforts. Still, the yawls, manned alternatively by a number of officers, including Lieutenant Francis and Detective Crawford, did unearth a number of unrelated items aside from the calico. Detective Crawford proved "most successful in bringing to the surface the mysteries of the river bottom," included among them: a boiler head, a shovel, a hoopskirt, and a waterlogged plank.[18] Although the crew remained somewhat optimistic about the possibility of recovering Gaines's remains, recent investigations suggested otherwise. Earlier that year, when a man fell off the bridge and drowned, his body was located some eight miles away, opposite Fort Delaware. The preceding year when a man fell from the bridge close to where Wilson allegedly dumped the remains, his body was discovered roughly a mile away, along Christian Street. Further complicating the search that day were the high winds that had begun to pick up, adding chop to the water.[19]

Although efforts to drag the river failed, investigators were making great progress in locating material evidence from the search of Wilson's home and place of employment. At 1241 Lombard Street, Wilson's aunt's home and his residence, investigators found a trunk that appeared to contain clothing related to the case. Specifically, the trunk contained an old pair of pantaloons that were covered with blood, reportedly with "splotches from the bottom to the knees." Investigators also found a light coat and vest in similar condition. Additionally, heavy cord that matched that of the torso wrapping was discovered. As if the discovery of these items did not appear to seal the case against Wilson, the police also recovered a bloody meat saw. Fine toothed and roughly ten inches in length, the saw could have easily cut through human tissue. In this case, it fit the description of possible weapons that could have severed Gaines's limbs and head.[20]

Just as the case seemed airtight, Wilson's family and friends rallied around him and provided an alibi that made it all but impossible for him to have been involved in the crime. The first step in the effort to save Wilson came when his family retained George S. Costa to represent him. Costa was, at twenty-six, a relatively young man and a native-white Philadelphian, though his father emigrated from England. Costa grew up around South Fifteenth Street at 1418 Ellsworth Street. His father was a salesman, while his mother stayed at home. His younger brother worked as a servant at the same time that the family had a boarder from Ireland, Susan Cannon.[21]

Almost immediately upon taking the case, Costa told the media that he had "indisputable evidence" that, on the day of the murder, Wilson was hard at work. Essential to this defense would be the information given by Wilson's employers, Joseph Mattheas and William Lee, who ran the upholstery shop on the first floor of 1241 Lombard Street, downstairs from Wilson and his aunt Martha Wallace. When they learned of Wilson's training in caning, a skill he learned at the House of Refuge, they decided to employ the young man. Intelligent and hard-working, Mattheas, described as a mulatto, migrated to Philadelphia from Bangor, Maine. He possessed a high school diploma as well as his trade skills in upholstery. He started working in upholstery in 1879 and by 1882 had established his own business on Lombard Street. Lee joined the partnership two years later and, like Mattheas, he proved to be intellectually talented and industrious. With their impeccable reputations in the city, the men counted among their clients a bank president, a surgeon, and the posh Bellevue Hotel. This would prove especially important, as their statements would place them at odds with police and many in the general public.[22]

Although initially telling investigators that they were uncertain as to Wilson's whereabouts, Mattheas and Lee would later state unequivocally that on the day in question Wilson was at work in the shop from 8:30 a.m. until 6:30 p.m. They would assert that it was virtually impossible for him to have committed or participated in the brutal slaying. Lee would claim that he had not taken his eyes off Wilson from at least 10 a.m. until 6:20 p.m. He went so far as to state, "If I were on the stand in court and George Wilson were to take the stand before me and say 'I killed Wake Gaines' on Wednesday and carried away his arms, legs, and head and threw them in the Schuylkill River,' I would still be compelled to swear that from ten o'clock Wednesday morning until twenty minutes past six Wednesday night George Wilson was not out of my sight but for fifteen minutes, when he was downstairs below my workshop eating dinner." Mattheas told a similar story and added that a letter carrier came into the shop somewhat confused because he had mail addressed to someone he did not believe lived at that particular address.[23]

This confusion would align with the fact that Wilson had only moved in with his aunt a month or so earlier, as he testified at his arraignment. Before residing at 1241 Lombard he lived on Helmuth Street, around the corner from the Tabbs's residence. Mattheas explained to the carrier, "The address is right; there's the man at work." According to Mattheas, the letter carrier handed the postal card directly to Wilson and thus would serve as an additional witness. The carrier would be extremely important for the defense because unlike Mattheas and Lee, whom many suspected of lying to protect Wilson, the carrier had no reason to fabricate an alibi. Despite suspicions about his and Lee's motives, Mattheas tried to make clear that it did not matter to him "whether Wilson is guilty or not. The boy was employed by me and that is all I have to do with him, but I am bound to tell the truth. I am not concerned in clearing him further than this, and when I am put upon the witness stand and have taken an oath, I will tell only the truth, and the truth is exactly as I have said to you." Moreover, in addition to the letter carrier, both Mattheas and Lee told reporters that one of their customers who was having a chair reupholstered "saw George Wilson here and will be able to testify to that effect."[24]

Further, Herbert Galloway of 1236 Anita Street told reporters that on February 16, "I had some work that I could not do myself, as it was, not exactly in my line, so I took it to Mattheas & Lee's place, at

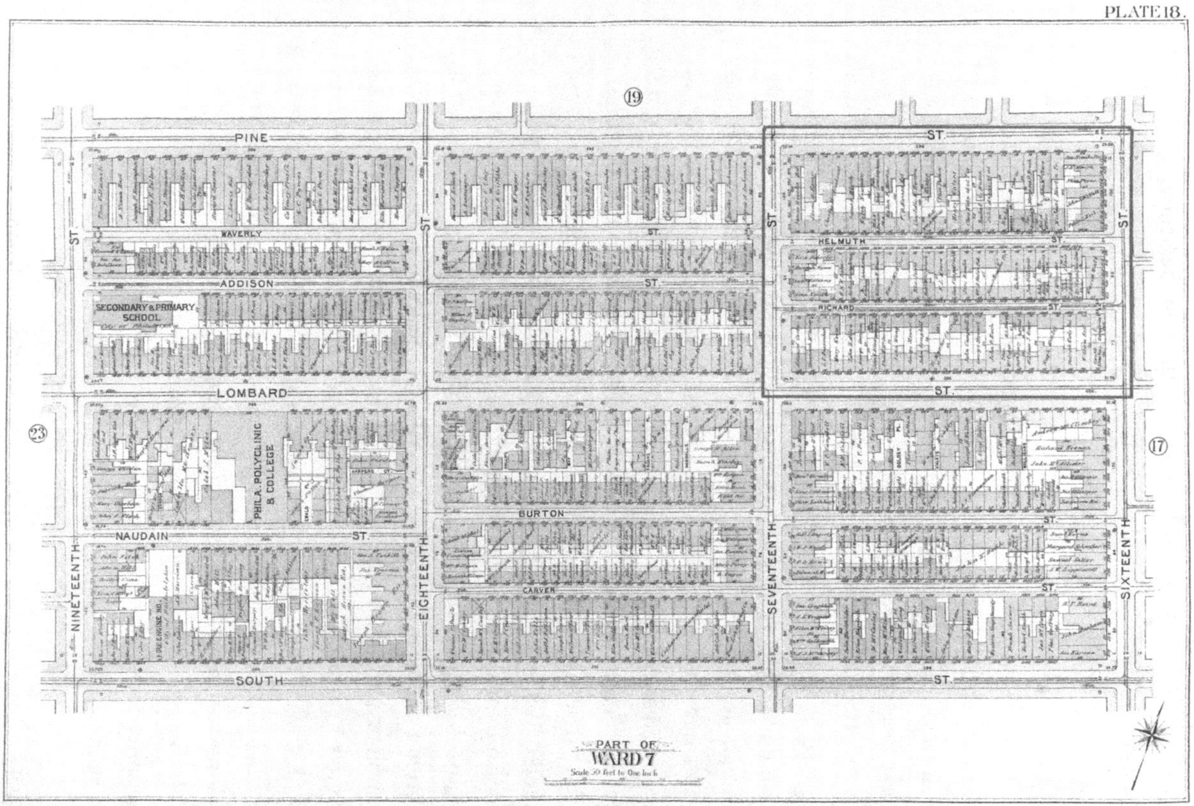

Figure 4.3. Map: Richard and Helmuth Streets. 7th Ward. Philadelphia. From *Atlas of the City of Philadelphia*. Courtesy of the Historical Society of Pennsylvania (Call #O-728 v. 2.1896).

1241 Lombard Street, as I knew I could do it there. While there I saw George Wilson at work, and I am ready and willing to swear to it." Reporters would later track down the letter carrier, John Delaney. He explained, "I am positive as to its being Wednesday when I delivered the card, because that was the only day I worked that week. Mr. Mattheas came to the door, and I asked if he had a George Wilson there, as I had another George Wilson on my route, on Lombard Street near Broad. He said, 'Yes, George Wilson is inside now.' I am positive of this and can swear it."[25]

But what of the bloody clothes and potential murder weapon that investigators recovered from Wilson's home? Wilson's employers mentioned that before he worked for them, he worked in the abbatoir as a butcher and may well have stained his clothes "in a legitimate way while he was engaged in that work." Further, the men seemed to undermine the effort of the investigators, stating that the police did not recover the coat in some old trunk. Rather Lee himself brought the coat to the authorities and pointed out the questionable stains on it. Lee also told reporters that he directed the investigators to the saws that they use. He explained, "I showed them these marks and said, 'This may be blood,' but in all probability they were glue marks. It would be a hard matter for anyone to tell the difference between blood marks and those of glue marks." The men also denied reports that a cleaver had been missing from their shop stating, "We never had any cleaver and so none could be missing." Still, neither Mattheas nor Lee could make sense of why Wilson would be confessing to the crime and participating in police searches.[26]

They did, however, make note of the fact that Wilson was somewhat simple, or "weak-minded," as other relatives alleged. Concerns about Wilson's mental fitness surfaced fairly early, as the court asked the prison physician who treated him for his seizure whether his mind was strong. Dr. Angney replied, "I would not like to say that he is an imbecile or insane, but he certainly does not look bright mentally."[27] Lee stated that Wilson was "a boy whom I would say is just not right, and he was very fond of notoriety. Mrs. Tabbs may possess some strong influence over him, and this may account for the way he is acting." Lee also took issue with the way that the press and authorities were using Wilson's time at the House of Refuge against him. He pointed out that George Wilson was placed in that institution as a nine year old not because of criminal activities or violence but because "he did not go to school and [his aunt] was very poor and could not take care of him." Lee added that he came out of the institution some two years ago and "has been a good boy since."[28]

Reports would surface on Saturday, February 26, 1887, that Wilson, from his cell, remarked that there was "not one word of truth in the confession" and that he had been tortured into a "nervous fit" by the detectives who coerced the statement from him. The physician who treated Wilson also stated that "he was probably in an extremely nervous fit from the effects of fright."[29] According to Wilson, he acquiesced "to save myself from being deviled to death." He added, "I admitted everything they charged me with. I went to Callowhill Street Bridge just to get a bit of fresh air." The *Evening Bulletin* claimed to have an informant who reportedly said that "Detective Crawford went to Wilson in his cell at the Fifth District Police Station and told the prisoner that he (Crawford) knew that Wilson knew all about the murder and had disposed of the head and limbs." The unnamed source claimed that Wilson told of being questioned repeatedly as to whether he threw the remains over the Chestnut Street Bridge and then the Market Street Bridge. Finally, when they got to the Callowhill Street Bridge Wilson said that he would say no more—tiring from the questions—and that it was Crawford who leaped to the conclusion that he was answering in the affirmative. Crawford called in Detective Tate who pursued the line of questioning more ardently, the two thinking that they were on to something about the Callowhill

Street Bridge. Then, in a fit of exasperation Wilson responded saying, "Well, if you will have it that way, I guess you will find them there."[30]

The anonymous informant, possibly a member of the defense team leaking crucial information to discredit the prosecution's case, further charged that once the head was recovered it would show that "a pistol ball, or keen knife across the throat of the victim, had caused death." The account noted that the male informant also lingered on the fact that Tabbs had lied a number of times in her purported confession, specifically about giving Wilson the victim's clothes to pawn—clothes that police discovered that Tabbs herself had pawned with the help of her young neighbor, Hattie Armstrong.[31]

Wilson's family and friends were not the only ones speaking to the press on his behalf. William F. Church, the assistant superintendent at the House of Refuge, would also share his opinion of the young man publicly. Church said that he "distinctly remembered" Wilson as a very industrious boy who was generally well behaved, but who had a "fierce temper." Still, he hastened to add that from his recollection, "Wilson was never guilty of any acts of violence as a result of this strong temper."[32] Records of Wilson's time at the House of Refuge are fairly scant, yet the few documents remaining provide a glimpse into the difficult circumstances of his childhood and the nature of cyclical incarceration.

Established in 1828, Philadelphia's House of Refuge was the third specialized institution for juveniles, following those founded in New York in 1825 and Boston in 1826. Its inmates—children who were more often "neglected than depraved"—were pressed into apprenticeships, placed in orphanages, or, worse, incarcerated with adult offenders. Whereas the institution in New York, and to a lesser extent the one in Boston, actually tried to serve as a refuge for impoverished and neglected youth, Philadelphia's House of Refuge functioned as little more than a prison in design and principle. It did, however, offer some schooling and training in certain trades.[33] As the institution initially served only white children, by 1850 the city had opened a House of Refuge for Colored Children. Located on Williams Street, below College Avenue, the institution was a "neat structure of plain brick," with approximately 102 "cells or dormitories, two schoolrooms, two large dining-rooms, and a kitchen," in addition to a chapel and an infirmary. Its establishment marked the evolution of the city's local black community as much as it mapped their struggle with poverty.[34]

At the time of its founding, antebellum Philadelphia had begun to witness the growing presence of free blacks. Largely the result of the state's 1780 Act for the Gradual Abolition of Slavery, the statute mandated that the children of enslaved blacks born after its passage would be indentured servants until freed in their mid- to late twenties, depending on gender. While the numbers of freed blacks increased during and after 1808, blacks' social status followed a more turbulent trajectory. Black men were granted the right to vote in the 1790 constitution, yet, in the same year Philadelphia established the nation's first penitentiary. Not only would blacks be disproportionately represented at the Walnut Street Jail and Penitentiary House but they also would be overrepresented among the city's destitute masses. As racial turmoil flared in the antebellum city, blacks steadily lost ground. Black and white abolitionists especially suffered a devastating blow when their newly completed meetinghouse, Pennsylvania Hall, stood only a few days before a mob of racist whites burned it to the ground in 1838. By the 1840s black men in the state were effectively disenfranchised, while Pennsylvania and the rest of the nation granted white men universal suffrage.[35] Still, as early industrialization fueled the tide of European ethnic immigrants and urban expansion, native-born whites started to focus their attention on maintaining social order in an increasingly heterogeneous society, and a number of citizens viewed children as the "key to social control."[36]

In light of this objective, the program implemented in both houses of refuge aimed at retraining youth, educating them, and instilling

Protestant moral values—but also incarcerating those children deemed potentially dangerous or otherwise harmful to society.[37] Yet racism stunted educational and programming opportunities in the House of Refuge for Colored Children. Black children were primarily trained for menial labor and domestic service; some even cleaned the grounds of the House of Refuge designated for white children. Just how much benefit black children could reap remained a central concern, as most of the proponents of the institution saw black children as both uniquely debased and woefully underserved. As one pamphlet noted of black children, "opportunities for improvement in morals or useful learning of any kind, we know to be extremely limited... in the habits and associations of the lowest grade there is an assimilation to the irrational animals—which, if seen among whites, would excite universal commiseration." Still, if an intervention could be made early enough in a youth's life, white reformers believed that they could transform the children from potential criminals to law-abiding servants, particularly by removing them from homes and neighborhoods seen to foster lasciviousness and vice.[38]

However, the House of Refuge for Colored Youth quickly found itself overcrowded and often understaffed. Black children came to the facility by way of the court, but their own family members also committed a significant number of them, citing "incorrigibility" as the primary reason. Such was the case of George Wilson. But "incorrigibility" seems to have been coded language for black families, as the underlying reason for this type of confinement seemed principally to be abject poverty.[39] Given a choice, many black families used this option to spare children from hunger and homelessness. In Wilson's case, the need for this type of confinement spanned generations, as he was not the first in his family to be the beneficiary of this refuge.

Born in New Haven, Connecticut, around 1869, George Henry Francis Wilson was the illegitimate child of Mary Francis, a black woman, and George Wilson Sr., a white man. Mary Francis had been an inmate of the House of Refuge for Colored Children in Philadelphia before her release and subsequent relocation. Whatever the nature of her relationship with George's father, records indicate that he had separated from the family sometime after his son's birth and before Mary's death on January 3, 1876.[40] Young George then went to live with maternal relatives before being committed to the House of Refuge for the first time on November 22, 1876, by his aunt, then listed as Martha Salters. She charged that he was absent from school, engaged in "pilfering," and was generally incorrigible. Prior to his confinement, George had attended a school at the House of Industry, where he learned some reading and writing skills in addition to learning how to "cipher," or do arithmetic. George was an inmate for six years until he was released into the custody of his aunt on May 11, 1882. On June 6, 1883, Magistrate Findley recommitted Wilson to the House of Refuge based his aunt's complaint of incorrigibility again. He would serve another two years before being released again in his late teens into his aunt's custody on April 9, 1885.[41] By the time he left the House of Refuge permanently, George could read and write well and could multiply and do fractions. He also learned chair caning as a trade.[42] Despite press reports of epileptic seizures accounting for his being unconscious in his prison cell, early health records indicate that he was a fairly robust lad who, prior to being committed to the House of Refuge, was "always well," though he did suffer from whooping cough upon his initial arrival.[43]

While admissions rosters and health records do not allow for a more nuanced telling of an inmate's history, Wilson's life was clearly marked by hardship and loss. Although his father had not abandoned him entirely, he did not appear to be in a position to care for his son. George Wilson Sr. had died roughly a year before the torso case in a rented room at 531 Lombard Street. A report noted that in going through his father's personal items, Wilson discovered a "life insurance receipt book, but found that his father had only made two payments of dues and that it was worthless." In the end, George Wilson sold what little his father had for "thirty-five cents to a second-hand man."[44] Moreover, losing his mother so early in life likely left him with deep-seated emotional issues. His difficulties adjusting to life with his aunt immediately following his mother's death point to a child struggling with the pain of bereavement as well as the extended family's financial troubles. Being committed to the House of Refuge seems almost a cruel irony though, given his mother's former placement.]

Mary Francis would have been among the first wave of black youth to enter the newly established facility. The House of Refuge for Colored Children was so overcrowded in its first years of operation that the managers immediately appealed for money to add another 125 beds. Even after this goal was met, overcrowding plagued the institution, contributing to a disproportionately high death rate for black children. In 1858, eight black children died from what administrators attributed to the "law of climate" and presumably their weakened constitutions resulting from "intermixture" of the races.[45] Some twenty years later, George Wilson, like his mother, would also witness the deaths of classmates as his record noted that a schoolmate in 1879 "died of consumption."[46]

The children also endured a fairly strenuous regimen. They rose at 7 a.m. during winter months and 5 a.m. during the summer. They had a breakfast of rye-coffee with milk and molasses before working for the better part of the morning. After a noon lunch of meat and vegetables, they worked again from one until four. They received supper, mostly mush and molasses, and then attended school until bedtime at eight. The austerity of the program did not proceed without contest, as many of the inmates disobeyed the rules, ran away, and occasionally took to setting small fires. In response to such behavior teachers and administrators deployed a variety of punishments, including flogging, isolation in dark cells, and being forced to stand during meals. In 1875, the institution was investigated for "cruelties and abuses," and many children testified to having been whipped and denied meals.[47]

How formative this kind of seasoning was is reflected in the records of roughly 30 percent of the recidivists at Eastern State Penitentiary, many of whom listed the House of Refuge as their first form of confinement. Moreover, some magistrates harbored deep concerns about the House of Refuge and worried "that the term during which children must remain in the House, i.e. until twenty-one years of age, is so long as to inflict an undue penalty for small misdemeanors."[48] It did for a time appear to have some benefit for Wilson, as he left the refuge literate and equipped with a trade that allowed him to find work with Mattheas and Lee.

While a battery of reputable men and women who supported Wilson's timeline of events bolstered the defense, Mattheas and Lee also had information that linked Wilson to Tabbs. Although Wilson was at work on the day of the murder, Mattheas recalled that roughly a week before, Wilson had returned "with a woman's coat and hat, which he said his girl in Darby had given him to give to Emmy, his cousin. He gave this coat and hat to Emmy, but afterward took them from her and hid them. I have given them to the detectives."[49] The story seemed to confirm Hannah Mary Tabbs's account of having given Wilson clothing that she believed was going to her niece, but which Wilson apparently kept for women in his family. This suggested that Wilson may have been exploiting Tabbs, and this connection did in fact tie him to the case.

Amid what appeared to be an evolving set of circumstances, Hannah Mary Tabbs and George Wilson returned to court on Monday, February 28, 1887. As at their preliminary hearing, their second appearance drew significant numbers of everyday citizens, especially from the Seventh Ward and around the blocks where Tabbs and Wilson resided. To manage the anticipated crowd, court officers moved the trial time from its initial morning slot to that afternoon.

Accounts noted that scores of African Americans, described as "denizens of Lombard, Richard, and other small streets," were most disappointed. They had arrived before 9 a.m., hoping to secure good seats in the courtroom and they hovered at Fifth and Chestnut Streets outside Central Station. By the time the big hands of the statehouse clock indicated a quarter to the hour a sizable crowd stood poised to enter. Blacks, reportedly wearing "their Sunday best," had taken the day off to witness the spectacle. The guard at the front door called for reinforcements to disperse the crowd as the prospective audience was initially unwilling to move.[50]

Although a few wandered away, the vast majority of would-be spectators waited until 2 p.m. to catch a glimpse of the alleged murderers and to take in the lurid details of the case. Rather than dissuading large crowds, the delay allowed time for newcomers to get in line. By all accounts, they were not disappointed. The hearing would include a glimpse of the chair allegedly used in the commission of the crime, in addition to bloody clothes, saws, and cleavers. The volleying between the state and the defense was probably the most exciting feature, however. Based on defense preliminaries, Wilson appeared to have an almost airtight alibi, thanks to the statements provided by his employers and that of a number of corroborating witnesses. Plus, Wilson's claims of police brutality undermined the credibility of his now-infamous confession.[51]

Yet suspicions about the boy lingered. His work in the abattoir coupled with his purported knowledge of the whereabouts of Tabbs's niece clung to him—indeed, the whole convoluted business did not look good. Moreover, Wilson's whiteness somehow was taken as evidence against him. Whereas crime reports typically invoked whiteness to indicate innocence, with victims often described as lighter than assailants, for Wilson it stirred doubt and an undercurrent of hostility. That he "possessed scarcely one feature to attest [to] his African descent" made him appear duplicitous.[52] Scores of papers would similarly note, with alarm and incredulity, "As has been said, he looked more like a Hebrew than a negro, and his hair, while curly and black, is still not so tightly curled as is that of the negro."[53] Additionally, accounts depicted him as shabby, yet with a curious, almost aloof disposition. As one piece noted, "The whiteness, or at least, the lightness of his skin and the vacant, uninterested expression of his face were the most noticeable features about him."[54]

Anxieties about white blacks moving around undetected undoubtedly ratcheted up as one such representative now stood accused of a most heinous crime. Moreover, Wilson's evident ability to pass even made its way into his published, albeit hotly contested, confession. After he allegedly dumped the arms and legs, it said Wilson returned to Seventeenth Street and "stood around there a while with some white fellows" before going home around eleven.[55] This line about Wilson circulating among whites, whatever its origin, effectively implicated him in another kind of deception that played on white fears of infiltration. What made Wilson's whiteness so worrisome was that it not only troubled white racial authority but also it meant that he had at his disposal the ability to "mobilize race for various self-authorized ends."[56]

Further, although his allegations of coercion cast doubt on the veracity of the confession and a number of decent, hard-working men and women were set to provide him with an alibi, there was one significant hitch. Mary Bailey, who lived almost directly across from Hannah Mary Tabbs on Richard Street, testified that she saw Wilson leaving Tabbs's home on the day Gaines died. She told the court:

On Wednesday, the day of the murder, I was washing. I know it was Wednesday, because I always wash on that day and on no other. My front door was open and I could see right over to Mrs. Tabbs's house. From 9 o'clock until half past nine, I saw Gaines, whom I knew by sight, sitting at the window reading a paper. A little while before that I saw him go out with a pitcher as though going for beer. I heard no noise of a quarrel, and know nothing further than that sometime after ten o'clock, I think between eleven and twelve, I saw George Wilson come out of the house carrying a bundle which was carried with light brown paper. He carried it by the string and away from him, instead of in his arms.

I have often seen George Wilson and known him to speak to. He lived for some time in the neighborhood and this is the way I know him. When he came out of the house he looked neither to the right or the left, but started up Richard street towards Seventeenth. I saw no one else about Mrs. Tabbs's house that day.[57]

Bailey's testimony linked Wilson to the crime and sounded fairly credible, given her memory of the day relating to her weekly household chores and the fact that she knew Wilson from the neighborhood—not just on Richard Street, but from Helmuth Street where they had both lived.[58]

Bailey was not the only resident from Richard Street to take the stand. Hattie Armstrong would also offer crucial information into evidence. In addition to describing the first trip to the pawnshop on Tabbs's behalf, she also explained:

Wednesday afternoon Mrs. Tabbs sent for me to do an errand. I went to her house and she gave me a bundle, telling me to pawn it and get $2. I took it to Cohen's pawnshop at Seventeenth and Bainbridge streets, where it was opened. It contained a blue vest, a blue pair of pantaloons, also a brown pair, a short, black coat, and an overcoat. I got $1.50 on them and gave it to Mrs. Tabbs. She gave me a quarter for my trouble. When I went into her house everything seemed to be in disorder. I thought she had been washing. She kept rubbing her eyes nervously. On Thursday she sent for me again and gave me a pair of men's shoes and a blue silk dress, telling me to pawn them. She gave me a basket to carry them in and a pitcher to carry to look as though I were going for milk. She then took me to the gate and let me out the alleyway. I took the things to Hunt's pawnshop, at Sixteenth and Bainbridge, and got ten cents on the hatchet, fifty cents on the shoes and sixty cents on the dress. I took this back to Mrs. Tabbs and she gave me ten cents. The hatchet was new and the dress was a very nice one.

Monday morning she came to the court here and called "Hattie! Hattie!" before I was out of bed. I got up and went out to her and she told me she wanted me to pawn something for her. She took me over to her house and gave me a blue silk dress. "I have got to go into the country," she said, "to see about Wake Gaines. Something is the matter with him and George Wilson is the cause of it." I pawned the dress and got two dollars for it. This is all I knew about the matter.[59]

Hattie's testimony certainly tied Tabbs to the crime and it also raised suspicion about Tabbs's conduct. Clearly, she was getting rid of evidence related to the crime as well as concealing her role in it. Tabbs's attempt to raise money to return to Eddington also points to a deliberate and perhaps desperate attempt to implicate Wilson.

While distancing herself from the murder, Tabbs could have been trying to lay the groundwork to implicate the actual guilty party, except that she had a pattern of blaming others for her actions. When she went to Eddington she told reporters that she believed George Redding had something to do with her niece's disappearance, though later interviews would reveal that Annie Richardson ran away from Tabbs out of fear for her safety. Armstrong's testimony, then, could point to a pattern of Tabbs leveling false accusations in an effort to shift blame—especially to those men whom she might have perceived as crossing the line when it came to her niece. Recall that Wilson seemed to be scamming Tabbs for money and clothes that he had no intention of giving to Annie Richardson and Tabbs's interview in Eddington implicating George Redding in the girl's disappearance contained statements suggesting that he was critical of how Tabbs reared her niece.[60]

On the day of the second hearing, Tabbs had to accomplish two tasks. At noon Detectives Miller and Tate removed her from her cell and escorted her to the local coroner's office to identify the exhumed torso as that of Wakefield Gaines. The detectives had taken preemptive measures in the hopes of avoiding crowds, but their decision to usher her out the side entrance through Independence Square and up Sansom Street proved futile. The trio had scarcely gone one hundred feet before people filled the block. Pushing through the throng of reportedly "several hundred colored men and women," the detectives managed to deliver Tabbs to the office, where she identified both the torso and the shawl strap that she used to carry the gruesome bundle. Tabbs also identified the piece of dress as having belonged to her niece Annie Richardson.[61]

Upon making the identification, the detectives, with the help of four stalwart officers, once again made their way with Wilson and Tabbs in tow. Once in the hearing room Tabbs was seated at the prisoner's dock at the western end of the bench; Wilson sat at the other end, leaving some six feet of distance between them. The media examined every aspect of the duo. Accounts noted that Tabbs was neatly dressed in deep black, as though in mourning, and looked like anything "but a person likely to commit so horrible a crime as that which she is accused." Tabbs seemed a combination of timidity and frailty. She remained with her eyes cast down.[62]

Her counterpart, however, appeared to be fascinated with the attention. Reports described him as looking around, taking in the packed courtroom with "a half curious way as though to learn the effect his presence was creating."[63] At the same time, he seemed not to comprehend fully the gravity of his situation. The *Evening Bulletin* perhaps best described it: "There was an utter absence of seriousness in his appearance, and if for one moment he appreciated the terrible nature of the charge pending against him, he effectually concealed it."[64] From the start of the hearing until its conclusion, Wilson gazed around the room from his seat on the bench wearing an expression interpreted by many as nonchalance. The repulsive nature of the crime and his predicament notwithstanding, he seemed to have an "unconcerned manner," and his chewing of tobacco during the proceedings conveyed either cluelessness or arrogance. Neither of which helped his cause.[65]

Wilson's wonderment and odd fascination with what was taking place was matched not only by the crowds of African Americans—a great many Wilson's neighbors—eager to learn the lurid details of the crime but also by a broad cross section of law enforcement officers and local politicians. Newspapers noted with surprise that "the entire detective service, a goodly portion of the reserve corps, numerous lawyers and a score or more of Councilmen" were in attendance.[66]

The principal actors—one a black southern migrant and one a northern mulatto light enough to pass—embodied the complicated dynamics that the country, just twenty-two years removed from slavery, still struggled to negotiate. Tabbs, with her browner skin, pronounced southern drawl, and deferential manner in court had the potential to set white people at ease; possibly tapping into a type of nostalgia for bygone days, as Philadelphia popular culture, somewhat ironically given its location and Union affiliation, displayed a fascination with romantic notions of plantation life. Wilson, on the other hand, seemed poised to invoke everything that disturbed so many in the late nineteenth century—from his inscrutable blackness and seamless mobility between black and white spaces in the city to his unconcerned, almost haughty manner.[67] Though the pair occupied arguably the lowest rungs in society, their employment found them in close proximity to mainstream whites and, in Tabbs's case, middle- and upper-class white homes. Even Wilson, by virtue of employment with Mattheas and Lee, had come into contact with a diverse clientele of individual patrons as well as upscale hotels and businesses.

Yes, this case had something for everyone. Race, place, and gender aside, the more lurid aspects of the crime had the makings of a soap opera: the affair between Tabbs and Gaines, the missing niece, the turbulent rows between surreptitious lovers—even the blurry connection between Tabbs and Wilson promised an exposition of otherwise prohibited passions. For law enforcement officers the case was exciting from a purely investigative standpoint; what the authorities in Bucks and Philadelphia Counties were able to accomplish considering the initial obstacles and challenges was of profound interest.[68]

Those interests, however, would not yet be satisfied. With a packed courtroom and more crowds outside, there was a fairly brief exchange between the prosecutor and the defense. Magistrate Smith took his place and then commanded, "George Wilson, stand up." Smith then turned to Tabbs and instructed her to stand also. Both complied, and Smith called out, "Chief Detective Kelly." Chief Kelly rose and took his place in the witness box.

Kelly, in a voice hoarse with cold, asked the magistrate "to hold the two prisoners to await the action of the Coroner. The inquest will be held on Wednesday morning next at 11 o'clock." The magistrate agreed and then asked, "Mrs. Tabbs, you have no counsel?"

Tabbs replied, "No, sir."

Turning from Tabbs to I. Newton Brown, another attorney who signed on to Wilson's defense, Magistrate Smith inquired, "You represent Wilson, do you not?" He responded, "Yes sir. Mr. George Da Costa [sic] and myself are his counsel."

With that, Magistrate Smith concluded the hearing by announcing, "Both prisoners are remanded to prison to await the action of the Coroner."

Papers noted that Tabbs answered, "Yes sir!" Wilson said nothing, "but continued to chew his tobacco."[69] With that, police hastened to usher the two out of the courtroom.

Despite accounts of Wilson's supposed nonchalance, his actions after the hearing suggest that he did indeed grasp the severity of his predicament. Detective Tate, charged with taking him to the county prison, escorted Wilson outside. Tate walked Wilson up Sixth Street to Minor Street to obtain transportation. As they waited for a car, Wilson seized on the opportunity to break away from Tate and started heading down Minor Street as fast as he could. The detective gave chase and so, too, did a large group of spectators—all following close at his heels and yelling. At Fifth Street a worker from Smith's brewery ran out and hit Wilson on the head with a bung driver. Wilson was knocked to the ground, giving Tate the time to catch up and put "nippers on the prisoner's hands." Detective Tate then got Wilson in the car where he reportedly sat "sullenly with his hands before his face."[70]

The entire scene displayed Wilson's impulsiveness, fear, and desperation as he sensed that his only true chance to avoid being sent down for the crime was to flee. Although Wilson seemed to be on the precipice of despair, his attorneys were in no way ready to surrender. Releasing a statement to the press, Costa and Brown assured reporters that "as counsel for Wilson, we are not prepared to admit or deny anything, but when the Commonwealth bring proof or allegations to warrant a defense, we will be prepared to meet such proof or allegations."[71]

There were a great many people who wanted to help Wilson. Most did not believe that he was primarily responsible for Gaines's death, particularly those in the black community. Without hesitation or the usual trepidation blacks had when dealing with police, almost all pointed to Tabbs. If her history demonstrated anything, however, it was that Hannah Mary Tabbs was formidable and she possessed a fine-tuned understanding of race, power, and the politics of representation.

Chapter Five

Held for Trial

For a long time there has not been, in this city, a murder case with so many elements of the sensational kind, and with so much mystery surrounding it, as the Gaines case.

—*Evening Bulletin*, March 2, 1887

Located on the southwest corner of Seventh and Chestnut Streets, the coroner's office played a pivotal role in homicide investigations in Philadelphia after it was established in 1860. The coroner was tasked with investigating "all sudden, violent, or possibly suspicious deaths and, if circumstances warranted, to hold an inquest, eliciting medical and other testimony to determine the cause."[1] An elected official, the coroner worked in tandem with licensed physicians. These partnerships operated on a case-by-case basis before the coroner's physician became a staff position in the 1870s, though many of the appointed physicians also maintained private practices.[2] Inquests would typically be held at the coroner's office and a six-man jury would be convened to review evidence and hear testimony both from the attending physician and any other parties called. Verdicts would be forwarded to the courts and, if an outcome warranted, the coroner, usually working with the district attorney, would forward a case to the grand jury.[3]

The two men primarily in charge of the Gaines investigation were both dynamic, though infamy followed one, honor distinguished the other. Samuel Ashbridge, the coroner for the torso case, was a thirty-eight-year-old native Philadelphian. He had been educated in the city's public schools and after graduation "entered mercantile life as a clerk in a coal office" before becoming a coal dealer in his own right. Ashbridge ingratiated himself in public affairs and secured an appointment as deputy coroner in 1883 before being elected coroner three years later. His tenure lasted until 1899, when he was elected mayor of Philadelphia.[4] Known as "Stars-and-Stripes Sam," Ashbridge would go on to become one of the most corrupt leaders in the city. His mayoralty was so notorious that it not only garnered him substantial treatment in Lincoln Steffens's turn-of-the-century exposé, *The Shame of the Cities*, but also this epitaph from the Municipal League of Philadelphia when he left office: "The four years of the Ashbridge administration have passed into history, leaving behind them a scar on the fame and reputation of our city which will be a long time healing. Never before, and let us hope never again, will there be such brazen defiance of public opinion, such flagrant disregard of public interest, such abuse of powers and responsibilities for private ends."[5]

Unlike his employer, Dr. Henry Formad, the coroner's physician, proved to be a man of some distinction. Born in eastern Europe in 1847, Formad studied medicine at the University of Heidelberg before immigrating to America in 1875. He earned his medical degree from the University of Pennsylvania in 1877, and as a microscopist and pathologist, he began his work alongside Ashbridge in 1884. Throughout his time as the coroner's physician, Formad served as "Demonstrator of Morbid Anatomy and Pathological History and Lecturer on Experimental Pathology" at his alma mater.[6] Formad devoted his life to research and teaching, and his work on homicide investigations profoundly impacted both.[7] His 1888 book, *Comparative Studies of Mammalian Blood, with Special Reference to the Microscopical Diagnosis of Blood Stains in Criminal Cases*, contains lengthy discussions about distinguishing between animal and human blood as well as diagnosing dried blood at crime scenes, which he would draw on for his testimony during the Gaines case.[8]

Perhaps not surprising, the coroner's inquest on March 2 would ultimately lead to the grand jury indictment of both Tabbs and Wilson. The hearing, eagerly awaited by many, had doubled as a form of popular entertainment.[9] Almost as much as the courtroom functioned as a site for the administration of justice in the late nineteenth century, it also existed as a kind of stage or public platform featuring real-life morality plays. Often the validity of facts, or a given side's story, rested substantially on how well witnesses and defendants executed, frequently to dramatic effect, mainstream notions of race, gender, and sexuality—at least as determined by the white men tasked with rendering verdicts.[10] [As daunting as appearing before whites in a court of law could be for black men and women, offering testimony nonetheless gave blacks a chance to address the court as citizens and, in the process, potentially contest racist caricatures about black people.]

Even so, other factors impacted how witnesses would present to juries. Authorities could significantly mark suspects by how they guarded, transported, and either withheld prisoners from or exposed them to the press; such actions conveyed messages about guilt and innocence for the court and the public. Indeed, the hearings appeared to be a kind of synchronized performance enacted by police, spectators, witnesses, lawyers, juries, the judge, and the press. Even the accused played their respective parts; though Wilson proved a poor study opposite Hannah Mary Tabbs's starring role.

[Despite the fact that almost all of the parties involved in the Gaines murder were "colored," their comportment in terms of gender and in relation to whiteness and white authority weighed heavily on the proceedings. To begin with, all blacks battled commonly held assumptions about their criminality and general untrustworthiness. Black women especially had difficulty convincing whites of their innocence. Philadelphia juries had a long history of finding them guilty, as 72 percent of black women tried were found guilty and juries dismissed fewer of their cases—more so than any other group in the city. Even so, if they understood their respective places, or could appear to, they stood a better chance of being read as decent or honest.[12] Most who testified seemed keenly aware of this.]

[Wilson, however, came off almost immediately as a kind of affront to whiteness because the "taint of black blood" in him was so well hidden, though its presence nonetheless told of inherited impurities.]] Moreover, Chief Kelly and his men worked to make him the public face of the gruesome murder[In addition to associating him with passing and prior confinement, Kelly and his men handled and transported Wilson in a manner that cast him as guilty. Rather than bringing Wilson in through a side door, quickly and quietly, as they had Hannah Mary Tabbs roughly an hour earlier, police paraded Wilson before a restless crowd of several hundred people. Many craned their necks to see him, perhaps in a desperate bid to, as one report charged, "repay them for their trouble or lost time."[14] The spectators, both black and white, closed ranks, as Wilson was essentially "perp walked," flanked by a detective and a patrolman, directly through the throng to the front door of the coroner's office] Many of the onlookers taunted and shouted at him as he passed. Reportedly, Wilson ignored the jeers. The *Evening Bulletin* noted that he looked "as cool and unconcerned as possible"—press commentary reserved for the most unrepentant of criminals.[15]

Officers had barred laypersons from observing the inquest, though reporters, law enforcement, and witnesses filled the room roughly half an hour in advance of the proceedings. Silas Hibbs and a handful of Eddington witnesses attended. Chief Kelly and the investigating detectives were present, as were relatives of both Tabbs and Wilson. District Attorney George S. Graham and counsel for Wilson, attorneys Costa and Brown, garnered great interest from the crowd too. In addition to Tabbs and Wilson, the witnesses who met with greatest curiosity were Hattie Armstrong, rumored "to know much more than she will tell," along with Jane Cannon (Gaines's sister) and Mrs. Williams

(Gaines's landlady).[16] Wilson had been given a seat on the east side of the inquest room, and Reserve Officer Grace was detailed to watch him. Given Wilson's earlier attempt to flee, this extra precaution made sense though it likely further positioned him as dangerous, and perhaps by extension guilty. Wilson's demeanor would again become the subject of much speculation. According to press accounts, he sat back in his chair during much of the hearing exuding what many perceived as "the utmost indifference." His occasional chewing of tobacco, supplied by one of the detectives no less, also seemed off-putting to many.[17]

Jane Cannon took the stand first and epitomized virtuous womanhood. Despite giving testimony about the violence and adultery that punctuated her brother's relationship with Tabbs, Cannon embodied femininity and frailty. For example, she required assistance from her husband as she walked to the stand. Her lips twitched convulsively and, with great effort, "she raised the Bible to her lips" and, in a weak voice, explained that Wakefield Gaines was her brother and that he had been married in Seaford, Delaware.[18] She told the court about the last time she saw her brother alive. Apparently, Gaines had been excited about the election and had come to talk with her about it. Cannon asked about Tabbs and warned, "You had better look out or she will catch up with you."[19]

Coroner Ashbridge interrupted her testimony to ask: "What did you mean by catch up with him?"[20]

Mrs. Cannon explained: "Why, she had sent a letter saying that she would catch up with him if it took ten years. She fought with him the last night of December. She chased him into my house. She was at my house for him the same night earlier, and said that she had work for my brother." Cannon's testimony only added to the growing sentiment among residents of the Seventh Ward that Hannah Mary Tabbs was the real culprit. Moreover, Cannon's trauma over the loss of her brother was palpable and undoubtedly stirred strong emotions in many who witnessed the proceedings. At the conclusion of her testimony, "the witness was half carried from the stand by her husband, as she was too weak to walk."[21] The brutal nature of the crime and Cannon's obvious shock at her painful loss seemed to transcend customary racial boundaries in the media, in the sense that Cannon was treated sympathetically and her womanhood was highlighted. Typical coverage of black women, even those who were victims, usually followed a kind of racist stereotyping that depicted all black women as savage, sexually lascivious "colored amazons"—hulking, jet-black figures who jeopardized white urban life. Cannon managed to avoid this by embodying frailty and vulnerability.[22]

Silas Hibbs was next to take the stand and would, probably for the hundredth time since that day, recount the details of his ghastly find. He explained that he saw the package on the bank, half floating in water at about half past seven in the morning. Hibbs described his efforts to get the package, stating that once he secured and opened it: "I found it to contain the trunk of the body of a colored man, and sent for Squire Vandegrift and remained with the body until the Coroner took it away." Slightly more embellished than his earlier renditions, Hibbs's recollection of that day had evolved from shock and frenzied calls for help to one that depicted a more stoic commitment to safeguarding the disembodied torso—not leaving its side until it was in the hands of the proper authorities.[23] Perhaps Hibbs felt the need to showcase the caliber and mettle of folks from Eddington as the coroner's proceedings in Philadelphia seemed to all but eclipse the involvement of the first wave of investigators—men largely responsible for cracking the case.

Rather than hearing next from Coroner Silbert or Constable Jackson, the coroner's clerk, John Donal, took the stand and stated that he had traveled to Bristol to receive the trunk from the Bristol authorities. That trunk would later be identified by Hannah Mary Tabbs as that of Wakefield Gaines. Upon positive identification Donal gave the remains to Deputy Coroner Powers.[24] Chief Kelly was next on the stand, and his testimony also abridged the investigative efforts of the Bristol team. He explained:

> Having seen accounts in the papers of the body found at Eddington I watched the case closely. On the Saturday following Conductor Swain, of the Pennsylvania Railroad, came to me and told me about a woman who had gone up on his train on the night before the body was found. I thought the woman had something to do with it, and took steps to see who the woman was, and what became of her. I sent Detective Geyer to Eddington and Bristol to learn what he could about her. At the same time I received information from Mrs. Cannon that her brother had been missing since the Tuesday previous to the day when the body was found in Eddington. She also said that the body found at Eddington resembled that of her brother. She said that she suspected a Mrs. Tabbs of killing her brother. I took steps to secure this woman.[25]

Kelly then described his interview of Mrs. Tabbs, her confession, and subsequently that of Wilson:

> She said that she had gone to Eddington to see about her niece, which contradicted her statement made to Mrs. Williams, at 207 Schell Street, where Gaines boarded before she went to Eddington. She told Mrs. Williams that she was going to Bristol to see about Wake, as she thought the body found there must be his. I said nothing further to her that night. The next day Mrs. Tabbs sent for me, saying that she had a statement to make. I went at once to her and she made a statement implicating George Wilson, who was arrested at his home, 1241 Lombard Street. He denied all knowledge of the affair at first, but the day following his arrest made a partial statement to me, saying that he was at

Mrs. Tabbs's house, and had had a fight with Gaines and struck him on the head with a chair. He said that he then went away, leaving Gaines sitting on a settee, and had subsequently come back and received from Mrs. Tabbs what he thought to be the head of the murdered man, wrapped in paper, and afterwards got the arms and legs in the same way, Mrs. Tabbs telling him to throw them into the river. He said that he had thrown them into the Schuylkill River at Callowhill Street Bridge. Two days later he made a full statement in the presence of witnesses.[26]

The coroner inquired as to whether the chief and his men had recovered any other additional body parts. They had not. Following this line of questioning, the coroner asked, "In what points do the statement of the two prisoners disagree?" Chief Kelly explained, "While both agree as to the cause, time and place of the quarrel, they disagree as to the killing, Wilson denying that he killed the man."[27] Again, stating that Wilson had denied the murder, rather than stating that both Wilson and Tabbs had denied responsibility for the act, Kelly managed to link Wilson, more than Tabbs, to the murder.

Coroner Silbert and Dr. Evan J. Groom would then testify about being notified of the discovery of the torso. Silbert told of having the remains sent to Mr. Rue's undertaking establishment, where Dr. Groom performed a postmortem examination. They interred the body, only to subsequently exhume it and have it transferred to the Philadelphia coroner. The only additional information provided by Groom was that the flesh of the limbs had been cut with a knife and "the bones sawed." He testified that the killer or killers had to be accustomed to using a knife and a "saw of fine teeth."[28] Beyond this, Groom testified that the organs were healthy and in good condition.

Perhaps the most powerful testimony came from Conductor Swain, who told the coroner that on the date in question he "had a passenger who kept the window open. I asked her if she was sick. She said 'No.' She had two bundles, the large one enclosed in soft stiff; the smaller one I did not notice much."[29]

"Have you seen the woman since that time?" Coroner Ashbridge asked.

"Yes, once," Swain answered.

Ashbridge continued, "Do you see her in this room?" At this moment the room was deadly silent as the "people held their breath and craned their necks."[30]

"To the best of my knowledge and belief that is the woman." As Swain gestured toward her, Tabbs rose before him. Even as she stood in the courtroom accused of discarding a human torso, Tabbs did so in an unassuming manner. She was clad again in a deep black dress, "with both eyes on the floor."[31] By keeping her eyes cast downward Tabbs could at once signify female modesty (a direct gaze was considered forward) and racial deference—even after slavery southern blacks avoided eye contact with whites lest their behavior be considered inappropriate or uppity.[32] After Swain's identification, she sat a few short feet from Wilson. Although Wilson had remained somewhat impassive throughout the day's testimony, he seemed anxious to catch Tabbs's attention. As the *Times* reported, "The lad cast several wistful glances at her as though desirous of speaking to her."[33] Whatever his intentions, Tabbs never indulged him. She sat quietly through all of the testimony with her eyes "continually on the floor."[34] By maintaining this posture from earlier court appearances, Tabbs continued to situate herself as an aggrieved, troubled woman.

After Detectives Crawford and Geyer testified to witnessing Tabbs and Wilson give their statements at the stationhouse, Hattie Armstrong took the stand.[35] Hers was highly anticipated testimony, as many had come to believe that the teen held valuable clues about the inner workings of Tabbs's household and about the murder since it was widely known that she had visited the crime scene shortly after Gaines's demise.[36] Yet Armstrong's testimony offered little more than her previous police statements. She testified to having been contacted by Tabbs on two occasions to pawn clothing and a hatchet. She again testified that Tabbs asked her to hide some of the items in a pitcher so that "people would think I was going to market." However, Armstrong did add that she "never saw George Wilson there but once and that was two or three weeks ago."[37] After Armstrong's testimony, Coroner Ashbridge had a lengthy consultation with District Attorney Graham and Chief Kelly. Afterward, Graham rose and announced:

> As prosecuting attorney in this case and representing the com-
> monwealth, I ask you to hold the prisoners for the murder of
> Wakefield Gaines. Enough testimony has been produced, I think,
> to make a *prima facie case*, and in order that justice may be satis-
> fied, I ask that no further witnesses be called at this stage of the
> proceedings, as it is desirable that the testimony be not made
> public until the case comes into court.[38]

Coroner Ashbridge instructed the jury that it was their duty, "from the testimony produced," to find a verdict against the two prisoners. On cue, the six jurymen talked among themselves for a few moments before the foreman announced that "the jury find that Wakefield Gaines came to his death from blows inflicted by George H. Wilson, and that Hannah Mary Tabbs was an accessory to the act."[39] With that, Ashbridge made it official, stating for the record, "I will hold George H. Wilson [,] to await the action of the Grand Jury, on the charge of murdering Wakefield Gaines, and will also hold Hannah Mary Tabbs as an accessory to the crime." In some respects, it appeared as if Tabbs was already largely off the hook in spite of her motive and past attempts on the victim's life.[40]

By the time the hearing concluded, Seventh Street had been ren-dered impassable by a sea of policemen and spectators. Detectives Miller and Tate, however, slipped the prisoners out of the Chestnut

Street entrance and hurriedly walked toward Sixth Street. Though a group of men and boys briefly caught up to them, the party managed to return to the county prison without much fanfare.[41] This would be in stark contrast to the groundswell of press coverage that now followed the case. The days leading up to the trial witnessed Philadelphia's newspapers, and those from New York to Missouri, churning out a variety of articles aimed both at keeping the story alive and also educating the public about the next steps in the judicial process.[42] Most cases in Philadelphia at the time were investigated and adjudicated within roughly a week's time; more complicated cases lasted as long as a month. The Gaines case had already exceeded this period and aroused widespread curiosity about the legal proceedings themselves.[43]

Articles and opinion pieces began discussing the specifics of the case. One in particular, penned by local attorney William Conway, took great pains to clarify the legal application of the phrase *corpus delicti*. After explaining that it referred to "the body of the offense," Conway delved deeply into the case's more controversial aspects, such as the viability of the homicide based on a headless, limbless torso and Tabbs's hotly contested "confession." He conceded that a "mere confession" alone would not suffice, but that with corroboration and identification of the remaining body parts a charge could stand. Citing the 1882 Pennsylvania Supreme Court verdict in *Gray v. Commonwealth*, he explained that the principle spoke directly to the Gaines case, as the court held "that the *corpus delicti* was sufficiently proven by the finding of a human skull and jaw bone near the residence of the victim and evidence that a lock of hair still attached to the skull was similar to the hair of the deceased, while the jawbone was identified... by persons who recognized peculiarities in its structure." The ruling paralleled the positive identification given by Tabbs and Cannon, both describing Gaines as having peculiarly high shoulders. Yet the court in *Gray v. Commonwealth* also found that jurors needed to be certain that the *corpus delicti* had been established beyond a reasonable doubt before deliberating on other evidence such as confessions. Here Conway noted that confessions in general should be "received with great caution," because many had been made based on "ignorance, fear, hope and insane delusions."[44]

Aside from highlighting that sad fact, Conway's discussion ultimately touched upon two interrelated themes: even with the positive identification of the torso, authorities and the public alike remained uneasy about the missing remains; and *Gray v. Commonwealth* and the Gaines case both served as chilling reminders of the fragility of urban life, particularly that it was not terribly uncommon to find only bits and pieces of what was once a living human being. This troubling reality surfaced again in the days following Conway's legal treatise. On Saturday, March 12, 1887, the *Evening Bulletin* printed a story titled "The Gaines Remains." Coroner Ashbridge received a package of "flesh believed to be that of a human." The package was discovered on the preceding Wednesday by a locksmith who was making repairs on a small house—the location of which was withheld by the coroner. The former family living there was rumored to have moved out the day Tabbs made her confession, though other information suggested they were acting on orders to vacate by the owner. The property in question was one of a dozen owned by a prosperous real estate agent in the city. According to accounts, as workmen entered the house they immediately smelled a foul odor and, in an attempt to discern where the smell was coming from, located the package. Upon discovering the source of the stench they contacted the authorities and the coroner began an investigation.[45]

The package had been held together tightly with twine, similar to that used in the wrapping of the trunk, though these particular remains had been dumped into an old salt sack. Dr. Formad performed microscopic investigations to determine if the flesh was human and, if so, "whether or not it is that of a white man or a colored man." Coroner Ashbridge was fairly confident that they had located human remains; reportedly a good portion of the windpipe was intact despite the rest of the contents being badly decomposed. Moreover, according to the information already gathered, the coroner believed that Hannah Mary Tabbs had visited the previous residents frequently though they had not resided in the house for any great length of time. Apparently, their departure "was conducted with great secrecy, and none of the neighbors know whither they have gone." More than likely, the surrounding neighbors thought it best not to get involved.[46]

The listing agent was also particularly invested in keeping the whole ordeal quiet as he worried that "if the information should get abroad he would be unable ever to find tenants for the house, because of the wide spread superstition that exists amongst the colored population." While the agent fretted, the coroner concluded his search and found no additional evidence or clues as to the identity of the flesh.[47] But the discovery exists as ominous evidence just the same— namely that another black person had met a violent end and, in this instance, with no concerns about whether the victim was white, the case would probably go unsolved. This makes visible the true rarity of the Gaines case—that any sort of justice was an option at all.

On May 16, 1887, the grand jury indicted both Wilson and Tabbs for "MURDER." Mr. Costa appeared for Wilson and by this time Tabbs had also secured counsel, twenty-four-year-old Robert Ralston, Esquire, and twenty-eight-year-old Alfred Guillou, Esquire. Both were new attorneys; Ralston had completed his law degree at the University of Pennsylvania in 1885, the same year he was admitted to the bar. Tabbs and Wilson both pleaded not guilty.[48] Wilson would be tried first and, as the star witness in his case, Tabbs aimed to paint him as principally responsible for Gaines's death. To do so effectively, she would need to be credible, which meant appearing respectable in some manner. It would be a challenging feat considering her current predicament and a mountain of evidence to the contrary. Clothing and comportment, omission and outright lies would be the primary tools Tabbs would use to recast her image.

As officers ushered in the pair, Hannah Mary Tabbs was seated on a bench in front of the dock, and George Wilson sat to her left. Both received thorough scrutiny from reporters and everyone else who managed to cram into the courtroom. Throughout the impaneling of the jury Hannah Mary Tabbs, wearing a black worsted dress and a trimmed black straw hat, seemed to be tiring of her otherwise downward gazing facade as she reportedly sat with her head inclined to the right, showing an expression of "solid indifference."[49] Meanwhile, accounts never tired of marveling over Wilson's whiteness, as he reportedly looked more like "a Spaniard than a negro."[50] His attire received scathing coverage, with one article noting that Wilson wore dark clothes, described as "well worn and seedy," with a polka-dot necktie, "which throughout the morning was making strenuous endeavors to climb up over his collar."[51] He remained seated, as usual, chewing tobacco. Unlike accounts from previous hearings, reports from this event depicted Wilson as keenly interested in the jury selection and the challenges taking place. I. Newton Brown handled the jury selection and questioned the potential jurors during voire dire.

After two and a half hours the juror selection process concluded with the placement of twelve white, predominantly working-class men. Two of the men were painters, and another two were laborers. Also included in their ranks were two clerks, a local merchant, and a real estate broker. The jurors lived in a cross section of wards in the city, men such as George Gibbons, a blacksmith living in the Third Ward at 815 Seventh Street, and Harry S. Huhn, a salesman from the Twenty-Fifth Ward living at 2117 Clementine Street. After the jury was sworn in, the court took a recess until 2:30 p.m.[52]

The trial began fifteen minutes later and District Attorney Graham opened by saying that "seldom in history was one called upon to try a case in which there were so many elements of brutality." Graham explained that Gaines had gone to "pay a friendly visit to the house of Hannah Tabbs." At that time, "Wakefield Gaines was in the possession of his health … yet never came forth from that house again alive." Even though most of the particulars discussed were now common knowledge, Graham's words captivated the courtroom. He explained that there were a number of issues to work out in the resolution—specifically, "whether Wakefield Gaines was murdered—killed unlawfully—and if so, who committed the murder, or did the unlawful killing." He walked the jury through the discovery of the body and the investigation led by Kelly and his men, pointing out that, "one link in the chain after another was found and one circumstance after another was discovered until finally Mrs. Tabbs and the prisoner, George H. Wilson[,] were arrested."[53]

Graham did not shy away from noting that both Tabbs and Wilson had lied to police about their knowledge of the case and the whereabouts of Wakefield Gaines. He discussed how both made statements to police regarding the crime, each presenting himself or herself as least culpable. Even so, in Wilson's case, Graham carefully noted "The important fact, however, was that he himself admitted the identity of the body and his personal presence in Mrs. Tabbs's house on the day the man was slain."[54] Perhaps most important, during his opening statement, Graham concluded with the commonwealth's most disturbing allegation, namely that Wilson in severing the head had caused Gaines's death. Graham told the court, "We will show by scientific testimony that Wakefield Gaines was dismembered while there was yet life in the body."[55]

The following lineup of witnesses was almost identical to those who had gone before the coroner weeks earlier. Silas Hibbs would again testify to having made the gruesome discovery on his way to work, though in this hearing Bucks County coroner Silbert would describe his investigation and the events leading up to the discovery of Frank Swain. Conductor Swain would testify about his encounter with the odd black woman on the night before the torso surfaced and to later identifying that woman as Hannah Mary Tabbs. Tabbs was next to take the stand, where she gave "a thrilling account of the murder."[56] She began her testimony by stating that she was married and that she lived with her husband on Richard Street. She then described the terrifying quarrel between Wilson and Gaines. She reiterated that Wilson had killed and dismembered Gaines and she "told how she threw the remains into the water." However, Tabbs's testimony differed somewhat from her initial police statement. On the stand she described several meetings with Wilson on the day of the murder as well as after she failed to fully dispose of the body part. She testified that on Thursday she told him she "was scared to death" and "couldn't sleep all night." According to Tabbs, on Friday morning Wilson came to her house again after the discovery of the trunk appeared in the paper. He "lighted his pipe and told me to say nothing about it as it would be as bad for me as it would be for him." She said he came to her house again Sunday. She also told of "what hard work she had to keep the secret." The court adjourned after Tabbs's testimony.[57]

It's difficult to tell how much of Tabbs's sentiment, if any, was genuine but the tone is similar to an exchange she had with Mrs. F. P. Nicholson, a prison reformer who visited her at the county prison in March. At that time, Tabbs asked Mrs. Nicholson to pray for her and, when questioned as to how she could have played a role in such a horrendous murder, Hannah Mary wept and exclaimed, "Only God knows." During a second visit, Tabbs appeared distraught declaring, "If I could only live my life over again I would not be in this cell."[58] Tabbs may well have been confronting the full gravity of her situation and, faced with the prospect of a lengthy stint, the prison conditions probably weighed heavily on her. Not only were the cells rank but also the punishments were severe; prisoners were denied meals and confined to the "dark cell" for infractions.

Though the only time Tabbs appeared in the prison matron's diary was to note that on May 31, 1887: "Mary H. Tabbs went to trial." Indeed, she did and she managed to blame Wilson for the most serious aspects of the crime. At the same time, she was able to subtly cast her complicity in dumping the torso and her struggle to remain quiet about it as attributable to her being a kind of "fallen woman." This idea of a virtuous woman being led astray typically only applied to white women because it rested on the preexistence of virtue and it possessed the possibility of rehabilitation—all traits usually believed to be beyond the scope of black womanhood. In this sense, Tabbs's approach was both savvy and risky because it allowed her to advance a more sympathetic rendering of herself in a way that would be legible to white male jurors. Though if she laid it on too heavily, it could be read as her trying to "play the lady" and put herself on the same level with white women.[59]

By Wednesday, June 1, 1887, the scene outside of the courthouse had become a familiar one. A surging crowd hovered while stalwart officers blocked the front gate and "refused admission to the usual court loungers." But spectators' efforts to observe Tabbs and Wilson were not in vain. Rather than taking defensive measures or more clandestine maneuvers to get the prisoners into court without an early morning scene, guards instead escorted Wilson in just before 10 a.m. He seemed in good spirits and reportedly "stepped jauntily up the steps through the trap door and took his place in the corner of the large dock." Tabbs followed closely behind, but her mood was far less light. She took her same seat in front of the south dock. She was clad in the same somber black and, because of the damp, chilly atmosphere, also wore "a light black shawl over her shoulders." Tabbs continued to keep her eyes downcast and maintained a somber demeanor. Chief Kelly arrived, and District Attorney Graham entered somewhat late, at 10:10 a.m.[60]

Although idle spectators were excluded from the proceedings, most investigators and interested law officers found seats. On the second day of trial even Mrs. Carrie Kilgore, the only female practitioner admitted to the Philadelphia Bar Association, attended. Wilson's attorney, I. Newton Brown, arrived later, and Mrs. Tabbs's counsel was also detained. At roughly 10:15 a.m., the court was called into session, and Judge Hare took his seat on the bench. He consulted briefly with District Attorney Graham while the jurors filed in and answered to their names. With Tabbs back on the stand, Graham opened his questions by asking her to identify articles of clothing that belonged to the victim, worn on the day he was murdered. Tabbs studied the blue vest and trousers and a pair of men's shoes before testifying that they were among the articles pawned on Wednesday and the following day.[61]

The district attorney then showed Tabbs a relatively new hatchet and asked, "Did you ever see that hatchet before?"

She answered, "I saw one just like it."

"Can you identify this as the one you saw?"

"To the best of my knowledge and belief that is the same hatchet. Yes sir."

Defense attorney Brown objected but his motion was overruled. The district attorney continued, "When did you see the hatchet?"

Tabbs replied, "On the first day and the second day." Graham followed up, "Where did you see it?"

"I saw it on the cellar steps, a few steps from the bottom on the first morning."

"What became of it then?"

Tabbs explained, "It staid there until the second morning, when I gave it to Hattie Armstrong with the other things to pawn." She also told the jury that Armstrong had returned to her with the money and the pawn tickets, which she tore up and threw away in the coalscuttle.[62] Graham asked Tabbs to step down and take a closer look at the clothing and other items. Wearing black gloves, she turned to examine them. After carefully inspecting the evidence, she testified that those were the items. After Tabbs's identification, Graham's next line of questioning concerned blood evidence at the crime scene.[63]

With respect to the bloodstained carpeting, Graham asked whether Tabbs knew where Gaines had been bleeding from at the time of the incident. She said that she did not know; "his body had blood on it, but I didn't see where the blood on the carpet came from."[64] Graham asked about the quantity of blood on the carpet, on the paper beneath it, and on the floor. Tabbs tried to explain, "There was some blood on the edge of the middle piece of the rag carpet and I wiped it off with a wet cloth and hung it up to dry. I didn't see where the blood came from. Gaines's head had blood on it but I didn't see what part it came from. The thickest of the blood was on the newspaper beneath the carpet and it had stained the floor underneath. The stain was about two feet long. I did not wash up the floor until the next morning."[65] After providing this testimony, Tabbs was subjected to a rigorous cross-examination.[66]

I. Newton Brown wasted no time asking sensitive questions that would both illuminate the nature of the affair between Tabbs and Gaines and further associate her with disrepute. He could never have known, however, that Tabbs was as slippery as she was hot-tempered. Just about every answer hedged on her memory and best recollections. When asked about introducing herself as Mary Sheppard, she replied, "To the best of my knowledge I was never known by any other name than Hannah Mary Tabbs since my marriage." In response to allegations that she introduced herself as a relative of Gaines's, she stated plainly, "Wakefield Gaines was not related in any way to me; I had only known him for a year; to the best of my knowledge I never introduced Gaines to Mrs. Bailey, nor Mrs. Jenkins, nor anyone, as my nephew or cousin." Brown persisted, asking about neighbor after neighbor who claimed that Gaines was all but living with her. Again, Tabbs maintained her composure and explained that she did not know all of her neighbors' names but that while Gaines visited her, "Gaines didn't live at my house…he never slept at my house; he lived in a street between Eighth and Ninth and Race and Vine with Mrs. Williams; the only time he kept clothing at my house was when he was going to leave Mrs. Williams; that was a little after New Year's."[67]

Though the questions alone were damning, Tabbs responded handily, if not honestly. She explained to the jury that the additional clothes she gave to Hattie Armstrong—Gaines's clothing that was in her closet—"he brought at that time." Rather than confirming that she was having an illicit affair with the victim, Tabbs sounded as if she merely had helped a friend. Telling the jury that initially Gaines was going to leave Mrs. Williams's boarding house, "but he owed her some money, and said if I would get his clothes and take them to my house he would not give her any money, and would take them from my house to his service place in West Philadelphia."[68] Tabbs further charged, perhaps to the incredulity of all who knew her, "I never quarreled with him in my life, to my knowledge." To shore up what surely sounded like backpedaling, Tabbs assured the court, "I am as positive of that as of anything I have sworn to here, to the best of my knowledge."[69]

Brown moved on to question her about the day of the murder, asking Tabbs to describe Wilson's alleged visits to her on Wednesday, February 16, 1887. In recounting the ugly events of the day, Tabbs testified that Wilson swore as he fought Gaines. She also told the jury, "I didn't make an outcry or say anything while the men were fighting." She answered a number of questions about the scene, noting that despite the blood on the carpet, the chair, and Gaines's clothing, she saw "none on Wilson's."[70] Perhaps Brown was trying to highlight the holes in her story by asking her about the state of Wilson's clothes, given her description of the crime scene; it seems hard to believe that Wilson would not have gotten any blood on himself. Tabbs also managed to avoid discussing the most heinous aspect of the case by stating, "I didn't see anything that took place in the cellar except the clothes taken from the body from the waist upwards."[71] This differed from her original police statement, where she described seeing Wilson take off Gaines's clothes, after which time she had gone "down in the cellar and we stood and looked at the body."[72] [She had carefully phrased answers to stay true to the confession on record but at the same time she put a measured distance between herself and the actual murder and dismemberment and decreased her proximity to and familiarity with Gaines's body.]

During her testimony Tabbs tried to lay down a rough timeline of events. She recalled that Wilson had gone out and come back at least three times on Wednesday after the quarrel and dismemberment: between 10 a.m. and 11 a.m., again between 11 a.m. and 12 p.m., and then again sometime after 5 p.m. During one instance he was gone about ten minutes and returned with a hatchet. He was then in the basement for approximately half an hour. At that time, Tabbs "was in the second story when he came up then and called me, and I went down to the kitchen where he was and then we went into the cellar, and I stood on the steps a few minutes and I came up stairs and he came up behind me." She described how he would go back to the cellar and that in the following instances he came back with parts wrapped in paper. He brought up bundles and she said she was uncertain as to what all of the bundles contained. The rest of her testimony described her taking the two bundles to Eddington. Tabbs claimed that one contained clothing, clothing she was afraid to dump because "I had done Gaines's washing, and that is how I knew he had his name on his shirt band; nearly all of his things were marked."[73] With that, Tabbs left the stand and Hattie Armstrong was called.

Armstrong's testimony remained the same but she did shed more light on the crime scene and, in particular, what Tabbs's physical and mental state was shortly after the murder. During cross-examination, she said that she saw no one else in Tabbs's house and she testified: "I asked her what was the matter with her eye, and she said she had been hanging pictures, and standing on a box, and that the box had upset, and she had struck her eye on a bed-post." Armstrong again described a room in chaos, with chairs askew and the "settee was all rumpled up, as if someone had torn it up."[74] Armstrong's testimony about the black eye and the absence of anyone else at the crime scene may well have given the jury pause but Wilson's attorneys did not effectively exploit the holes in Tabbs's story—namely that the cause of the black eye had undergone a number of renditions over the course of the police investigation.

Moreover, the commonwealth had a new witness to present: John Loughran, a pawnbroker from 1704 South Street. Loughran would testify that on the day of the murder a young man came into his shop between 12 p.m. and 12:30 p.m. asking if they had a cleaver to sell. Loughran's son, who had stopped in from school, also witnessed the incident. They did not have a cleaver so the man left. Loughran testified that he subsequently saw that man in custody at Central Station and would identify him again in court as George Wilson.[75] Wilson's defense cross-examined the witness, asking for him to describe what Wilson was wearing, to which Loughran explained, "He had on rough clothes, but I didn't take much notice whether he had a vest on, or his coat was buttoned up."[76] He concluded by stating that he saw the coat and vest again when he identified Wilson at the police station as "it was as light in the cell then as it is now."[77]

The commonwealth next summoned Mrs. Mary Bailey. She would again identify Wilson as the young man she saw leaving Tabbs's house between 10 a.m. and 11 a.m., stating that he had a brown paper package with him and that "he held it out from him."[78] On cross-examination, however, Bailey also revealed, "I heard loud noise like quarreling before Wilson went into the house." She would add, "I saw Mrs. Tabbs passing to and fro in the rooms after Wilson went in and I saw her looking through the bowed windows at 1 o'clock." Bailey also testified that Tabbs did not have a black eye on the day of the murder but that "she had [one] on the day after the murder." Bailey also said that, in addition to seeing Gaines, Wilson, and Armstrong go into Tabbs's house, she also saw a young boy enter the dwelling. Tabbs would be recalled, and she amended her testimony, explaining, "I sent a boy for Hattie Armstrong that day."[79] Bailey proved to be a most formidable witness, though her testimony differed slightly from earlier statements in that she had not made mention of having seen Hattie Armstrong or the boy Tabbs summoned. Moreover, while she may have damaged Tabbs's credibility, her testimony did not exactly exonerate Wilson. If anything, she seemed more certain about the goings-on at 1642 Richard Street than the residents themselves.

Dr. Groom would again testify about the postmortem examination he conducted in Bucks County. Next, Dr. Formad took the stand. Defense attorneys initially objected to Dr. Formad's testimony because he asserted that the torso was that of Wakefield Gaines. Their objections were overruled, and Formad proceeded. He produced photographs of the torso and of his examination. He testified that "the blood vessels showed under the microscope a contraction that only could occur during life and nothing else." He explained, "The contraction of the muscles found in this case might have been found if the cutting had been done a minute after death, but it could not if the cutting were done 6 or 7 minutes after death."[80] His testimony shocked many who, up until this time, had believed that Gaines died from a blow to the head, not from being dismembered while still alive. Moreover, Formad testified that the substance found on Wilson's shoes and on the recovered hatchet was human blood. Defense attorneys wasted no time in questioning Formad about how he came to those conclusions. Formad explained, "I came to the conclusion that the blood upon the shoes and the hatchet was human blood by measurements of the corpuscles and chemical tests."[81] A preeminent scholar in this area, Formad proved an impressive witness. The court adjourned shortly after his testimony.

The third day of the trial found Wilson nervous and excited, per-haps anxious for his defense to begin. Accounts described the young man as sitting on the bench biting his nails and offering a smile to the officer who guarded him and got him water when he requested it. Even after Tabbs and Wilson were present, it took some time for the rest of the court to assemble. The trial resumed at roughly 10:30 a.m.[82] After Formad left the stand, Kelly's men were called next.

Detective Tate gave testimony about the trips that he and Wilson took to the potential dump sites in search of the rest of Gaines's re-mains. As he was about to explain that Wilson pointed out a particu-lar spot along the Callowhill Bridge, Wilson's defense objected. The court ruled that if the statement was made voluntarily it was admis-sible. As if on cue, the district attorney asked, "Was anything said either to menace the prisoner, intimidate, coax or persuade him?"

"No sir," Tate responded.

"He made his statement of his own motive and voluntarily?"

Tate replied, "Yes sir," and proceeded to describe how Wilson led them to a spot between two lamps on the bridge where he claimed to have thrown the bundle. The bundle, tied together and weighted, contained the head, arms, and legs of Wakefield Gaines. This portion of the testimony seemed to make Wilson somewhat restless and per-haps uncomfortable. He sat at the prisoner's dock, "with one arm on the railing and one foot on the round of his chair, giving him a some-what awkward and dwarfish appearance." He watched the exchange between Detective Tate and District Attorney Graham closely. Press coverage remarked that he showed no sign of "nervousness, save in the fact that he used the cuspidor in the dock continually."[83]

Brown went on the offensive and immediately asked the detective whether he was charged by his superior with the task of "extorting a confession" from Wilson. He asked specifically about visits that Tate made to Wilson's cell during his incarceration at the Fifth District sta-tionhouse. Graham objected to questions about the witness's motives, charging that questions related to his actions or conversations alone were admissible. When questioned again, Tate answered that he and Miller went to Wilson on their own.[84]

Brown followed up by asking, "What object, if any, had you in visiting the prisoner?"[85]

Tate testified that he had no particular aim. "I stopped in the station house and the sergeant asked me to take Wilson's dinner to him, but Wilson did not say anything in reference to it."[86] Tate stated that that was the only conversation he had with Wilson in the Fifth District stationhouse before taking him to the bridge. He testified that later he spoke to Wilson when he was in his cell at Central Station. In a rather perfunctory conversation, Tate inquired as to how Wilson was doing, and the latter responded and asked for a match to light his pipe.[87]

Brown then asked, "Was there anything said to the prisoner when he was on the boat?"

Tate answered, "We talked in a general way about the searching for remains, the freshet in the river, etc."

"Did you give him anything?"

"I gave him a cigar and Officer Miller gave him a little liquor. I don't know whether it was whiskey or not."

"Was that all you gave him?"

"That was all. No, I remember, I gave him a newspaper."

Brown pressed, "Did it contain an alleged statement or confession of Mrs. Tabbs?"

"I think it did."

"He was given that to read; isn't that a fact?"

"Yes sir."

"He read it in your presence?"

"He read it to himself," answered Tate.

"Do you remember whether there were any comments made at the time in relation to that statement?"

Tate explained, "I asked him what he thought of it and he said there was a great deal of it true and a great deal of it not true."

"Did he tell you what parts of it were true and what parts of it were untrue?"

"No sir. I will say to you he mentioned at that time striking with the chair."

"Did you ask him why he had struck with the chair?"

"No sir."

"Were there no questions asked?"

"No sir, I am sure of that."

On re-examination the witness said that Wilson asked for the liquor on the boat before it was given to him: "It was a cold and chilly day and the others there were taking a little stimulant." The prosecution then offered into evidence the chair, the hatchet, the shoes, and clothing related to the case. With that the commonwealth rested its case.[88]

The prosecution's case, with little contradiction, largely affirmed Hannah Mary Tabbs's confession and the theory of the crime Chief Kelly and his men had put forward. In brief, Wilson and Gaines fought at Tabbs's house, with Wilson using a chair to strike Gaines unconscious before he took the body to the cellar for dismemberment. The twist was that the victim was alive at the time of dismemberment—a shocking revelation by all accounts. While Hannah Mary Tabbs did her best at trial to portray herself as demure and virtuous, at the time of adjournment it was unclear how successful this had been, particularly as the defense attorneys were gunning for her. They had fairly good ammunition too—the affair, evidence of her prior altercations with the victim (including on the morning of the murder), her aliases, and her lies about the nature of her relationship with Gaines.

Still, few could deny that when the defense team presented their opening statements, it was Wilson's life on the line.

Chapter Six

A Most Revolting Deed

Dr. Formad, the Coroner's physician…concluded that the
deceased had been butchered while still alive.

—*Evening Bulletin*, Thursday, June 2, 1887

George S. Costa opened for the defense. He was both aggressive and
precise in his attack on the commonwealth's case. He implored the
jury to be impartial and told the men that Hannah Mary Tabbs was
not to be trusted, as she was the primary reason that the police
arrested Wilson—an arrest made, he pointed out, without a proper
warrant. Costa went on to make more serious allegations against
Francis Kelly and his men. He told the jury about Wilson's interrogation in Kelly's office and detailed how police insulted and berated his
client to extract a confession. Detectives called Wilson a "liar and a—
fool," asserting that his "——hard head would be the cause of his
neck being stretched." They pressured Wilson saying that if he told
them what they wanted to hear, "they would make it easier for him,
and if not they would make it harder." Although Wilson had denied
their allegations, Costa explained that Detectives Geyer and Crawford
had hounded him for a statement. Costa further highlighted how
authorities took advantage of the young, frightened Wilson by taking
him out to search for the missing remains while plying him with
whiskey—a drink to which he was unaccustomed. It was at this time,
when he was under the influence and particularly vulnerable, that
they showed him copies of Tabbs's confession in the papers. He

insisted that nothing in it was true but authorities again intimidated Wilson into incriminating himself.[1] The defense also attempted to cement his alibi with a bevy of witnesses who countered the prosecution's theory and perhaps because so many of the witnesses were from the black community, they might challenge negative connotations associated with Wilson's proximity to whiteness and his juvenile record.

[Even so, Costa had taken a bold step by calling the honor of white lawmen into question on behalf of a black man. This tactic was risky because it remained unclear whether the jurors would afford a black man—any black man, but especially one such as Wilson—the same consideration or impartiality extended to one of their own race. Moreover, the jurors were not the only men to consider.]

The Honorable John Innes Clark Hare was a seminal fixture in the city's legal landscape. He authored two volumes on constitutional law, taught the subject at the Law Department at the University of Pennsylvania, and he had been practicing law for almost fifty years.[2] Described as the "personification of high-bred courtesy," Hare was regarded by many as "the most learned lawyer that ever administered justice in the courts of Philadelphia."[3] He was not above imbibing between cases nor was it uncommon for Judge Hare to cross the street from the courthouse and take "a drink of whiskey at a neighboring public bar [before] returning to his judicial duties."[4] He may well have needed that drink to help stomach the shenanigans taking place in court since the next round of testimony seemed coached, each witness prepared to offer whatever evidence suited the aims of their respective side. Ultimately, however, Judge Hare's instructions to the jury would powerfully demonstrate how much his own beliefs and biases shaped justice.[5] They would also serve as an ironic testament to the true genius of Hannah Mary Tabbs.

The defense recalled Mattheas, who would again testify to seeing Wilson working in the shop on the day in question. Wilson's relatives—

two aunts and two cousins—would testify to overhearing detectives threaten and intimidate Wilson, and a number of clients from Mattheas's and Lee's shop (approximately eight) took the stand. However, these witnesses may have done more harm than good. The most unshakable were Wilson's relatives; the most impartial, patrons such as Mrs. Mary Frances Carr, a black woman who had no motive to lie, but in trade proved unreliable. Mrs. Carr, who resided at 1236 Lombard Street, testified that she saw Wilson in the shop for the better part of the day. She said, "Good morning, George," to Wilson, whom she had known for three years from around the neighborhood. She returned again later that afternoon, sometime around 2 p.m., and testified that Wilson let her in. However, on cross-examination, Graham got her to admit that it was, in fact, Coleman Boyer who let her in, thus damaging her credibility. Jennie Wilson, also black, testified that she saw Wilson in the shop on the day of the murder. However, on cross-examination, she admitted to being "doubtful about the day."[6]

Arguably the most devastating blow would come on Friday, June 3, when the defense aimed to call their strongest alibi witness, letter carrier John H. Delany. A resident of 723 South Eighth Street, Delany was expected to testify that he delivered a postcard to Wilson at the shop on Wednesday, February 16, on the day and time that the murder supposedly took place. Delany would explain that he remembered the day so clearly because he was initially confused by the fact that someone named George Wilson would be receiving mail at that particular address. He knew that Mattheas and Lee worked out of 1241 Lombard Street—they had done so for many years—but as Delany told the court, "I called out that address and inquired," he was abruptly and somewhat dramatically interrupted by District Attorney Graham, who exclaimed, "Never mind what you inquired, I object to that."[7] It is not clear on what grounds Graham raised his objection, however, the account notes that though I. Newton Brown protested, Judge Hare sustained the objection. In the end, Delany concluded his testimony stating that he "delivered the postal card to Mr. Mattheas."[8]

Attempts to make Wilson appear more sympathetic were also stymied by Graham's rigorous cross-examination, particularly on those questions posed about why Wilson was placed in the House of Refuge. His aunt skirted whether Wilson had been "incorrigible" by answering simply, "I had put him there; he had no mother at that time." Graham also asked about Wilson's employment history, where-upon she explained that since his release two years ago he had held a number of jobs such as caning chairs in the market and also "he worked in the abattoir."[9] It was becoming increasingly clear that the defense needed to discredit Graham's key witness, Hannah Mary Tabbs. It would not be easy.

[Tabbs had already shown herself to be fairly crafty on the stand. She had managed to deny the more incriminating allegations about her conduct with the victim, while steadfastly pointing the finger at Wilson. She had also made a show of apologizing to her husband in court for not heeding him and, as a result, bringing their family to this low place. Here she struck a delicate balance between denying adulterous sex outright and appearing to take responsibility for her mistakes. She took the performance of contrite wife to another level, however, by abandoning what likely amounted to a cover story anyway, when she actively referred to Annie Richardson as her "little girl." Presenting herself as a mother, which would spotlight her womanhood that much more, would be advantageous because prevailing notions regarded women as the "repositories of virtue." It might also allow her to tap into the chivalry that helped keep similarly situated white women out of prison—such as the aforementioned Annie Gaskin who ended up in an asylum rather than the penitentiary for butchering an infant in 1885. Ultimately, Tabbs continued to straddle the performance of womanly remorse and racial deference.[1]

Still, as the defense witnesses lined up, Tabbs's best efforts would not go unchallenged. Mrs. Emily Raynald, a resident of 1645 Lombard Street, went first. Her husband rented the home on Richard Street to the Tabbs family. She explained to the court:

> I know Hannah Mary Tabbs. I was subpoenaed to attend this trial. My husband owns the house that Mrs. Tabbs lived in. I saw her on election day in our yard for water. Her eyes were the same as mine at the present moment. I saw her on the next day, Wednesday. She was washing and came in the yard for water, but before I could speak to her she turned her back and avoided me. That was about two o'clock. She was washing a counter-pale. On Thursday she came in for water, and avoided me on that day. On Friday I went to her house, but she pretended to be out, and I know that she was in. I saw her in my yard on Saturday and she tried to avoid me. I said "Mrs. Tabbs, don't run away." She turned around and said: "I'm not very well." I said, "My gracious! Whatever has happened to your face since I saw you?" She said "I have been sick for two or three days from the face-ache and toothache." I said "I never saw such a face in my life from the toothache." She said it had made her face black. I have seen Gaines there forty-times a day. My house is so situated that I could see into her house all the time. I spoke to her about having this young man there, and she said "I never heard the like— that young man is my brother and this house is his home."[11]

As if her words were not damning enough, Raynald added, "They were constantly quarrelling." Naturally, the prosecution aimed to shake her testimony under cross-examination. However, Mrs. Raynald held her ground and explained, "I came here to tell the facts. I was a little vexed. She had her head tied around with an opening on the cheek, and her eye was bloodshot. The yards on our houses are one. I had seen Gaines there all day long. I first saw him there in August last."[12] Raynald's testimony effectively rivaled Tabbs's story.

District Attorney Graham's problems with Raynald, however, proved to be just the beginning. Mrs. Elizabeth Williams, Gaines's landlady, also African American, took the stand next. She told the court that she did not know anyone named "Hannah Mary Tabbs." Rather the woman sitting in the court, who stood up to be identified, had introduced herself using the surname "Sheppard" and claimed that Gaines was her nephew. Williams also testified that, while "Gaines paid for his room the first week...all after that was paid by Mrs. Sheppard [Mrs. Tabbs]." She told the jury that Gaines boarded with her starting the week of the previous Thanksgiving and that "Mrs. Sheppard came there every Saturday night." According to Mrs. Williams, Tabbs also did his washing and even dropped off weekly provisions.[13] Williams's sister, Mrs. Phoebe Ann Wells, also a resident of 207 Schell Street, corroborated her sister's statements by swearing before the court that she did not know a Mrs. Tabbs but "Mary Sheppard. That is [her] sitting over there. That is the name she gave. That was the first week Wakey was at 207 Schell Street. She said she was Wake's aunt."[14]

Tabbs's neighbor at 1640 Richard Street, a black woman named Rachel A. Flynn, testified that she knew Tabbs and Gaines by sight. Regarding the day in question, Flynn told the court, "I think I was home all day. I didn't hear any noise in Mrs. Tabbs's house that day in particular that I noticed. There was always so much noise there that I didn't notice."[15] The defense also recalled Mary Bailey. She restated that she knew Tabbs for five or six years and that she had heard Tabbs "tell people that Wakefield Gaines was her brother and to others that he was her nephew." Bailey stated that she had not heard Tabbs threaten the victim but that she had "heard [Tabbs's] character discussed for truth and veracity and it was very bad." She told the court again that she had herself quarreled with Tabbs and had heard that

Tabbs and Gaines quarreled but had not witnessed this herself. The defense attempted to show that Mrs. Tabbs had threatened to kill Mrs. Bailey but the court overruled their effort. With that the defense rested their case.[16]

The prosecution recalled Kelly and a number of the detectives. Detective Miller, also recalled to the stand, denied having made the threatening "remarks attributed to him at the station house, when he had a conversation with Wilson." But Miller may well have had a pattern of intimidation and coercion when it came to eliciting confessions. In 1906, Henrietta Cook, another black plaintiff, would make similar allegations against him. She charged that Detective Miller and one of his colleagues visited her at the hospital, where she was taken following her arrest. After questioning her, they made her sign a piece of paper without letting her read it and before she received medical treatment.[17] Still, one by one, the officers denied allegations that Wilson had been coerced in any way. The prosecution also called the clerk, John B. Moffitt. Moffitt testified to being present when Wilson gave his official statement, and he stated that "he read the statement to the prisoner, word for word, as it was written, and he assented to its being correct and signed it." On cross-examination, Moffitt admitted that Wilson "was not represented by counsel," and that he "saw the prisoner when he was suffering a fit...it was the first day he was brought to the Central." Moffitt told the court that Dr. Angney was present and that ultimately "the paper was signed on the following day." Graham attempted to then enter Wilson's confession into evidence. The defense objected because the statement was "written on disconnected sheets of paper and signed only on one, and because it was irrelevant and inadmissible." Judge Hare overruled the objection.[18]

Francis Kelly was then questioned about his interactions with Mr. Mattheas regarding Wilson's alibi. Kelly told the court that when he asked Mattheas about Wilson's whereabouts on Tuesday, February 15, Matheas responded, "he was working in our shop all day." When he asked if he was certain, Mr. Lee corroborated Mattheas's information. However, when asked about Wednesday, Mattheas told Kelly, "I sent him for cane, but he was away all day and did not come back until night, and then said he had been to Darby."[19]

After making these statements, Mattheas and Lee came back to see Kelly on the following Thursday. They claimed that they had made a mistake, "that the boy had been at work on Wednesday, and it was Tuesday he was away."[20]

Chief Kelly then told the court that he responded, "You fellows are lying; I have a statement the boy has made."[21]

Further, Graham called Mrs. Alice Hines, an African American woman who testified that "on the morning of February 14th last, I saw Mrs. Tabbs at 1713 Burton Street, where I lived; she had a black mark on her eye; the skin was black as if bruised."[22] Hines's testimony was undoubtedly an attempt to neutralize the doubt the defense raised about Tabbs's involvement in the murder of Wakefield Gaines. During her cross-examination though, Hines admitted that she had not seen Hannah Mary Tabbs for a year before, but that Tabbs told her that she fell, "but didn't tell me how, when or where." After Hines's cross-examination the commonwealth closed its case.[23]

The defense then asked "to consult as to whether they should call more witnesses, as they had been surprised by the admission of the prisoner's statement in rebuttal when it had not been offered in chief."[24] Judge Hare refused the application and, with that, District Attorney Graham began his summation. He spoke to the jurymen for roughly an hour and fifteen minutes. He stressed that "the prisoner was educated in the abattoir...that was how he knew how to cut and hack the body." He directed the jury to take notice that "the prisoner had a legal and moral right to take the stand, but he did not do so. His mouth remains closed." Graham also held to the notion that some kind of argument transpired between the two men over Tabbs's niece, Annie Richardson. It was certainly plausible, but somewhat weak

considering the history of violent confrontations between Tabbs and
the victim, and the fact that Wilson was himself reportedly engaged
to another black girl named Louisa Wren. Graham concluded at 6:45
p.m., and the court adjourned until Saturday morning.[25]

On June 4, I. Newton Brown presented three hours of closing
arguments, summarizing alibi witness testimony, reiterating police
and investigative misconduct, and questioning the veracity of Hannah
Mary Tabbs's statements. After defense counsel made their closing
statements, Judge Hare provided lengthy instructions to the jury,
which were partially preserved:

> This story of Mrs. Tabbs, standing alone, would be the story of a
> party to the crime and, therefore, it ought to be received with
> caution: not to be rejected or accepted blindly, but to be judged
> by such light as may be obtained collaterally, by the manner of its
> relation, its plausibility. To my mind this woman told her story
> with great coherence from beginning to end, and I am not aware
> that there is any point of time that she is necessarily contradicted
> by any other evidence in the case; and, moreover, there are some
> circumstances in it which might lead one to believe that she
> spoke truthfully because while she told the story in a way that
> exonerated her in the actual homicide, yet if a quarrel took place
> more likely the two men quarrelled [sic] then the woman came
> in and took a part, and if she did take part it is not easy to see
> what room there was for her intervention.[26]

That Judge Hare took this position, one recognizing Tabbs as a
woman in a truly feminine sense, is fairly remarkable. Typically,
black women in Philadelphia courts were judged with little regard to
gender. In fact, black women were more disproportionately represented than their black male counterparts in Philadelphia's Eastern
State Penitentiary—black women accounted for roughly 40 percent

of female prisoners, nearly twice the percentage of black males among male inmates. Black women on average also served longer prison sentences than their white female counterparts for comparable crimes.[?] Still, Judge Hare acknowledged that this was only his opinion and that they should draw their own conclusions. Then he added:

> It is, however, proper that, in speaking of the testimony of Mrs. Tabbs, to advert [sic] to the statement or confession made by the prisoner himself. On four different occasions he made a statement concerning this case, and the last one, at the Central Station, was reduced to writing. Now it is to be observed that, if these statements were made under circumstances which give them place as evidence in the case, they corroborate Mrs. Tabbs, and I do not know that they contradict her anywhere, except while she states that three successive blows followed, he spoke only of one. Taking the two stories together, and treating both as evidence, leaving out such denial, it would seem that there is substantial basis to rest our belief that a quarrel ensued from jealousy on Gaines' part in reference to Mrs. Tabbs or the girl, and in consequence of that he inflicted an unprovoked blow on Wilson; that a scuffle ensued: and that, as a result of it, Wilson, with a blow from a chair, felled Gaines to the floor, where he lay lifeless, or, perhaps, not to give any signs of life.[28]

With reference to Wilson's confession he said:

> Naturally a man telling his own tale, with a heavy burden over him, what he says in his own behalf may be accepted with some degree of doubt, but what he says against himself, according to the rules of human conduct, would be more readily accepted. And so it is in regard to Mrs. Tabbs testimony, and it is a question

for the jury to say what part of it was perverted, what was to be believed and what was not to be believed.[29]

But Judge Hare was not yet finished with the jury. He also instructed them as to the defense's case and he reviewed their testimony. He told the jury that if they had reasonable doubt "such as should hold a mind in suspense, that what all the witnesses, for the Commonwealth had said in regard to Wilson's being at the house on the day in question was false, and they believed the testimony of witnesses for the defense then they should acquit."[30] Following these instructions, he explained the parameters of the law with respect to murder in the first degree, second degree, and manslaughter. Hare told the jurymen that the circumstances of the butchery and carrying away body parts were shocking, but at the same time if the man was dead it would not be murder in the first degree under the facts in this case:

> However wrong the purpose, it was not a specific offense of homicide with intent to take life. On the other hand it was just as true that if this prostrate man was alive, and the prisoner, knowing that he was alive, proceeded to cut the man up and dispose of him to escape punishment for the initial assault, it would take no argument to show that it was murder in the first degree. On the question whether he was alive or not the jury had heard the testimony, and they had the significant phrase of Mrs. Tabbs, "I don't know whether he was dead or not."[31]

Hare remarked that Dr. Formad had given scientific testimony on the subject, but added that the jury was not necessarily bound by that. He explained that even with Dr. Formad's testimony that the victim was alive when dismembered, it was for them to decide whether the prisoner knew it. According to the judge, "If he believed that he was dead and in his ignorance arrived at that conclusion, then it would not amount to a case of murder in the first degree," because Wilson could not have intended to take what he believed was not there. "On the other hand, if he had reason to suppose that Gaines was still alive and recklessly went on, without ascertaining whether he was alive or not, then, I think, in the eye of morality, common sense, of humanity and in the law, there is a case in which a verdict of murder in the first degree could probably—I will not say must—be rendered."[32]

Judge Hare further advised that if the jury believed that Wilson did not inflict the third blow, except in the heat of passion, carried by a torrent of rage and anger, then the man was only guilty of manslaughter. But Hare added that "under all the evidence" he did "not think he could be acquitted of this offense." Following these instructions the jury recessed at 7 p.m.[33]

After the hearing closed, officers transported Wilson and Tabbs to the county prison but just before 9 p.m. the jury sent word that they had reached a verdict. Given that most deliberations were less than forty-five minutes in the nineteenth century, two hours was fairly lengthy.[34] Judge Hare was summoned and Wilson was brought back to court. At 9:30 p.m., when Judge Hare returned and the jurymen entered, Wilson had already arrived. The court rendered a verdict of guilty—murder in the first degree. Stunned, the defense counsel asked to poll the jury. All of the jurors believed that Wilson was guilty of murder. However, of the twelve, nine believed he was guilty of murder in the first degree, while three believed he had committed murder in the second degree.[35] The verdict was received in "perfect silence." Wilson reportedly received the verdict calmly.[36]

The defense immediately motioned for a new trial. Judge Hare accepted the motion and agreed to rule after hearing their arguments. Before Wilson was removed from the deck, his defense lawyers shook hands with him. Brown told him, "We did all we could, but we will do more. You are not dead yet. Keep a stiff upper lip."[37]

By June 8, 1887, Costa and Brown had filed two motions.[38] One was a two-page document in which they asserted that their client had been subjected to a miscarriage of justice. In large part, the men argued that the verdict was illegal in that it was not supported by the evidence presented, but also they argued that "there was not sufficient evidence to establish the *corpus delicti*."[39] Costa and Brown also had taken serious issue with how Judge Hare adjudicated the case, noting that "the learned Judge erred in permitting the Commonwealth to prove by witnesses, declarations and statements alleged to have been made by the prisoner, different from what was contained in his written statement although objected to by defense counsel." Their final argument in the first motion was that "the learned Judge erred in admitting in evidence in rebuttal the written statement signed by the prisoner at the end of five pages of detached paper—which statement if evidence against the prisoner, could only have been used to refresh the memory of the witness who heard the same made and wrote it down."[40]

In the second filing, "The defendant by his counsel George S. Costa and I. Newton Brown, Esqs. moves the Court for a rule for a new trial."[41] Costa and Brown proceeded to build on the arguments made in the first motion to essentially set aside the verdict. In addition to charging that the verdict was against the law and the weight of the evidence, they broadened their attack on Judge Hare's rulings on evidence and testimony and his instructions to the jury. In particular, Costa and Brown took issue with the judge's instructions to the jury regarding the consistency of Hannah Mary Tabbs's story, his own supposition as to the likelihood that the men fought over one of the women involved, and his opinion that Wilson could not be acquitted. Their critiques were not without merit.[42]

The defense presented these arguments in court before Hare and District Attorney Graham on July 1, 1887. The motion for a new trial was granted.[43] However, there seems to have been some negotiating behind closed doors because, almost immediately after that allowance, Wilson, who was also present, took a plea—guilty of murder in the second degree.[44] Judge Hare then sentenced him:

> You were convicted of this crime before me last month of murder in the first degree in killing Wakefield Gaines, by a most intelligent jury, who arrived at that conclusion on evidence that justified the verdict, and as the matter then stood, could not have led to anything else. That evidence was circumstantial upon two vital points—first, that your victim was alive, but possibly unconscious when you dismembered him, and next that you were cognizant that he was alive. There was no direct proof on these points, and your knowledge that he was alive was inferred from the evidence. Since then circumstances have come to the knowledge of the District Attorney, and through him to the court, which leaves room for doubt whether you knew him to be alive when you dismembered him. Under the mercy of the law I granted you a new trial, though the probability is that another trial under the same evidence, the verdict would be the same. You have tendered a plea of guilty of murder in the second degree, a crime only next in enormity to that of which you were convicted. In view of your youth, and the fact that you were convicted on the testimony of an accomplice and circumstantial evidence that may leave a doubt as to whether you knew your victim was alive when you cut up his body, and a sense of mercy, which a judge should always feel, I have accepted your plea, and I now impose the extreme penalty of the law upon it. I sentence you to twelve years in the Eastern Penitentiary at separate and solitary confinement.[45]

Wilson's conviction did not mark the end of the saga, however, as the fate of Hannah Mary Tabbs had yet to be determined. She had been held in the county prison during Wilson's trial, his conviction, his defense attorney's wrangling for a new trial, and for nearly two months after his plea deal—presumably while she and her counsel hammered out the final details of their own deal, as plea bargaining had become a fairly standard practice in urban criminal courts in the late nineteenth century.[46]

On September 28, Hannah Mary Tabbs again appeared in court. She pleaded guilty as an accessory after the fact. District Attorney Graham was first to address the court:

> May it please your Honor, I desire now to move for judgment upon this plea. I am very glad to be able to call this case before your Honor, knowing that you are entirely familiar with all the facts and the testimony, having sat patiently during the trial of George H. Wilson, who was convicted of causing the death of Wakefield Gaines. It is unnecessary for me to rehearse all the facts and the testimony. Wakefield Gaines, you will remember, was killed in the house of this woman, and was subsequently dismembered, and part of his body was carried by Hannah Tabbs into an adjoining county and thrown into a creek, whence it was taken and identified. The details, of course, are not such as to invite a recapitulation.[47]

Tabbs's counsel then spoke on her behalf, asking the judge to have pity on her given that she was "unfortunately, against her will, a witness to the killing."[48] He reminded the court of Tabbs's first exclamation after the murder, "George Wilson, you have done a terrible thing."[49] He argued that out of fear and frenzy she succumbed to Wilson's will and helped him dispose of the remains. But he also asked the court to recall that she had repented for her actions.[50] Counsel argued that she had shown sincere remorse and that her actions demonstrated that she "was heartily sorry for what she had done."[51] He therefore asked for leniency in her sentencing.[52]

In making his ruling, Judge Hare told the court that "the woman was a passive witness of the killing, but she made herself an accomplice after the fact by aiding Wilson to dispose of the corpse."[53] Although it was not murder, she had participated in what Hare characterized as "a most revolting deed."[54] In light of this, he sentenced her to two years—the full extent of the law.[55] However, on October 3, 1887, Hare adjusted Tabbs's sentence, "so that the imprisonment of two years imposed on her should take effect from 30th of June, instead of the 28th of September, the date of her sentence."[56] Tabbs did not appear in court again. Her name did show up in the press one more time in an October 28, 1887, article noting that in the original indictment, "The charge of murder against Hannah Tabbs as accessory in the Wilson case was technically disposed of to clear the docket."[57]

On a different matter, Coroner Ashbridge felt satisfied that the skull, yet another, found on Friday night on the banks of the Schuylkill River at Bainbridge Street wharf was not that of Wakefield Gaines. Rather, Ashbridge believed that the skull was one of many that medical students had committed to a watery grave.[58]

With the final verdict and sentences, and the prisoners committed to Eastern State Penitentiary to serve out their respective terms, the torso case faded from public view. So, too, did the primary figures involved. Under Pennsylvania's commutation law, which reduced prisoner's sentences annually for time served, George Wilson served a total of nine years and three months before being released on October 1, 1896, with $7.56 earned working in the penitentiary over the years.[59] That he survived his sentence was itself an accomplishment, as many prisoners died from illness, and the institution was investigated for abuses and brutality against the inmates in 1897.[60] Wilson likely experienced significant difficulties adjusting to the outside world. He becomes somewhat difficult to trace following his release, though it appears he did marry. Mary, his bride, was about eight years younger than he. Wilson found low-income jobs, such as being a peddler of "rags" in 1920 and later he worked as a "Teamster" in the "Junk" industry. He and Mary were lodgers on Rodman Street in the Seventh Ward as late as 1930.[61]

For her part Hannah Mary Tabbs was released on April 30, 1889. With commutation, she ended up serving one year and one month. She worked on the inside, sewing stockings, and departed the facility with $18.04. Her intended destination was Philadelphia.[62] It would not be a happy homecoming necessarily, as John Tabbs had died four days before her release. He was buried on May 1, 1889, in Lebanon Cemetery. Prior to his death, John had moved from their home at 1642 Richard Street to 933 Lombard Street—still in the heart of the Seventh Ward. He had been working as a waiter until he succumbed to what Dr. Thomas Merrick listed as his cause of death: the "Retention of Urine." He was fifty-four years old.[63]

Hannah Mary Tabbs returned to Maryland, living with her brother Augustus Smith and his wife at 226 Carlton Street in Baltimore. She found work as a domestic and, after successfully applying for it, lived off of her wages and widow's pension. Although her initial pension application was denied—due to some difficulty in proving residency at first and also some questions arose about whether John had served as a member of ground troops or on a ship—Tabbs was eventually awarded $8 per month beginning on February 16, 1891. On December 29, 1910, a special examiner from the pension office, E. M. Taber, apparently checked up on Tabbs and certified that "I have this day personally interviewed the above named pensioner [Hannah A. Tabbs], and I am satisfied that she is the pensioner that she represents herself to be." It is not clear whether this certification was routine or the result of suspicion about Tabbs's case. She was dropped as a pensioner just over five years later on July 5, 1916, after she notified the Department of the Interior of a change in marital status. She wrote, "I am marriage & want my pension stop right away. I am marriage to James H. Anderson. I am now stopping it 2538 May

Street, Balto Md." A follow-up letter reminded the office that she was "entitled to payment from June 4th to June 12th, 1916, will thank you to send a voucher therefore, for execution, etc." It was signed "hannah a tabbs now hannah a anderson."[64]

At first blush, it seemed that Hannah Mary had decided it best to live on the straight and narrow. But if history tells us anything, it's that such a path did not exist for women such as she. Historical records indicate that there was in fact a James H. Anderson, age fifty-five, living in Baltimore at 2538 Mace (not May) Street, with his fifty-six-year-old wife, Mary E. Anderson, and a daughter, age sixteen, named Lucy Scott. Anderson rented the home and worked as a "Jobber" while his wife and Lucy worked as laundresses. The age is somewhat off and the name is not a perfect match, but Hannah Ann Smith was somewhat of a chameleon, among other things. The information about her marriage is from the 1910 U.S. federal census, six years earlier than when she notified the pension office—and according to that census data she had been married for two years at that point; though coincidentally, 1910 is the same year that Hannah was recertified as still being eligible for the Widow's Pension she had been collecting since 1891. Moreover, James H. Anderson may have been her third husband because she was identified as Mary E. Scott when she wed James H. Anderson on February 6, 1908. In 1920, James H. Anderson was still living at 2538 Mace Street, though with a lodger named Charlie Hawkins rather than his wife and Lucy. Whether his wife died or the pair separated is unclear; there are a number of women with the name Mary E. Anderson who died in the Baltimore area between 1915 and 1950, including one who was laid to rest in Anne Arundel County.[65]

* * *

Hannah Mary Tabbs possessed extraordinary physical and intellectual abilities. Violence, lies, and intimidation allowed her to create a space for her own ambitions whether she sought personal pleasure, bloody revenge, or aimed to get away with murder. Even so, Tabbs was not a cold-blooded killer in the coolest sense. Though her brutality is well documented, her actions on the day of the murder and in the days immediately after revealed someone completely unnerved as she left a trail of witnesses for the authorities and even returned to the scene of the crime. Still, her capacity to mimic mainstream mores and manipulate others was extraordinary. What may be most haunting about Tabbs is that her unsettling methods worked so effectively. It is as if somewhere along the way, she embraced the nihilism of the era; she accepted that the rules were fixed and that if she really wanted to live, in any remote sense of that word, as a working-class black woman in that time, she would have to adopt a duplicitous relationship with the tenets of morality—particularly the moral rhetoric dictated by those who had arguably benefied the most from violence, avarice, and unapologetic individual pursuits. She managed to remain intimately acquainted with the social expectations in both the black and white communities, though significantly detached from them.

She also understood that northern whites wanted to be reassured about the boundaries of whiteness and black subordination to it. Perhaps she acquiesced because she saw how it facilitated her own aims, in the sense that white supremacy kept blacks estranged from the justice system, isolated and unprotected; it created the void that permitted her bad behavior within the black community to go on largely unabated. Yet even when the state caught up to her, she could so skillfully mime race and gender conventions, without jeopardizing white women's centrality, that she transcended the otherwise-overwhelmingly damning narratives that typically condemned black women. Ultimately, her success belies the fallacies imbedded in those restrictive codes.[66]

Indeed, Hannah Mary Tabbs manipulated the criminal justice system exceedingly well—better than her accomplice and his attorneys and better than most black women who dealt with the Philadelphia authorities, before 1887 and quite possibly since.]

Epilogue

It is a history of an unrecoverable past; it is a narrative of what might
have been or could have been; it is a history written with and against
the archive.

—Saidiya Hartman, "Venus in Two Acts"

He was born Silas Wakefield Gaines in 1864 in Seaford, Sussex County,
Delaware. He was the second youngest of nine children. Silas and
his siblings lived with their parents, Emory and Charlotte (both
described in census data as mulattoes), and his grandmother, Hester
(listed in the census as black). His mother and grandmother were
born in Maryland, but his father was from Delaware.[1] Most likely
descended from slaves, if not formerly enslaved himself, Emory Gaines
had nonetheless managed to own land in Seaford valued at $800 in
1870, and he had acquired personal property worth $600. His wealth
was a substantial accomplishment given Seaford's history. During the
antebellum period, while much of the state had abandoned the peculiar institution, at the time of Silas's birth the majority of the state's
remaining enslaved blacks lived and labored in Sussex County. The
region's slave-owning holdouts were steadfastly committed to their
way of life—a lifestyle predicated on human chattel slavery and white
supremacy.[2]

With the close of the Civil War that world would be forever
changed. Blacks such as Emory and Charlotte (also known as Lottie)
strove to make better lives for themselves and their families, and both

learned to read, though neither could write. A successful farmer, Emory provided for the family while Lottie stayed at home. Their two oldest children, ages eighteen and seventeen, worked as well— the boy as a common laborer and the girl as a servant. At some point, Emory became a preacher. He also served as the witness for his son's marriage in 1882. Silas Wakefield Gaines, who was described as a "dark mulatto," married his eighteen-year-old bride, a "dark" girl named Maria Jane Connor, also from Seaford. The two moved to Philadelphia to start their lives together but unlike his parent's union, their partnership—plagued by conflict and infidelity—would be short-lived. Parting after two years, Wakefield would soon make the fateful acquaintance of Hannah Mary Tabbs.[3]

Although his death would leave citizens in Philadelphia, as well as those across the country, terrified, titillated, and preoccupied, for most of the public the life of Wakefield Gaines would remain largely unknown. Despite the things we know, we never fully see him. We know that he was the son of a farmer and preacher. We know where he was born. We know that he was described as a mulatto. We know that he had a wife and lovers. That he was fired for being drunk on the job suggests that he liked to drink, perhaps too much.[4] His wife's statement that they couldn't get along, when combined with witnesses attesting to his rows with Tabbs, would lead us to believe that he was no stranger to domestic strife. His sister's statement about him being excited about the election results indicates that he cared about politics. We know from his sister Jane Cannon's distress and sadness that he was loved. And we know he died, tragically and violently, too young. He passed prior to his father, who would die at age seventy-two in 1904 and his mother who died at age eighty-one in 1913.[5]

This history has indeed been "written with and against the archive."[6] The incomplete parts of Gaines's life powerfully map not only the horror that was his death but also the violence of history that should find those responsible for his murder better served by archival records because of their crimes against him. Even existing records fail, though, when it comes to knowing what exactly happened to him on his last day. I believe that Tabbs killed Gaines during a violent argument on February 16, 1887, and that this was the original cause of the bruising around her eye. I think Wilson either witnessed the altercation or perhaps intervened. I also believe that Wilson, who took Tabbs for money and clothes under the false pretense of supplying the items to Annie Richardson, ended up being either coerced or duped into helping Tabbs dismember and dispose of Gaines's body.

I also believe that, in addition to being manipulated by Tabbs, Wilson was threatened and intimidated by the police, who set him up to take the fall for the crime. In many respects, he and Gaines serve as foils—both demonstrating how whiteness could shape black men's access to justice. In the case of Gaines, that his race wasn't easily discernible—that is to say that he appeared to be something other than black—led to the case being taken so seriously in the first place. There was a feverish nature to the early parts of the investigation in both Eddington and Philadelphia. Gaines's inscrutable complexion permitted a measure of justice under the most unlikely of circumstances—namely, that a headless, limbless torso should be found and identified, that foul play would be detected, and that suspects would be arrested, tried, and sentenced in 1887—all without the benefit of fingerprints, DNA evidence, or well-placed surveillance cameras. This outcome starkly contrasts with the fate of the victims of the other severed limbs found in black areas during the investigation and trial; once it was clear that these were not part of the Gaines case, they faded into obscurity. For Wilson, whiteness made him the subject of fear, anxiety, and ultimately suspicion—enough to find him guilty of a crime for which he had no real motive, save the vague notion that perhaps the two men fought over Tabbs's niece, Annie, whom neither had seen for nearly a year.[7]

[Hannah Mary Tabbs, too, seemed to have had a complicated relationship with those light-complexioned blacks in her world. Her own vengeful behaviors toward Annie, Wakefield, and Wilson suggest a tangle of emotions—perhaps compulsion and revulsion related to whiteness, gender, sexuality, power, and, of course, violence.]

Violence in black women's history often marks both the beginning and the end point of black women's humanity, as violence is typically a black woman's undoing. For Tabbs though, whatever the unknowable violences or traumatic events that likely happened in her life—violences that seem to have significantly structured her worldview—it didn't mark the end of her; rather that she seems to have appropriated and deployed it so often and so effectively gestures toward different possibilities and outcomes. This is not to say that whatever events equipped Tabbs with the capacity to carry the bloodied, dismembered torso of her lover on a train so that she could throw it off a bridge is not downright horrifying; but also that perhaps this history instilled alternative properties and critical skills at the same time that it inspired a kind of brutal ferocity.[8]

Despite the tightly drawn parameters of black women's worlds, Tabbs found ways to move around and to reinvent herself—more than once. She manipulated and cajoled people, and she found ways to indulge in otherwise-forbidden pleasures. The lengths to which she would go to access those things is terrifying but also somehow aspirational. In many ways, much of Tabbs's behavior contests her "rightlessness" as a black woman and exists as a searing marker of it.[9] [Against the shadow of enslavement and the protracted denial of black citizenship by virtue of white racial violence, Tabbs somehow managed to see her own desires as worth fighting for.]This flies in the face of most social beliefs of the era; yet that she had to go to such lengths to have a measure of agency underscores the extent of her powerlessness.[10] Tabbs's prolific violence in her community, combined with her lack of criminal record, also marks the chasm between the black community and police protection. The fierceness with which she navigated her world ultimately reflects her own shadowy past and the ever-present dangers that haunted all black women. But the limitations of the archive are not the only reason for the missing moments in Tabbs's history.

Throughout the course of investigating this case it has become distressingly apparent that Tabbs took pains to obfuscate and hide her truths. Recall that she lied about where she was born, used aliases, and gave misleading addresses. Perhaps similarly to those black women who concealed their sexuality, she aimed to keep some small part of her interior life to herself rather than have it exposed to such a hostile world. Perhaps her efforts mark the behaviors of a wanted woman. Maybe the rumors were true that she had killed someone years before Gaines died in her Philadelphia home.[11]

Whatever the case, it's likely that this aspect of history is doomed to suffer the same fate as the missing head, arms, and legs of Wakefield Gaines—human remains irretrievable by design.

ACKNOWLEDGMENTS

Sylvia E. Neal (1917–2010), my grandmother, was one of my fiercest supporters and one of my fiercest role models. I mean the latter in every sense of the word. She did not "take tea for the fever," she was unabashedly progressive and cosmopolitan. As a young woman she loved jazz, cigarettes, and cocktails, and throughout her life she was unapologetic about standing up for herself. And she admired professional women immensely. My aunt, Judith Ann Lovell (1939–2013), was an ambitious woman with a gift for the accumulation of wealth at the same time that she maintained a passionate appreciation for thrift. She was an amazing cook, had a loud, contagious laugh, and she could cuss up a storm—stringing profanities together in truly poetic fashion. Respect ladies, and rest in peace.

June Maria Gross, my mother, has a quieter way, though no less intense. She has grounded and guided me through tight spots and stretched herself mentally, physically, and emotionally to get me through school. She did much of it alone. She continues to support me. She has an iron core and tackles systems fearlessly. More than once she pushed me forward when I did not think I could go on. Thanks Ma, I love you. Always.

My upbringing has imbued in me a profound reverence for black women who have, and have had, the ire to get their backs up and hold their heads high in a world that often aims to grind them down. It's a trait that I have nurtured and nourished by surrounding myself with kindred spirits, like-minded role models, sisters, scholars, friends, and extended family. I would like to offer a special thanks to some of those folks now: Mary Frances Berry, Stephanie M. H. Camp (rest in peace sisterfire), Cheryl Hicks, Tiffany Gill, Jessica Millward, Jacqueline Jones, Erica Armstrong, Daina Berry, Rhonda Frederick, Edward Baptist, Rebecca Cohen, Tera Hunter, Robin D. G. Kelley, Nicole Childers, and Nicole Burrowes. Sharon Harley and Francille R. Wilson, our Martha's Vineyard writer's retreat helped me put on the finishing touches—thank you for the support and additional sources. Inez Ramos and the Ramos family, Ross Johnson and the Johnson clan, and Lisa Bowleg, thanks for love, community, and laughs out loud! To Uncle Lincoln and the rest of the Lovell clan and to my baby brother Jacob, I love you.

When I stumbled across a German-language newspaper, printed in Maryland, that had covered the case, three students graciously translated the pieces for me: Alina Palimaru, Cooper Wyatt, and Christina Walter-Gensler—thank you.

I owe a special debt of gratitude to the archivists and staff at the Philadelphia City Archive: David Baugh, Angela Burton, Barbara Campbell, and Raven Darkholme. You all have gone above and beyond the call of duty for me more times than I can count. I would not have been able to complete this project without your kind, patient, expert assistance. Thank you very much.

Kylie Ladd, an archivist at the National Archives in Washington, D.C., also went out of her way to help find a crucial Civil War Pension file—thank you. I also want to thank Margaret Dunham, at the Delaware State Archives who helped comb through dozens of sources to find more information on African Americans in Seaford, Delaware, after Emancipation.

The Schomburg Center's Scholars-in-Residence fellowship supported my work and the cohort of scholars were extremely helpful and encouraging. I must thank Colin A. Palmer for his brilliant, steadfast leadership and guidance. Truly, I am indebted. Diana Lachatanere, you have always helped me and I love your spirit. Aisha al-Adawiya, I cannot thank you enough for your assistance. I am grateful to my cohort: Venus Green, Shannon King, Evie Schockley, Nicole Fleetwood, Johanna Fernandez, Malinda Lindquist, Ivor Lynn Miller, and Chad Williams. And I have to thank my tireless research assistant, a graduate student at the time, now Dr. Seth Markle.

My project also received funding from the Christian R. and Mary F. Lindback Foundation, for which I am truly grateful. I also benefited from a visiting research grant from the Virginia Historical Society, where I spent countless hours trying to locate "Hannah Sheppard."

Cecelia Cancellaro, my agent, helped make sure this project was signed and placed in most capable hands. She remained by my side throughout the final processes. Thank you. I am very grateful to Susan Ferber, my editor at Oxford, for the hardcore line-by-line editing. It has made me a better writer and the project is stronger for it. I am also grateful for your wise stewardship of the book. My personal editor and fact-checker Cynthia Gwynne Yaudes has been a godsend; I simply cannot thank you enough. Christian Purdy aka "Purdy" and the marketing team at OUP, Lauren Hill, Michelle Blankenship, Bonnie Blankenship, Jeff Catlow-Shea, and Carolyn Darr—thanks for working so hard to promote this project.

I would be remiss if I did not thank the women who have taken care of my child when I have had to work and travel. I owe a special debt to Leticia Flores and her brilliant, lovely daughter Cristina for their kind, loving care of my baby girl—thank you so much for teaching her and caring for her. I never worried when she was with you. Merilen Graham, not only have you taught my child in your class and tutored her on weekends but you have also been an important caregiver. Thank you.

To my daughter, Samanthi, thanks for your patient and impatient understanding, as I worked during family vacations and on weekends and weeknights. And thank you for pulling Mommy away from the computer, too. I love you very, very much and I thank God for you.

NOTES

Prologue

1. The story was carried in all the local Philadelphia papers and in other area
    papers, such as the *New York Police Gazette*, the *Richmond* (Va.) *Daily Times*, the
    Washington (D.C.) *National Republican*, the *Emporia* (Ky.) *Weekly News*, the
    Saint Paul (Minn.) *Daily Globe*, and the *Sedalia* (Mo.) *Weekly*. For a brief discus-
    sion of this case, see Kali N. Gross, *Colored Amazons: Crime, Violence, and Black
    Women in the City of Brotherly Love, 1880–1910* (Durham: Duke University Press,
    2006), 94–97. Throughout the historical accounts, the central character's name
    shifts between "Hannah Mary Tabbs" and "Mary Hannah Tabbs." I have elected
    to use Hannah Mary Tabbs consistently because this is the name Tabbs used
    when she signed official documents in 1891. See Hannah A. Tabbs, 1891, file
    no. 310974, United States Civil War Widows and Other Dependents Pension
    Files (National Archives and Records Administration, Washington, D.C.).
2. A number of works served as important models for approaching the text in this
    way, books such as Melton A. McLaurin, *Celia, A Slave* (New York: Avon, 1999);
    Patricia Cline Cohen, *The Murder of Helen Jewett* (New York: Vintage, 1999);
    Suzanne Lebsock, *A Murder in Virginia: Southern Justice on Trial* (New York:
    W. W. Norton, 2003); Heidi Ardizzone and Earl Lewis, *Love on Trial: An
    American Scandal in Black and White* (New York: W. W. Norton, 2002); and
    Timothy Gilfoyle, *A Pickpocket's Tale: The Underworld of Nineteenth-Century
    New York* (New York: W. W. Norton, 2007). While I understand that race is
    socially constructed, I use terms like "black" and "white" and "race," as these are
    terms used by the people in this account and because race, then as now, plays a
    powerful role in structuring society. On social constructions of race, see Michael

Omi and Howard Winant, *Racial Formation in the United States,* 3rd ed. (New York: Routledge, 2014), 106–9; David Morley and Kuan-Hsing Chen, eds., *Stuart Hall: Critical Dialogues in Cultural Studies* (New York: Routledge, 1996), 411–51; Jacqueline Jones, *A Dreadful Deceit: The Myth of Race from the Colonial Era to Obama's America* (New York: Basic, 2013), xi–xiii.

3. "Respectable" is defined as being chaste, moral/Christian, married, a good mother, and otherwise virtuous. For more detailed discussions of the politics of respectability, see Evelyn Brooks Higginbotham, *Righteous Discontent: The Women's Movement in the Black Baptist Church, 1880–1920* (Cambridge, Mass.: Harvard University Press, 1994), 14–15, 100, 145; Kevin K. Gaines, *Uplifting the Race: Black Leadership, Politics, and Culture in the Twentieth Century* (Chapel Hill: University of North Carolina Press, 1996), 45–46, 57, 76–83; E. Frances White, *Dark Continent of Our Bodies: Black Feminism and the Politics of Respectability* (Philadelphia: Temple University Press, 2001), 36–39, 122–23; and Victoria Wolcott, "Female Uplift Ideology, the Politics of Class, and Resettlement in Detroit," in *Remaking Respectability: African American Women in Interwar Detroit,* by Victoria Wolcott (Chapel Hill: University of North Carolina Press, 2000), 11–48. Tabbs is engaged in a similar kind of narrative/self-presentation balancing act as Mrs. Mary Seacole, who is discussed in Rhonda Frederick's work; see Rhonda Frederick, "Creole Performance in *Wonderful Adventures of Mrs. Seacole in Many Lands,*" *Gender and History* 15, no. 3 (November 2003): 494. Geography here builds on Frederick's work by referring to the historical ways that geographical spaces have been configured and contested via biased notions of race and gender. See Stephanie M. H. Camp, *Closer to Freedom: Enslaved Women and Everyday Resistance in the Plantation South* (Chapel Hill: University of North Carolina Press, 2004), 7–8.

4. In telling black women's stories, many scholars explore how to write against one-sided historical records. Works that I have found helpful are Saidiya Hartman, "Venus in Two Acts," *Small Axe* 12, no. 2 (June 2008): 1–14; Michel-Rolph Trouillot, *Silencing the Past: Power and the Production of History* (Boston: Beacon, 1995); Evelyn Brooks Higginbotham, "Beyond the Sound of Silence: Afro-American Women in History," *Gender and History* 1, no. 1 (1989): 50–67; Evelyn Brooks Higginbotham, "African-American Women's History and the Metalanguage of Race," *Signs* 17, no. 2 (Winter 1992): 251–74; Michele Mitchell, "Silences Broken, Silences Kept: Gender and Sexuality in African American Women's History," *Gender and History* 11, no. 3 (November 1999): 433–44.

5. Some of the works on slavery include Deborah Gray White, *Ar'n't I a Woman?: Female Slaves in the Plantation South* (New York: W. W. Norton, 1999); Daina Ramey Berry, *"Swing the Sickle for the Harvest Is Ripe": Gender and Slavery in Antebellum Georgia* (Urbana: University of Illinois Press, 2010); Camp, *Closer to Freedom*; Erica Armstrong Dunbar, *A Fragile Freedom: African American Women and Emancipation in the Antebellum City* (New Haven: Yale University Press,

2011); Amrita Chakrabarti Myers, *Forging Freedom: Black Women and the Pursuit of Liberty in Antebellum Charleston* (Chapel Hill: University of North Carolina Press, 2011); Nell Irvin Painter, *Sojourner Truth: A Life, A Symbol* (New York: W. W. Norton, 1997); Margaret Washington, *Sojourner Truth's America* (Urbana: University of Illinois Press, 2011); Thavolia Glymph, *Out of the House of Bondage: The Transformation of the Plantation Household* (Cambridge: Cambridge University Press, 2008). For works on the post-emancipation period, see Hannah Rosen, *Terror in the Heart of Freedom: Citizenship, Sexual Violence, and the Meaning of Race in the Postemancipation South* (Chapel Hill: University of North Carolina Press, 2008); Rosalyn Terborg-Penn, *African American Women in the Struggle for the Vote, 1850–1920* (Bloomington: Indiana University Press, 1998); Tera W. Hunter, *To 'Joy My Freedom: Southern Black Women's Lives and Labors after the Civil War* (Cambridge, Mass.: Harvard University Press, 1998); Jacqueline Jones, *Labor of Love, Labor of Sorrow: Black Women, Work, and the Family from Slavery to the Present* (New York: Basic, 2009); Sharon Harley, ed., *Sister Circle: Black Women and Work* (New Brunswick: Rutgers University Press, 2002); Mary Frances Berry, *My Face Is Black Is True: Callie House and the Struggle for Ex-Slave Reparations* (New York: Vintage, 2006); Noliwe Rooks, *Ladies' Pages: African American Women's Magazines and the Culture That Made Them* (New Brunswick: Rutgers University Press, 2004); Farah Jasmine Griffin, *"Who Set You Flowin'?": The African-American Migration Narrative* (New York: Oxford University Press, 1996); Kirsten Kai Buick, *Child of the Fire: Mary Edmonia Lewis and the Problem of Art History's Black and Indian Subject* (Durham: Duke University Press, 2010); Tiffany M. Gill, *Beauty Shop Politics: African American Women's Activism in the Beauty Industry* (Urbana: University of Illinois Press, 2010); Higginbotham, *Righteous Discontent*; Francille Rusan Wilson, *Segregated Scholars: Black Social Scientists and the Creation of Black Labor Studies, 1890–1950* (Charlottesville: University of Virginia Press, 2006). For works that explore black female crime and vice, see Cheryl D. Hicks, *Talk with You Like a Woman: African American Women, Justice, and Reform in New York, 1890–1935* (Chapel Hill: University of North Carolina Press, 2010); Cynthia M. Blair, *I've Got to Make My Livin': Black Women's Sex Work in Turn-of-the-Century Chicago* (Chicago: University of Chicago Press, 2010); Talitha LeFlouria, *Chained in Silence: Black Women and Convict Labor in the New South* (Chapel Hill: University of North Carolina Press, 2015). For works that explore the mid-to-late twentieth century, see Angela Y. Davis, *Blues Legacies and Black Feminism: Gertrude "Ma" Rainey, Bessie Smith, and Billie Holiday* (New York: Vintage, 1999); Dayo F. Gore, *Radicalism at the Crossroads: African American Women Activists in the Cold War* (New York: New York University Press, 2012); Jo Ann Robinson, *Montgomery Bus Boycott and the Women Who Started It: The Memoir of Jo Ann Gibson Robinson* (Knoxville: University of Tennessee Press, 1987); Chana Kai Lee, *For Freedom's Sake: The Life of Fannie Lou Hamer* (Urbana:

University of Illinois Press, 2005); Danielle L. McGuire, *At the Dark End of the Street: Black Women, Rape, and Resistance—A New History of the Civil Rights Movement from Rosa Parks to the Rise of Black Power* (New York: Vintage, 2011); Bettye Collier-Thomas, *Jesus, Jobs, and Justice: African American Women and Religion* (New York: Alfred A. Knopf, 2010); Elaine Brown, *A Taste of Power: A Black Woman's Story* (New York: Anchor, 1993); Bettye Collier-Thomas and V. P. Franklin, *Sisters in the Struggle: African-American Women in the Civil Rights–Black Power Movement* (New York: New York University Press, 2001); Barbara Ransby, *Ella Baker and the Black Freedom Movement: A Radical Democratic Vision* (Chapel Hill: University of North Carolina Press, 2005); Jeanne Theoharis, *The Rebellious Life of Mrs. Rosa Parks* (Boston: Beacon, 2013); Assata Shakur, *Assata: An Autobiography* (New York: Lawrence Hill, 2001). For surveys of black women's history, see Darlene Clark Hine and Kathleen Thompson, *A Shining Thread of Hope: The History of Black Women in America* (New York: Broadway, 1999); Paula Giddings, *When and Where I Enter: The Impact of Black Women on Race and Sex in America*, 2nd ed. (New York: Perennial, Harper Collins, 2001); Gerda Lerner, *Black Women in White America: A Documentary History* (New York: Vintage, 1992).

6. I am borrowing from Frank B. Wilderson III's notion of anti-blackness and violence. "Blackness is the site of absolute dereliction at the level of the Real, for in its magnetizing of bullets the Black body functions as the map of gratuitous violence through which civil society is possible." Frank B. Wilderson III, "The Prison Slave as Hegemony's (Silent) Scandal," *Social Justice* 30, no. 2 (2003): 18–27, esp. 25. Also, as Barbara Christian noted, storytelling is how we theorize. See Barbara Christian, "The Race for Theory," *Cultural Critique* 6 (Spring 1987): 52. I have found W. E. B. Du Bois's work helpful in that he acknowledged that discrimination in policing and the legal system distorts the nature of black offending. See W. E. B. Du Bois, *The Philadelphia Negro: A Social Study* (1896; repr., Philadelphia: University of Pennsylvania Press, 1996), 242.

7. Because whites ridiculed blacks in the dominant public spheres and denied them access to mainstream legal and public forums, African Americans were forced into their own enclave communities. See Kidada E. Williams, *They Left Great Marks on Me: African American Testimonies of Racial Violence from Emancipation to World War I* (New York: New York University Press, 2012), 104, 147. Many works have examined the sexual violence against black women during slavery and have highlighted how, even after emancipation, legal redress for black women was limited at best. See Rosen, *Terror in the Heart of Freedom*, 7–8, 9–11; Gross, *Colored Amazons*, 73–77, 79; Steven Wilf, *Law's Imagined Republic: Popular Politics and Criminal Justice in Revolutionary America* (Cambridge: Cambridge University Press, 2010), 121; Randolph Roth, *American Homicide* (New York: Belknap, 2012), 272; Kali Nicole Gross, "African American Women, Mass Incarceration, and the Politics of Protection," *Journal of American History* 102,

no. 1 (June 2015): 25–33. I am building on the work of Douglass Flowe, whose research on black men in turn-of-the-century New York argues that black men cultivated narratives of themselves as "bad niggers" as a means of staving off interracial violence. See Douglass Flowe, "'Dem niggas wuzn' skeered of nothing': Saloons, Dives, and Male-Centered Criminal Economy in Manhattan's Negro Bohemia, 1890–1910," paper delivered at the annual meeting of the Association of the Study of African American Life and History, Jacksonville, Florida, October 2013, p. 29. I am also interested in the work of Brendan O'Flaherty and Rajiv Sethi, who argue that "culture-of-violence" and "tail-of-the-distribution" theories inadequately address racial disparities. They argue that studies must take into account that murder can be preemptive, in that sometimes people—particularly those in areas that lack appropriate protection—"kill simply to avoid being killed." See Brendan O'Flaherty and Rajiv Sethi, "Homicide in Black and White," *Journal of Urban Economics* 68, no. 3 (November 2010): 215–30. I am also interested in engaging parts of Frantz Fanon's discussion of the role of violence for oppressed or colonized peoples: "At the individual level, violence is a cleansing force. It rids the colonized of their inferiority complex, of their passive and despairing attitude. It emboldens them, and restores their self confidence.... Violence hoists the people up to the level of the leader." See Frantz Fanon, *The Wretched of the Earth* (1961; repr., New York: Grove, 2005), 51.

Chapter 1

1. For the location of Eddington, Pennsylvania, see E. P. Noll and Co., *Combined Atlases of Bucks County, Pennsylvania, 1876–1891: Indexed* (Mt. Vernon, Ind.: Windmill Publications, 1992); *Philadelphia Public Ledger (PL)*, Feb. 19, 1887; and *Philadelphia Times (PT)*, Feb. 19, 1887. For information on Silas Hibbs and his family, see *1880 US Federal Census*. For Hibbs's daily route and actions that day, see *Philadelphia Evening Bulletin (EB)*, Feb. 18, 1887; *PL*, Feb. 19, 1887; *PT*, Feb. 19, 1887; and *Philadelphia Inquirer (PI)*, Feb. 19, 1887. On the ownership of the pond by Williams B. Mann, see *PL*, Feb. 19, 1887.

2. The headline was written and spaced in this manner in *EB*, Feb. 18, 1887.

3. Bills of Indictment, RG 21.46, No. 237, May Sessions, 1887, *Commonwealth v. Mary Hannah Tabbs*, MURDER., True Bill, May 16, 1887, see section titled "Witnesses."; No. 238, May Sessions, 1887, *Commonwealth v. George H. Wilson*, MURDER., True Bill, May 16, 1887, see section titled "Witnesses." Philadelphia City Archive, Philadelphia, PA (PCA); *EB*, Feb. 18, 1887; *PL*, Feb. 19, 1887; *Doylestown Intelligencer (DI)*, Feb. 18, 1887, Bensalem Twp., Eddington News, *DI*, 1886–1890, 1897–1900, Spruance Library, Mercer Museum, Doylestown, PA (SP).

4. *DI*, Feb. 18, 19, 1887; Post-Mortem Certification, Feb. 24, 1887, Bucks County Coroner's Report no. 1547, February 24, 1887, and the Coroner's Inquisition, no.

1547, March 2, 1887, Coroners Papers 1700–1900, Bucks County Archives (SP); *PT*, Feb. 19, 1887.

5. Howard O. Sprogle, *The Philadelphia Police: Past and Present* (Philadelphia: Howard O. Sprogle, 1887), 89–113; Allen Steinberg, *The Transformation of Criminal Justice: Philadelphia, 1800–1880* (Chapel Hill: University of North Carolina Press, 1989), 177–78, 187–88; Kali N. Gross, *Colored Amazons: Crime, Violence, and Black Women in the City of Brotherly Love, 1880–1910* (Durham: Duke University Press, 2006), 37. Craig B. Little, "The Criminal Courts in 'Young America': Bucks County, Pennsylvania, 1820–1860, with Some Comparisons to Massachusetts and South Carolina," *Social Science History* 15, no. 4 (Winter 1991): 457–78, esp. 458, 459.

6. Little, "Criminal Courts in 'Young America,'" 458; Craig B. Little, "Horse Thief Pursuing Companies of Nineteenth-Century Bucks County, Pennsylvania," *Mercer Mosiac* 3 (1986): 5–18; Craig B. Little and Christopher P. Sheffield, "Frontiers and Criminal Justice: English Private Prosecution Societies and American Vigilantism in the Eighteenth and Nineteenth Centuries," *American Sociological Review* 48 (1983): 796–808.

7. "A Vigilance Committee Wanted," *DI*, Mar. 3, 1898.

8. *PL*, Feb. 19, 1887; *PT*, Feb. 19, 1887; *PI*, Feb. 19, 1887; *EB*, Feb. 18, 1887. Newspapers note that Dr. William Winder, a physician from Andalusia, another village in Bensalem Township, also visited the site where the body was found. For William S. Silbert's occupation, see *1880 US Federal Census* and *1900 US Federal Census* available at Ancestry.com. On Evan J. Groom, see *1880 US Federal Census*.

9. Daniel Kilbride, "Southern Medical Students in Philadelphia, 1800–1861: Science and Sociability in the 'Republic of Medicine,'" *Journal of Southern History* 65, no. 4 (November 1999): 697–732, esp. 697–98. Founded in 1850, the Female Medical College of Pennsylvania was the first "medical school regularly organized for the exclusive purpose of training women to be physicians." See Sandra L. Chaff, "Images of Female Medical Students at the Turn of the Century," *Signs: Journal of Women in Culture and Society* 4, no. 1 (1978): 203–7, esp. 203.

10. Bucks County Coroner's Report no. 1547 and Coroner's Inquisition no. 1547, Coroners Papers 1700–1900 (SP); *EB*, Feb. 18, 1887; "The Bensalem Mystery," *Newtown (PA) Enterprise (NE)*, Feb. 26, 1887.

11. *EB*, Feb. 18, 1887; *DI*, Feb. 19, 1887; *PI*, Feb. 19, 1887.

12. *EB*, Feb. 18, 1887. There are three men named John Murray in the *1880 US Federal Census*: one in Bristol and two in Bensalem.

13. Frederick B. Jackson worked as a laborer before becoming constable. See *1880 US Federal Census*. *PT*, Feb. 19, 1887; *PI*, Feb. 19, 1887; *PL*, Feb. 19, 1887; *DI*, Feb. 18, 1887.

14. In Hugh B. Eastburn's statements to the press he seemed to be weighing the possibilities that a medical student could be responsible for the death, despite inves-

tigators' statements to the contrary. *EB*, Feb. 18, 1887. For Eastburn's background, see *1880 US Federal Census*. *DI*, Feb. 18, 1887.

15. *DI*, Feb. 21, 22, 1887.

16. *DI*, Feb. 21, 22, 1887. For information on the numbers of blacks in Bucks County, see William W. H. Davis, *The History of Bucks County, Pennsylvania from the Discovery of the Delaware to the Present Time*, vol. 2 (New York: Lewis, 1905), 2:13, 64, 162.

17. *PT*, Feb. 19, 1887.

18. *DI*, Feb. 18, 1887. One Frank T. Allen appears in the 1880 census in Bucks County and it lists a brother, but the names do not match. However, the newspaper article mentions that the two live on a farm and that is mentioned in the census. See *1880 US Federal Census*.

19. *EB*, Feb. 19, 1887.

20. *PT*, Feb. 19, 1887.

21. *EB*, Feb. 19, 1887. For the estimated weight and age of the victim, see *PL*, Feb. 19, 1887; and *PT*, Feb. 19, 1887.

22. Fears of "miscegenation" abounded, and in 1882 the US Supreme Court upheld laws prohibiting interracial sex, arguing that the laws were not discriminatory because the law was applied equally to both parties. *Pace v. Alabama*, 106 U.S. 583 (1883). See also Debra Thompson, "Racial Ideas and Gendered Intimacies: The Regulation of Interracial Relationships in North America," *Social and Legal Studies* 18, no. 3 (September 2009): 359. The rise of miscegenation laws also reflected reemerging science that stressed the importance of racial purity and regarded intermixing as catastrophic. See Peggy Pascoe, *What Comes Naturally: Miscegenation Law and the Making of Race in America* (Oxford: Oxford University Press, 2009), 6–7.

23. On the tensions and eventual expansion of whiteness to include European ethnic immigrants, see Nell Irvin Painter, *A History of White People* (New York: W. W. Norton, 2010), 201–11; Noel Ignatiev, *How the Irish Became White* (New York: Routledge, 1995), 3–4, 144–204; Matthew Frye Jacobson, *Whiteness of a Different Color: European Immigrants and the Alchemy of Race* (Cambridge, Mass.: Harvard University Press, 1998), 140–42; David Roediger, *The Wages of Whiteness: Race and the Making of the American Working Class* (New York: Verso, 1994); and David Roediger, *Toward the Abolition of Whiteness: Essays on Race, Politics, and Working-Class History* (New York: Verso, 1994); Frederick L. Hoffman, *Race Traits and Tendencies of the American Negro* (New York: Macmillan, 1896), 225.

24. Gross, *Colored Amazons*, 8–9, 133–38. Michael Sappol's work on Sammy Tubbs also points to the renewal of scientific interest. See Michael Sappol, *A Traffic of Dead Bodies: Anatomy and Embodied Social Identity in Nineteenth-Century America* (Princeton: Princeton University Press, 2002), 239–41. Nicole Hahn Rafter, *Creating Born Criminals* (Urbana: University of Illinois Press, 1998),

36–38, 57, 69–84, 86–89; Harriet A. Washington, *Medical Apartheid: The Dark History of Medical Experimentation on Black Americans from Colonial Times to the Present* (New York: Doubleday, 2006), 99–100.

25. Thomas Jefferson, *Notes on the State of Virginia* (Paris: n.p., 1783), 50, 138; Washington, *Medical Apartheid*, 98–99.

26. Concern about so-called white blacks emerged as early as the 1780s, but whether mulattoes were included is unclear. For my purposes I am including them in this discussion and group. Harriet A. Washington also notes that these "white blacks" were also regarded as popular spectacles and appeared in freak shows and traveling vaudeville acts. See Washington, *Medical Apartheid*, 94–95. Charles D. Martin, *The White African American Body: A Cultural and Literary Exploration* (New Brunswick: Rutgers University Press, 2002), 18–20, 21. Also see Allyson Hobbs, *A Chosen Exile: A History of Racial Passing in American Life* (Cambridge, Mass.; Harvard University Press, 2014), 9–10, 73–75. Helen MacDonald's work also explains the racialized theories of monogenists, who believed that man had a common origin with racial differences being a matter of degrees versus those polygenists who "held that the races were both distinct and immutable, and had different origins. For polygenists, there was no way that civilised men with good intentions could 'raise' the savage races." See Helen MacDonald, *Human Remains: Dissection and Its Histories* (New Haven: Yale University Press, 2005), 103–6.

27. Martin, *White African American Body*.

28. Kevin Gaines, *Uplifting the Race: Black Leadership, Politics, and Culture in the Twentieth Century* (Chapel Hill: University of North Carolina Press, 1996), 65–76; Gross, *Colored Amazons*, 107–8. Washington, *Medical Apartheid*, 98–99. Khalil Gibran Muhammad, *The Condemnation of Blackness: Race, Crime, and the Making of Modern Urban America* (Cambridge, Mass.: Harvard University Press, 2010), 16, 23–25; Joel Williamson, *New People: Miscegenation and Mulattoes in the United States* (Baton Rouge: Louisiana State University Press, 1995).

29. Leonard Richard Lempel, "The Mulatto in United States Race Relations: Changing Status and Attitudes, 1800–1940" (Ph diss., Syracuse University, 1979), 248, 264, 268, 271; Josiah C. Nott noted that "numerous attempts have been made to establish the intellectual equality of the dark races with white; and the history of the past has been ransacked for examples, but they are nowhere to be found." See Josiah C. Nott, *Two Lectures on the Connection between the Biblical and Physical History of Man* (New York: Bartlett and Welford, 1849), 31; Josiah C. Nott, *Two Lectures on the Natural History of the Caucasian and Negro Races* (Mobile: Dade and Thompson, 1884); and Josiah C. Nott, "The Mulatto a Hybrid—Probable Extermination of Two Races if the Whites and Blacks Are Allowed to Intermarry," *The American Journal of the Medical Sciences* 66 (July 1843): 252–56. J. C. Nott and Geo. R. Gliddon, *Types of Mankind: Or, Based upon the Ancient Monuments, Paintings, Sculptures, and Crania of Races, and upon Their*

Natural, Geographical, Philological and Biblical History (Philadelphia: Lippincott, Grambo & Co., 1854).

30. Pascoe, *What Comes Naturally*, 27–30; although the deterioration of whiteness may have been a greater concern (at least initially) to southern eugenicists than a black threat, strict antimiscegenation marriage laws were a part of their race-purity strategy. See Edward J. Larson, *Sex, Race, and Science: Eugenics in the Deep South* (Baltimore: Johns Hopkins University Press, 1995), 1–3, 22–24, 33–34.

31. *PT*, Jan. 3, 1898. Newspapers also reported on the devastating effects of being bitten by "blue gummed" Negroes. See "A 'Blue-Gummed' Negro Bite," *PT*, Mar. 17, 1890, roll no. 8.75: Miscellaneous 1889–1890, William H. Dorsey Scrapbook Collection (Cheyney University of Pennsylvania, Cheyney, Pa.); and "A Black White: A Beautiful Baby Made to Look Like a Negro," *Philadelphia Press*, Mar. 19, 1880, roll no. 6.60: Miscellaneous, 1868–1885, Dorsey Collection (CH). See also Roger Lane, *William Dorsey's Philadelphia and Ours: On the Past and Future of the Black City in America* (New York: Oxford University Press, 1991), 34; Gross, *Colored Amazons*, 134.

32. Stephen J. Gould, "American Polygeny and Craniometry before Darwin: Blacks and Indians as Separate, Inferior Species," in *The "Racial" Economy of Science: Toward a Democratic Future*, ed. Sandra Harding (Bloomington: Indiana University Press, 1993), 84–115; and Nancy Leys Stephan and Sander Gilman, "Appropriating the Idioms of Science: The Rejection of Scientific Racism," in *The "Racial" Economy of Science*, 173; Muhammad, *Condemnation of Blackness*, 22–34; MacDonald, *Human Remains*, 103–6. See also Charles Darwin, *The Origin of the Species by Means of Natural Selection* (London: John Murray, 1859). On the overall degeneracy and criminality of the black race, few works are more damning than Hoffman, *Race Traits and Tendencies of the American Negro*, 217, 225, 234–37.

33. Sydney Klaus, "A History of the Science of Pigmentation," in *The Pigmentary System: Physiology and Pathophysiology*, ed. James J. Nordlund et al. (New York: Oxford University Press, 1998), 5–6. Sidney Klaus notes three schools of thought on this subject: (1) the belief that the origins of skin color differences could be found in the epithelial cells of the epidermis, (2) that the origins lay in the connective tissues, and (3) that the origins stemmed from both epidermis and the connective tissues. See also H. E. Jordan, "A Comparative Microscopic Study of the Melanin Content of Pigmented Skins with Special Reference to the Question of Color Inheritance among Mulattos," *American Naturalist* 45, no. 536 (August 1911): 453–55.

34. Sappol, *Traffic of Dead Bodies*, 2; Robert L. Blakely and Judith M. Harrington, eds., *Bones in the Basement: Postmortem Racism in Nineteenth-Century Medical Training* (Washington, DC: Smithsonian Institution Press, 1997), 195–97.

35. A. R. Thomas, *A Practical Guide for Making Postmortem Examinations, and for the Study of Morbid Anatomy, with Directions for Embalming the Dead, and for the*

Preservation of Specimens of Morbid Anatomy (1873; repr., Lansing: University of Michigan Library, 2005), 312–13.

36. The slow acceptance of fingerprinting in turn-of-the-century police departments, despite flaws in the Bertillon System of Criminal Identification (an anthropometric identification system based on intricate measurements of the criminal anatomy), rather effectively demonstrates the reliance on visuals. See Simone Cole, *Suspect Identities: A History of Fingerprinting and Criminal Identification* (Cambridge, Mass.: Harvard University Press, 2001), 140–53.

37. *PT*, Feb. 19, 1887. *National Police Gazette* (*NPG*), Mar. 5, 1887; *PL*, Feb. 19, 1887; *PI*, Feb. 19, 1887.

38. Washington, *Medical Apartheid*, 99–100.

39. On the coroner's inquest, see *DI*, Feb. 18, 1887; and *PI*, Feb. 19, 1887. On Samuel Mill, see *1880 US Federal Census*; and *EB*, Feb. 19, 1887.

40. On Frank G. Swain, see *1880 US Federal Census*. *DI*, Feb. 21, 1887; *PL*, Feb. 21, 1887; *NE*, Feb. 26, 1887; *PT*, Feb. 20, 1887.

41. *NE*, Feb. 26, 1887; *EB*, Feb. 19, 1887; *PT*, Feb. 21, 1887; *PI*, Feb. 21, 1887.

42. *EB*, Feb. 19, 1887; *PT*, Feb. 20, 1887; *DI*, Feb. 21, 1887. For the rebate procedure, see *The District Reports of Cases Decided in all the Judicial Districts of the State of Pennsylvania, During the Year 1910, vol. 19* (Philadelphia: Howard W. Page, 700 West End Trust Building, 1910), 485.

43. *NE*, Feb. 26, 1887; *EB*, Feb. 19, 1887.

44. *EB*, Feb. 19, 1887; *PT*, Feb. 20, 1887; *PL*, Feb. 21, 1887.

45. *PT*, Feb. 20, 1887; *DI*, Feb. 21, 1887; *NE*, Feb. 26, 1887.

46. *PT*, Feb. 20, 1887; *DI*, Feb. 21, 1887.

47. On Mary Coursey, see *1880 US Federal Census*.

48. *NE*, Feb. 26, 1887; *PT*, Feb. 20, 1887; *PT*, Feb 21, 1887; *DI*, Feb. 21, 1887.

49. Kali Nicole Gross, "Exploring Crime and Violence in Early-Twentieth-Century Black Women's History," in *Contesting Archives: Finding Women in the Sources*, ed. Nupur Chaudhuri, Sherry J. Katz, and Mary Elizabeth Perry (Urbana: University of Illinois Press, 2010), 56; W. E. B. Du Bois, *The Philadelphia Negro: A Social Study* (1896; repr., Philadelphia: University of Pennsylvania Press, 1996).

50. *PT*, Feb. 21, 1887. On George Brock, see *1870 US Federal Census*; and *1880 US Federal Census*.

51. *PT*, Feb. 20, 1887; *DI*, Feb. 21, 1887.

52. On Hugh Eastburn's meeting with Francis Kelly, see *EB*, Feb. 18, 1887. *PT*, Feb. 21, 1887.

53. *PT*, Feb. 20, 1887; *EB*, Feb. 21, 1887.

54. *EB*, Feb. 21, 1887.

55. *EB*, Feb. 21, 1887. In early accounts, the name Waite Gaines appears as either "Gains" or "Gaines" and George Wilson is erroneously listed as John Wilson; I corrected the narrative to make it less confusing; and I use "Gaines" throughout the book because this is what appears in census data and on his marriage records.

See Delaware Marriage Record Index, Silas Wakefield Gaines (December 7, 1882); *1870 US Federal Census*.

56. *EB*, Feb. 21, 1887.
57. *PT*, Feb. 22, 1887.

Chapter 2

1. "Weather Bulletin," *Philadelphia Evening Bulletin (EB)*, Feb. 21, 1887. Hugh Eastburn had reached out to Francis Kelly earlier, but the substance of the dialogue is not clear. See *EB*, Feb. 18, 1887.
2. For the location of Central Station, see Howard O. Sprogle, *The Philadelphia Police: Past and Present* (Philadelphia: Howard O. Sprogle, 1887), 99, 253, 259, 283; and *EB*, Feb. 22, 1887.
3. Kelly had worked in the Secret Service and blended skills he learned as an operative with his training in Philadelphia. See Sprogle, *Philadelphia Police*, 256–58; David R. Johnson, *Policing the Urban Underworld: The Impact of Crime on the Development of the American Police, 1880–1887* (Philadelphia: Temple University Press, 1979), 104, 90–121.
4. Johnson, *Policing the Urban Underworld*, 103–4; Sprogle, *Philadelphia Police*, 204.
5. Johnson, *Policing the Urban Underworld*, 91–92, 114–15; Peter McCaffery, *When Bosses Ruled Philadelphia: The Emergence of the Republican Machine, 1867–1933* (University Park: Pennsylvania State University Press, 1993), 51–52.
6. Sprogle, *Philadelphia Police*, 189, 192–93.
7. Henry Boies, *Prisoners and Paupers: A Study of the Abnormal Increase of Criminals, and the Public Burden of Pauperism in the United States* (New York: Putnam, 1893), 73; W. E. B. Du Bois, *The Philadelphia Negro: A Social Study*, 1896; repr. (Philadelphia: University of Pennsylvania Press, 1996), 241; Frederick Hoffman, *Race Traits and Tendencies of the American Negro* (New York: Macmillan, 1896), 225, 234–37; Nicole Hahn Rafter, *Creating Born Criminals* (Urbana: University of Illinois Press, 1998), 86–89, 118–19; Khalil Gibran Muhammad, *Condemnation of Blackness: Race, Crime, and the Making of Modern Urban America* (Cambridge, Mass.: Harvard University Press, 2010), 16, 23–35; Kali Nicole Gross, *Colored Amazons: Crime, Violence, and Black Women in the City of Brotherly Love, 1880–1910* (Durham: Duke University Press, 2006), 65–66. David R. Johnson writes that physical violence was largely a normal part of police work, and that as long as "officers beat up lower-class criminals, the public seems to have been willing to condone their efforts." See Johnson, *Policing the Urban Underworld*, 103.
8. Sprogle, *Philadelphia Police*, 253–55.
9. Sprogle, *Philadelphia Police*, 256–58. "Counterfeit Trade Dollars," *New York Times*, Dec. 9, 1879; "Violation of the Federal Laws," *New York Times*, Dec. 11,

1879; "Four Counterfeiters Arrested," *New York Times*, June 6, 1882; Sprogle, *Philadelphia Police*, 258–61.

10. Sprogle, *Philadelphia Police*, 262–63. "Act for the Identification of Habitual Criminals," *Laws of the General Assembly of the State of Pennsylvania*, Harrisburg, Pennsylvania, 1881–1909, (1899), No. 109, Pennsylvania State Archives, Harrisbug, Pa. (PSA); Gross, *Colored Amazons*, 136–37; Simon A. Cole, *Suspect Identities: A History of Fingerprinting and Criminal Identification* (Cambridge, Mass.: Harvard University Press, 2002), 32–40.

11. Sprogle, *Philadelphia Police*, 262–63. The "professional criminals act" and those like it that developed elsewhere were not without contest. See "Professional Criminals: The Constitutionality of the Recent Act Sustained," *New York Times*, June 11, 1873. Also see Gross, *Colored Amazons*, 133–38.

12. Barra Foundation, *Philadelphia: A 300-Year History* (New York: W. W. Norton, 1982), 488–90; *The Peoples of Philadelphia: A History of Ethnic Groups and Lower-Class Life, 1790–1940*, ed. Allen F. Davis and Mark Haller (Philadelphia: Temple University Press, 1998), 13, 117, table 10.2.

13. Beggars, Vagrants, and Tramps, code no. 207, in *Patrolman's Manual: Bureau of Police of the City of Philadelphia* (Philadelphia: Department of Public Safety, 1913), reprinted in *Metropolitan Police Manuals, 1817, 1913*, ed. Richard C. Wade (New York: Arno, 1974), 62; Gross, *Colored Amazons*, 70.

14. For the quotations on early instances of racial profiling, see Roger Lane, *Roots of Violence in Black Philadelphia, 1860–1900* (Cambridge, Mass.: Harvard University Press, 1986), 87; Allen Steinberg, *The Transformation of Criminal Justice, Philadelphia, 1800–1880* (Chapel Hill: University of North Carolina Press, 1989), 129; David R. Johnson explains that "Philadelphia's police manual directed lieutenants to suspend any officers who failed to make an arrest whenever a crime occurred on their beats." See Johnson, *Policing the Urban Underworld*, 102. Eric H. Monkkonen's work points to police neglect of black communities as well. See Eric H. Monkkonen, *Police in Urban America, 1860–1920* (Cambridge: Cambridge University Press, 1981), 96–97.

15. "Seeing the Elephant," *National Police Gazette* (*NPG*), Nov. 21, 1885; Gross, *Colored Amazons*, 83–84; Chad Heap, *Slumming: Sexual and Racial Encounters in American Nightlife, 1885–1940* (Chicago: University of Chicago Press, 2010), 23–26, 271; Allen Steinberg noted that critics believed officers received bribes from tavern owners because so many watchmen sought patrols with these kinds of establishments. See Steinberg, *The Transformation of Criminal Justice*, 131.

16. Du Bois, *Philadelphia Negro*, 242–44. On police racial discrimination, see also Muhammad, *Condemnation of Blackness*, 39–55.

17. *Philadelphia Times* (*PT*), Feb. 21, 1887; *Philadelphia Inquirer* (*PI*), Feb. 21, 1887.

18. Sprogle, *Philadelphia Police*, 277–78, 280. For the arrests of James Watson and "Poodle Murphy" who appears in the docket as Henry Williams, see *Prisoners for Trial Docket of Philadelphia County (1790–1948)*, RG 38.38, Jan. 22, 23, 1885 (PCA). Timothy Gilfoyle discusses the arrest of two men in New York with very

similar names, though it's difficult to say with certainty whether the men are the same and using aliases or other pickpockets with comparable nicknames. See the arrests of Terrence "Poodle" Murphy and "Pretty Frank" Brooks in 1891 in Timothy Gilfoyle, *A Pickpocket's Tale: The Underworld of Nineteenth-Century New York* (New York: W. W. Norton, 2007), 213, 409n35.

19. Sprogle, *Philadelphia Police*, 280–81, 288–92; Johnson, *Policing the Urban Underworld*, 189–91, appendix 1. For examples of other arrests made by Thomas Crawford, see Oliver Woods, "Charged with Rape," *Prisoners for Trial Docket of Philadelphia County*, Aug. 28, 31, 1885 (PCA).

20. Sprogle, *Philadelphia Police*, 292–95.

21. Frank P. Geyer, *The Holmes-Pitezel Case: A History of the Greatest Crime of the Century and of the Search for the Missing Children* (Philadelphia: Publisher's Union, 1896), 233. Also see *Commonwealth v. Herman Mudgett, 1895, No. 466, Quarter Sessions Court Records, RG 21.5: Notes of Testimony 1877–1915* (PCA) and *Commonwealth v. Herman W. Mudgett* (1895) in *Pennsylvania State Reports, vol. 174, Containing Cases Adjudged in the Supreme Court of Pennsylvania, January Term, 1896* (New York: Banks & Brothers), 211.

22. Opening ceremonies for the Centennial International Exposition were held on May 10, 1876, and it closed on November 10, 1876. The international commemorative fair of America's first century was the result of years of planning, with the resolution to hold the event in Philadelphia's Fairmount Park being adopted in 1872. See J. S. Ingram, *The Centennial Exposition, Described and Illustrated* (Philadelphia: Hubbard Bros., 1876), 44–45.

23. Sprogle, *Philadelphia Police*, 295–96; "Charge of Murder against Mother," *Philadelphia Public Ledger (PL)*, Dec. 29, 1885. Annie Gaskin was sent to the state asylum in Norristown. See "Annie Gaskin," *Prisoners for Trial Docket of Philadelphia County*, Dec. 29, 1885; and Gross, *Colored Amazons*, 116–17.

24. Du Bois, *Philadelphia Negro*, 74, 58–62, 287–90; Gross, *Colored Amazons*, 51–53. For works that examine southern justice, see Edward L. Ayers, *Vengeance and Justice: Crime and Punishment in the Nineteenth-Century South* (New York: Oxford University Press, 1995), 238–55; David M. Oshinsky, *"Worse Than Slavery": Parchman Farm and the Ordeal of Jim Crow Justice* (New York: Free Press, 1997), 29, 32–55; Douglas A. Blackmon, *Slavery by Another Name: The Re-Enslavement of Black Americans from the Civil War to World War II* (New York: Anchor, 2009); and Talitha L. LeFlouria, *Chained in Silence: Convict Labor in the New South* (Chapel Hill: University of North Carolina Press, 2015), 27–30; Sarah Haley, "'Like I was a Man': Chain Gangs, Gender, and the Domestic Carceral Sphere in Jim Crow Georgia," *Signs* 39, no. 1 (Autumn 2013): 53–77.

25. John F. Sutherland, "Housing the Poor in the City of Homes," in *The Peoples of Philadelphia: A History of Ethnic Groups and Lower-Class Life, 1790–1950*, ed. Allen F. Davis and Mark H. Haller (Philadelphia: University of Pennsylvania Press, 1998), 181; Gross, *Colored Amazons*, 51–53.

56. *PT*, Feb. 23, 1887. On Hannah Mary Tabbs's confession as selective, she omitted information about her affair with the victim and also that Kelly believed she played a more "active part in the quarrel" from the "fact that one of her eyes had been blacked, evidently by a blow," see *PI*, Feb. 23, 1887.

57. *PT*, Feb. 23, 1887.

58. *EB*, Feb. 23, 1887; *PI*, Feb. 23, 1887; *PT*, Feb. 23, 1887; *DI*, Feb. 23, 1887. See also *Richmond (VA) Dispatch*, Feb. 23, 1887; and *Baltimore Sun (BS)*, Feb. 23, 1887.

59. *PT*, Feb. 23, 1887; *PI*, Feb. 23, 1887; *PL*, Feb. 23, 1887.

60. *PL*, Feb. 23, 1887.

61. *EB*, Feb. 23, 1887. For information on George and Harold McCalla, see *1880 US Federal Census*.

62. *EB*, Feb. 23, 1887.

63. *EB*, Feb. 23, 1887. See also "Charged on Oath of F. R. Kelly with Murder of Wakefield Gains," *Prisoners for Trial Docket*, Feb. 23, 1887, p. 475; and "George H. Wilson," Feb. 23, 1887, p. 475; Feb. 24, 1887.

64. *EB*, Feb. 23, 1887; *PT*, Feb. 22, 1887; *PT*, Feb. 24, 1887.

65. *PT*, Feb. 23, 1887.

Chapter 3

1. *Philadelphia Evening Bulletin (EB)*, Feb. 22, 23, 1887; *Philadelphia Record (PR)*, Feb. 24, 1887; *Doylestown Intelligencer (DI)*, Feb. 24, 1887. Hannah Mary Tabbs would also later identify the torso as being part of the body of Wakefield Gaines—which she discarded in a pond in Eddington, Pennsylvania. See *EB*, Feb. 28, 1887; and Post-Mortem Certification, Bucks County Coroner's Report no. 1547, Feb. 24, 1887, and Coroner's Inquisition no. 1547, March 2, 1887, Coroners Papers 1700–1900 (SP).

2. For an example of misleading information, see *Philadelphia Inquirer (PI)*, Feb. 21, 1887; *Philadelphia Times (PT)*, Feb. 22, 1887; *Baltimore Sun (BS)*, Feb. 24, 25, 1887. See also Richard Worthington, Election District 1, 1866–1867, MSA 105–8, Series: *Anne Arundel County Justice of the Peace* (Docket), 1833–1939 (MSA); George F. White, Election District 4, 1867–1874, MSA 105–40, ibid.; James H. Fowler, Election District 5, 1914–1916, MSA 105–62, ibid.; "01/1867–01/1868," MSA 2111–3, Series: Baltimore City Police Department (Criminal Docket, Eastern District) 1863–1959, ibid.; "01/1873–12/1873," MSA 2111–10, ibid.; "01/1867–01/1868," MSA 2113–1, Series: Baltimore City Police Department (Criminal Docket, Southern District) 1867–1960, ibid.; and "01/1876–01/1877," MSA 2113–2, ibid.

3. *Eastern State Penitentiary Convict Descriptive Register, 1829–1903*, RG 15, Department of Justice (PSA), September 28, 1887; *PT*, Feb. 22, 1887; *PR*, Feb. 22, 1887.

4. "Philadelphia Affairs: The Eddington Murder Mystery Cleared Up," *BS*, Feb. 23, 1887; John H. Tabbs, Marriage Index, Male, 1851–1885 (microfilm: reel CR 1682, Stoop to Underwood), Baltimore County Court of Common Pleas, Index Series MSA CM205 (MSA). Hannah A. Tabbs, deposition A, Oct. 12, 1893, file no. 310974, United States Civil War Widows and Other Dependents Pension Files, National Archives and Records Administration, Washington, DC (NA).

5. Barbara Jeanne Fields, *Slavery and Freedom on the Middle Ground: Maryland during the Nineteenth Century* (New Haven: Yale University Press, 1985), 2, table 1.2; Claudia Floyd, *Maryland Women in the Civil War: Unionists, Rebels, Slaves and Spies* (Charleston, S.C.: The History Press, 2013), 36.

6. Fields, *Slavery and Freedom on the Middle Ground*, 6.

7. Seth Rockman, *Scraping By: Wage Labor, Slavery, and Survival in Early Baltimore* (Baltimore: Johns Hopkins University Press, 2009), 3–4, 57–58.

8. Harriet Tubman was born in Dorchester County, Maryland. Sarah Bedford, *Harriet Tubman: The Moses of Her People* (1886; repr., Bedford, Mass.: Applewood, 1993), 108–11. Frederick Douglass was born in Talbot County, Maryland. See Frederick Douglass, *Narrative of the Life of Frederick Douglass, An American Slave* (Boston: Anti-slavery Office, 1845), 19, 23–25, 34–38. On the ways Tubman has been iconized, see Milton C. Sernett, *Harriet Tubman: Myth, Memory, and History* (Durham: Duke University Press, 2007), 3–9.

9. "Caroline Hammond," in *Slave Narratives: A Folk History of Slavery in the United States from Interviews with Former Slaves*, vol. 8: *Maryland Narratives*, comp. Federal Writers' Project (Washington, D.C.: Library of Congress Printing Office, 1941), 19–22. On housing conditions, see "Rezin Williams (Parson)," in *Slave Narratives*, 68–72.

10. "Rezin Williams (Parson)," in *Slave Narratives*, 68–72. James Revell, as the state attorney for Anne Arundel County, prosecuted a case against free blacks who entered the state "unlawfully, contrary to and in violation of the laws." See "To the Honorable Judges of the Orphans Court for Anne Arundel County," April 3, 1860, PAR number 20986043, *Race and Slavery Petitions Project*, http://libraryuncg.edu/slavery/petitions/details.aspx?pid=18103. Census data show a number of white male heads of household with the surname Revell dwelling in various districts in the county. See *1860 US Federal Census*, Daniel Revell, District 8, Anne Arundel County, Theodore Revell, District 3, Anne Arundel County, Martin Revell, Annapolis, Md.; also slave-holding whites with the surname Revell in *1860 US Slave Schedules*, see William T. Revell, *1850 US Slave Schedules*. Also the Simon J. Martenet, *Map of Anne Arundel County*, 1860, Library of Congress, lists a Dr. T. Revell in the Third District (suggesting Wm. T. Revell in the slave schedule is a relative or is the physician listed). For more on black women's early experiences in Maryland, see Jessica Millward, *Finding Charity's Folk: Enslaved and Free Black Women in Maryland* (Athens: University of Georgia Press, 2015).

11. Francis Fredic, *The Autobiography of Rev. Francis Fredic* (Baltimore: J. J. Woods Printer, 1869), 5; Wilma King, *Stolen Childhood: Slave Youth in Nineteenth-Century America*, 2nd ed. (Bloomington: Indiana University Press, 2011), 106, 116, 173–74, 223.

12. Fredic, *Autobiography of Rev. Francis Fredic*, 7.

13. Ariela Gross, *Double Character: Slavery and Mastery in the Antebellum Southern Courtroom* (Athens: University of Georgia Press, 2000), 109. On the evolution of James Henry Hammond's approach to mastery, see Drew Gilpin Faust, *James Henry Hammond and the Old South: A Design for Mastery* (Baton Rouge: Louisiana State University Press, 1982), 99–104; Edward Baptist, *The Half Has Never Been Told: Slavery and the Making of American Capitalism* (New York: Basic, 2014), 117–18.

14. Gross, *Double Character*, 105–6; Baptist, *The Half Has Never Been Told*, 346–47. For a discussion of the violence of white southern masters, also see Edward Baptist, "'My Mind Is to Drown You and Leave You Behind': 'Omie Wise,' Intimate Violence, and Masculinity," in *Over the Threshold: Intimate Violence in Early America*, ed. Christine Daniels and Michael V. Kennedy (New York: Routledge, 1999), 94–95.

15. Douglass, *Narrative of the Life of Frederick Douglass*, 34–38; Faust, *James Henry Hammond and the Old South*, 313–16; E. Frances White, *Dark Continent of Our Bodies: Black Feminism and the Politics of Respectability* (Philadelphia: Temple University Press, 2001), 40–42.

16. Steven Wilf, *Law's Imagined Republic: Popular Politics and Criminal Justice in Revolutionary America* (Cambridge: Cambridge University Press, 2010), 121; Kali Nicole Gross, "African American Women, Mass Incarceration, and the Politics of Protection," *Journal of American History* 102, no. 1 (June 2015): 26–28. Some legislation explicitly negated rape as a crime that might occur between blacks. See *George v. State of Mississippi*, 39 M. 570, 2 Mor. St. Cas. 1404 (1859); and Paula C. Johnson, *Inner Lives: Voices of African American Women in Prison* (New York: New York University Press, 2003), 22–23. Although sex crimes against black women were not punished, Darlene Clark Hine and Kathleen Thompson also note that British common law treated rape as an act against property, and therefore masters could not be considered as raping their own property. See Hine and Thompson, *Shining Thread of Hope* (New York: Broadway, 1998), 170–71; and Deborah Gray White, *Ar'n't I a Woman?: Female Slaves in the Plantation South* (New York: W. W. Norton, 1999), 78; Jennifer Morgan, *Laboring Women: Reproduction and Gender in New World Slavery* (Philadelphia: University of Pennsylvania Press, 2004), 12, 68–72.

17. White, *Dark Continent of Our Bodies*, 30–38; Harriet Jacobs, *Incidents in the Life of a Slave Girl* (Boston: Harriet Jacobs, 1861), 96; Thomas A. Foster, "The Sexual Abuse of Black Men under American Slavery," *Journal of the History of Sexuality* 20, no. 3 (September 2011): 445–64, 447.

18. "Mrs. Nancy Howard," in *The Refugee: Or the Narratives of Fugitive Slaves in Canada. Related by Themselves, with an Account of the History and Condition of the Colored Population of Upper Canada*, by Benjamin Drew (Boston: John P. Jewett and Company, 1856), 50–51. Also see "Mrs. Henry Brant," in *The Refugee*, 346–47.

19. Fields, *Slavery and Freedom on the Middle Ground*, 77–80. For earlier Maryland statutes that aimed to criminalize free blacks, see James D. Rice, "The Criminal Trial before and after the Lawyers: Authority, Law, and Culture in Maryland Jury Trials, 1681–1837," *American Journal of Legal History* 40, no. 4 (October 1996): 427.

20. "Philadelphia Affairs," *BS*, Feb. 23, 24, 1887. Hannah A. Tabbs, deposition B, Oct. 12, 1893, file no. 310974, United States Civil War Widows and Other Dependents Pension Files. Statement made by Rosella Smith (NA).

21. Intake records make no mention of the physical scarring. See *Eastern State Penitentiary Convict Descriptive Register, 1829–1903*, September 28, 1887 (PSA). Also in 1856 a formerly enslaved woman from Maryland noted of her experience that even though she suffered the "worst kind of usage: that of being held as a slave...I was fortunately among those who did not beat and bruise me." See "Mrs. Henry Brant," in *The Refugee*, 356.

22. *PI*, Feb. 23, 1887; *PT*, Feb. 22, 1887; *PT*, Jun. 2, 1887.

23. *Baltimore Der Deutsche Correspondent (DC)*, Feb. 25, 1887; *PR*, Feb. 23, 1887. For enslaved cooks, see Daina Ramey Berry and Deleso A. Alford, *Enslaved Women in America: An Encyclopedia* (Santa Barbara, Calif.: Greenwood, 2011), 38–39, 69, 98–99, 165; Keith Barton, "'Good Cooks and Washers': Slave Hiring, Domestic Labor, and the Market in Bourbon County, Kentucky," *Journal of American History* 84, no. 2 (September 1997): 436–60.

24. Joseph Sheppard, legal representative of Elizabeth Sheppard, appears in the Election District 8. See *Anne Arundel County Commissioner of Slave Statistics, 1864*, MSA C0142–1 (MSA).

25. Floyd, *Maryland Women in the Civil War*, 50–58; Harry A. Ezratty, *Baltimore in the Civil War: The Pratt Street Riot and a City Occupied* (Charleston, S.C.: The History Press, 2010), 17–18.

26. White, *Dark Continents of Our Bodies*, 164; Tera W. Hunter, *To 'Joy My Freedom: Southern Black Women's Lives and Labors after the Civil War* (Cambridge, Mass.: Harvard University Press, 1998), 19–20; Thavolia Glymph, *Out of the House of Bondage: The Transformation of the Plantation Household* (Cambridge: Cambridge University Press, 2008), 131–34; Drew Faust, *This Republic of Suffering: Death and the American Civil War* (New York: Vintage 2009), 27.

27. Antietam, Boonsboro, Folck's Mill, Hancock, Monocacy, South Mountain, and Williamsport were locations of battles. Antietam was the bloodiest; Monocacy sustained an estimated 2,359 casualties, South Mountain saw roughly 4,500 deaths, and Williamsport suffered an estimated 1,730. See the database "Civil War Battle Summaries by State," *The American Battlefield Protection Program*,

http://www.nps.gov/abpp/battles/bystate.htm. Drew Faust discusses the difficulties in burying the bodies and the coping methods soldiers deployed. See Faust, *This Republic of Suffering*, 66–69.

28. E. Harris testimony, July 1, 1871, *Testimony Taken by the Joint Select Committee to Inquire into the Condition of Affairs in the Late Insurrectionary States: North Carolina* (Washington, D.C.: Government Printing Office, 1872), 100, cited in Elsa Barkley Brown, "Negotiating and Transforming the Public Sphere: African American Political Life in the Transition from Slavery to Freedom," *Public Culture* 7 (Fall 1994): 108–12; Glymph, *Out of the House of Bondage*, 132.

29. Floyd, *Maryland Women in the Civil War*, 48; Benson J. Lossing, *Pictorial History of the Civil War in the United States of America*, vol. 3 (Hartford, Conn.: T. Belknap, 1868, reprint by Applewood Books), 346n4.

30. Expanding on an earlier notion that black female violence provides important clues about the perpetrator's own historical experiences with and of violence. See Gross, *Colored Amazons*, 76–81 Nell Irvin Painter, *Southern History across the Color Line* (Chapel Hill: University of North Carolina Press, 2002), 15–39.

31. Brown, "Negotiating and Transforming the Public Sphere," 111–12, 115; Hannah Rosen, *Terror in the Heart of Freedom: Citizenship, Sexual Violence, and the Meaning of Race in the Postemancipation South* (Chapel Hill: University of North Carolina Press, 2008); Catherine Clinton, "Reconstructing Freedwomen," in *Divided Houses: Gender and the Civil War*, ed. Catherine Clinton and Nina Silber (New York: Oxford University Press, 1992), 306–19.

32. Brown, "Negotiating and Transforming the Public Sphere," 108–12, 115, 144; Darlene Clark Hine, "Rape in the Inner Lives of Black Women in the Middle West: Preliminary Thoughts on the Culture of Dissemblance," in Darlene Clark Hine, "Rape in the Inner Lives of Black Women in the Middle West: Preliminary Thoughts on the Culture of Dissemblance," in *Signs* 14, no. 4 (Summer 1989): 912–20.

33. *EB*, Mar. 3, 1887. For example, Ida B. Wells's parents and infant brother died in 1878. See Ida B. Wells, *Crusade for Justice: The Autobiography of Ida B. Wells* (Chicago: University of Chicago Press, 1991); Paula Giddings, *Ida: A Sword among Lions: Ida B. Wells and the Campaign against Lynching* (New York: Harper Paperbacks, 2009), 4; Mia Bay, *To Tell the Truth Freely: The Life of Ida B. Wells* (New York: Hill and Wang, 2010), 4. Some accounts estimated that Annie Richardson was near the age of twenty. See *PR*, Feb. 22, 1887.

34. *Philadelphia Public Ledger* (*PL*), Mar. 2, 1887.

35. The description is a quotation from John Tabbs. See *PR*, Feb. 22, 1887.

36. The names Hannah Smith and John H. Tabbs appear on the marriage certificate. See Marriage Index, Baltimore County Court of Common Pleas. But when Hannah Mary met Gaines's landlady, she introduced herself as Mary Sheppard. See *EB*, Jun. 3, 1887; *Woods' Baltimore City Directory 1865–1866* (Baltimore: John

W. Woods, 1866); *Woods' Baltimore City Directory 1870* (Baltimore: John W. Woods, 1870); and wedding certificate, African Methodist Episcopal Church, Hannah A. Tabbs, deposition A, Oct. 1893, file no. 310974, United States Widows and Other Dependents Pension Files (NA).

37. *Compiled Military Service Records of Volunteer Union Soldiers Who Served with the United States Colored Troops: 1st through 5th United States Colored Cavalry, 5th Massachusetts Cavalry (Colored), 6th United States Colored Cavalry*, publication M1817 (microfilm, 107 reels, National Archives and Records Administration), reel 91; Pension no. 502 985, general affidavit, United States Civil War Widows and Other Dependents Pension Files (NA).

38. *PR*, Mar. 3, 1887.

39. *EB*, Feb. 23, 1887. The actual account misspells the street as "Rayburg," but the Baltimore city directory and a street map confirm that there was a "Rayborg Street"; however, I have been unable to find the school John H. Tabbs references as it may have been held in a church or sponsored by another kind of black organization.

40. *PR*, Feb. 23, 1887. For the assertion that "[Hannah Mary] Tabbs was a capable cook and easily found service," see *DC*, Feb. 25, 1887.

41. Larry Tye, *Rising from the Rails: Pullman Porters and the Making of the Black Middle Class* (New York: Owl Books, Henry Holt, 2005), 36–38; Melinda Chateauvert, *Marching Together: Women of the Brotherhood of Sleeping Car Porters* (Urbana: University of Illinois Press, 1998), 24–30.

42. Marriage records in 1873 list his occupation as a porter, see John H. Tabbs, Marriage Index, Male, 1851–1885 (microfilm: reel CR 1682, Stoop to Underwood), Baltimore County Court of Common Pleas, Index Series MSA CM205 (MSA). For John Tabbs's various positions, see *Wood's Baltimore City Directory* for 1871, 1872, 1873, and 1875. His name does not appear in the directory for the years 1874 or 1876.

43. Dorothy Gondos Beers, "The Centennial City, 1865–1876," in *Philadelphia: A 300-Year History*, ed. Russell F. Weigley (New York: W. W. Norton, 1982), 420.

44. Roger Lane, *Roots of Violence in Black Philadelphia, 1860–1900* (Cambridge, Mass.: Harvard University Press, 1986), 13.

45. Authorities claimed that George Wilson said some of these were sites where he discarded the limbs of Wakefield Gaines. See *PT*, Feb. 24, 1887; *PI*, Feb. 24, 1887; *EB*, Feb. 24, 1887; and *DI*, Feb. 24, 1887.

46. *EB*, Mar. 3, 1887.

47. *PT*, Feb. 26, 1887; *PI*, Mar. 4, 1887; *PR*, Mar. 3, 1887; see Silas Gaines, *1870 US Federal Census*; Silas Wakefield Gaines, Return of Marriage, Seaford of Delaware, Sussex County, December 7, 1882, Marriage Records, Vol. 74, p. 218; Vol. 89, p. 59 (DPA).

48. *PT*, Feb. 22, 1887. I build on the arguments that Elsa Barkley Brown makes about black women appearing to adhere to expected gender mores politically while

exerting their own ideas and opinions intraracially. See Brown, "Negotiating and Transforming the Public Sphere," 108–12.

49. *EB*, Feb. 24, 1887.

50. That African Americans received inequitable justice is fairly well documented but for some discussions of this, see Mary Frances Berry, *Black Resistance, White Law: A History of Constitutional Racism in America* (New York: Penguin, 1994), 81–96; A. Leon Higginbotham, *In the Matter of Color: Race and the American Legal Process. The Colonial Period* (New York: Oxford University Press, 1980), 267–313. For works that discuss black women's inability to receive police protection from abusive partners, see Jeffrey S. Adler, "'I Loved Joe, but I Had to Shoot Him': Homicide by Women in Turn-of-the-Century Chicago," *Journal of Criminal Law and Criminology* 92, no. 3 (Spring–Summer 2002): 892; Randolph Roth, *American Homicide* (New York: Belknap, 2012), 272; Gross, "African American Women," 26–28, 30–31. On shifting police and prosecutorial practices, see Allen Steinberg, *The Transformation of Criminal Justice, Philadelphia, 1800–1880* (Chapel Hill: University of North Carolina Press, 1989), 1–9, 26, 196–232; Roger Lane, *Murder in America: A History* (Columbus: Ohio State University Press, 1997), 194–97.

51. It is impossible to completely transfer psychological terms from the twentieth and twenty-first centuries to illnesses and behaviors enacted by people from the nineteenth century. That said, a broad, expansive definition of trauma such as the one Cathy Caruth sketches is helpful for thinking about Tabbs's violence. Caruth explains that the "pathology consists, rather, solely in the structure of its experience or reception: the event is not assimilated or experienced fully at the time, but only belatedly, in its repeated possession of the one who experiences it. To be traumatized is precisely to be possessed by an image or event." See Cathy Caruth, *Trauma: Explorations in Memory* (Baltimore: Johns Hopkins University Press, 1995), 4. For works that consider this type of violence as an artifice of black vulnerability, see Douglass Flowe, "'Dem niggas wuzn' skeered of nothing': Saloons, Dives, and Male-Centered Criminal Economy in Manhattan's Negro Bohemia, 1890–1910," paper delivered at the annual meeting of the Association of the Study of African American Life and History, Jacksonville, Fla., October 2013, 29; Gross, *Colored Amazons*, 88–89; Cornel West, *Race Matters* (New York: Vintage, 1994), 14–15. Many scholars have written about black women's lack of protection, but I found Randolph Roth's summation particularly useful: black women "were better prepared to defend themselves, because they knew that they could not rely on law enforcement and the courts." He is speaking specifically of domestic violence, but I would argue that this holds true for most violent crime against black women. See Roth, *American Homicide* (New York: Belknap, 2012), 272. For more examples of historical black intraracial violence, see Jeffrey Adler, "'Bessie Done Cut Her Old Man': Race, Common-Law Marriage, and Homicide in New Orleans, 1925–1945," *Journal of Social History* 44 (Fall 2010): 123–43.

52. "Colored Woman Horsewhipped by Three Whites," *Cleveland Gazette*, April 4, 1887. For examples of black women carrying knives, see Gross, *Colored Amazons*, 88–89, 114. After a drunken white man assaulted her and her date on a streetcar and followed her after she exited the car, Bessie Banks stabbed the man. He died, and she was charged with murder. See *Commonwealth v. Bessie Elizabeth Minor Banks*, Jan. 6, 1911, testimony notes, case no. 307, August 1910 Sessions files, Quarter Sessions Court records, RG 21.5: Notes of Testimony 1877–1915 (PCA).

53. Although Hannah Mary Tabbs did drink, John Tabbs could only recall one instance where she was "badly intoxicated," so it is unlikely that her violence was fueled by alcohol. See *EB*, Feb. 24, 1887. His account contradicted that of his niece in that he alleged that Tabbs met Gaines at the Brock residence, and he further charged that he had never seen Gaines.

54. "What the Neighbors Say," *EB*, Feb. 23, 28, 1887.

55. The letter was sent to George Wilson during his imprisonment at the Philadelphia County Jail. *EB*, Mar. 1, 1887. This was likely a crank letter, but whoever sent it had some knowledge of Hannah Mary Tabbs's purported history—because in addition to mentioning Richmond they also connected her to "the Meadow," which I believe is a reference to either the Meadows, a section in Prince George County, Maryland, or the Meadowland, which is a section in Baltimore County, Maryland, where Tabbs lived before migrating to Philadelphia.

56. Census data do list a farmer with the last name of Schenek, however Jacob R. Schenek and his wife, Anna, lived in Raritan, Hunterdon, New Jersey, together with the children, a servant, and a boarder. See *1880 US Federal Census*. The 1895 census shows the Scheneks residing in Hudson County, and there are a number of Annie Richardsons listed in New Jersey, but only two in Hudson County.

57. *EB*, Mar. 3, 1887.

58. *EB*, Mar. 3, 4, 1887. "Annie Richardson" is listed as an inmate in a Philadelphia almshouse, but the dates are a bit off, so it is probably not Hannah Mary Tabbs's niece. See *1880 US Federal Census*, Schedules of the Defective, Dependent, and Delinquent Classes, No. 17. Also she does not appear in the existing intake records for the *House of Refuge, Colored Female Department, 1883–1889*. Historical Society Pennsylvania, Philadelphia, PA (HSP).

59. *EB*, Feb. 23, 1887; *PR*, Mar. 3, 1887.

60. *EB*, Jun. 1, 1887; *PR*, Feb. 23, 24, 1887. For the second anonymous letter, see *PT*, Mar. 2, 1887. The letter stated that Tabbs had killed Annie Richardson and had thrown her body in the river, but by the time the correspondence arrived, Richardson had already surfaced.

61. African American women masked their sexuality to stave off sexual assaults and to counter racist myths about black female morality, or lack thereof. For more on dissemblance, see Hine, "Rape in the Inner Lives of Black Women in the Middle West." Michele Mitchell's work also discusses notions of respectability, sexuality, and social purity. See Mitchell, *Righteous Propagation: African Americans and the*

Politics of Racial Destiny after Reconstruction (Chapel Hill: University of North Carolina Press, 2004), 85–90, 127, 139, 208.

62. *PT*, Feb. 25, 1887; *EB*, Feb. 24, 1887. Hannah A. Tabbs, deposition A, Oct. 12, 1893, file no. 310974, United States Civil War Widows and Other Dependents Pension Files (NA); Hine, "Rape and the Inner-Lives of Black Women in the Middle West," 380–82; Hortense J. Spillers, *Black, White, and in Color: Essays on American Literature and Culture* (Chicago: University of Chicago Press, 2003), 153–66. Tabbs offers a rare glimpse of black female sexual desire. As scholars have noted, black women's history is still wanting for these types of examples. See Evelynn M. Hammonds, "Toward a Genealogy of Black Female Sexuality: The Problematic of Silence," in *Feminist Genealogies, Colonial Legacies, Democratic Futures*, ed. M. Jacqui Alexander and Chandra Talpade Mohanty (New York: Routledge, 1997); Hortense Spillers, "Interstices: A Small Drama of Words," in *Pleasure and Danger: Exploring Female Sexuality*, ed. Carole S. Vance (New York: Routledge, 1984).

63. W. E. B. Du Bois, *Philadelphia Negro: A Social Study* (1896; repr., Philadelphia: University of Pennsylvania Press, 1996), 67–72; Mitchell, *Righteous Propagation*, 85–90; Hazel Carby, "Policing the Black Woman's Body in an Urban Context." *Critical Inquiry* 18, no. 4 (Summer 1992): 738–55; Higginbotham, *Righteous Discontent*, 99–100. See also Hunter, *To 'Joy My Freedom*, 38–40.

64. Tabbs led the Brocks to believe that she had arrived from Richmond, Virginia, but there is no evidence to support this. To the contrary, Annie Richardson told reporters that she lied, to play the Brocks. See *PR*, Mar. 3, 1887.

65. *EB*, Jun. 3, 1887.

66. *PR*, Mar. 3, 1887.

67. *EB*, Feb. 24, 1887; *PI*, Feb. 25, 1887.

68. *EB*, Feb. 23, 1887; *PT*, Feb. 24, 1887.

69. *EB*, Feb. 23, 1887; *PR*, Feb. 24, 1887.

70. *EB*, Feb. 23, 1887; *PR*, Feb. 24, 1887.

71. One newspaper noted that Gaines is a black man who lived in back of 1031 Lemon Street and worked at Einstein's livery stable, at 913 Green Street. See *PR*, Feb 24, 1887. According to the city directory he did live at the residence, and he worked as a "hastier." See *Gopsill's Philadelphia City Directory for 1887: A Complete and Accurate Index to the Residents of the Entire City—Their Names, Business, and Location. With an Appendix Containing Useful Information as to Banks, Insurance Companies, Churches, City, State, and Miscellaneous Records, Carefully Selected and Compiled. Also a Valuable Street Index or Guide, as Furnished by the City Survey Department* (Philadelphia: James Gopsill's Sons, 1887).

72. *PR*, Feb. 24, 1887.

73. *PR*, Feb. 24, 1887. See Silas Wakefield Gaines, Delaware Marriage Records, 1806–1933, Sussex County, 1883 (DPA). On the marital discord, see *PI*, Feb. 26, 1887.

74. *PT*, Feb. 24, 1887.
75. *PT*, Feb. 24, 1887.
76. On Gaines looking ashen, see *PI*, Feb. 25, 1887; *EB*, Feb. 25, 1887; *PR*, Feb. 25, 1887; *PL*, Feb. 25, 1887; and *BS*, Feb. 25, 1887.
77. *PT*, Feb. 25, 1887; *BS*, Feb. 25, 1887.
78. *BS*, Feb. 25, 1887.
79. *EB*, Feb. 24, 1887; *PT*, Feb. 25, 1887.

Chapter 4

1. Maimie Pinzer, *The Maimie Papers: Letters from an Ex-Prostitute*. Edited by Ruth Rosen and Susan Davidson (New York: Feminist, 1996), 193–94. On Tabbs's and Wilson's night in their holding cells, see *Philadelphia Inquirer* (*PI*), Feb. 23, 24, 1887; and *Philadelphia Times* (*PT*), Feb. 23, 24, 1887.
2. *Philadelphia Evening Bulletin* (*EB*), Feb. 23, 1887.
3. *EB*, Feb. 23, 1887. "B, Mary Tabbs, committed February 23, 1887; Charged on Oath of F. R. Kelly with Murder of Wakefield Gains," *Prisoners for Trial Docket*, 475; "#78, B, George H. Wilson, committed February 24, 1887, Charged on Oath of F. R. Kelly with Murder of Wakefield Gaines," ibid., 477 (PCA).
4. *PT*, Feb. 24, 1887.
5. On mulattoes having better educations and employment, see Theodore Hershberg, "Mulattoes and Blacks: Intra-Group Differences and Social Stratifications in Nineteenth-Century Philadelphia," in *Philadelphia: Work, Space, Family, and Group Experience in the Nineteenth Century: Essays Toward an Interdisciplinary History of the City*, ed. Theodore Hershberg (New York: Oxford University Press, 1981); Leonard Richard Lempel, "The Mulatto in United States Race Relations: Changing Status and Attitude, 1800–1940" (Ph diss., Syracuse University, 1979), 248–49, 253. Despite believing that white blood contributed to mulattoes being smarter than pure-blooded Negroes, E. W. Gilliam ultimately concluded that "the blending of different white blood makes, in every way, a stronger race; but every instance of blending between white and black has proven adverse, creating in the end, a half-breed race below the pure African ancestry." See E. W. Gilliam, "The African Problem," *North American Review* 139, no. 336 (November 1884): 417–30, esp. 425; Nell Painter also discusses how these ideas permeated American Anthropology. See Painter, *A History of White People* (New York: W. W. Norton, 2010), 198–202.
6. These fears were particularly strident in the South, but those notions did not remain in that region. Rather, "southern attitudes about race had a high power in the North." See Joel Williamson, *New People: Miscegenation and Mulattoes in the United States* (New York: Free, 1980), 95, 109; Lempel, "Mulatto in United States Race Relations," 248–49, 255, 271; Harriet A. Washington, *Medical Apartheid:*

The Dark History of Medical Experimentation on Black Americans from Colonial Times to the Present (New York: Doubleday, 2006), 144–45. Nell Painter also makes reference to "the invisible taint of black blood," which is what so rattled mainstream Philadelphians observing Wilson for the first time. See Painter, *A History of White People*, 129. Also see Grace Elizabeth Hale, *Making Whiteness: The Culture of Segregation in the South, 1890–1940* (New York: Vintage, 1999), 27, 66–74.

7. *PT*, Feb. 23, 24, 1887; *PI*, Feb. 24, 1887.
8. Writings of men such as Josiah C. Nott found that "mulattoes, (i.e.) those born of parents one being African and the other white of Caucasian, are the *shortest lived of any class of the human race.*" See Nott, *Two Lectures on the Natural History of the Caucasian and Negro Race* (Mobile, Ala. Dade and Thompson, 1844), 30. See also Werner Sollors, *Neither Black nor White, yet Both: Thematic Explorations of Interracial Literature* (Cambridge, Mass.: Harvard University Press, 1997), 129–35. On the laws prohibiting unions, given the threat of the progeny, see Sollors, *Neither Black nor White, yet Both*, 399–407. The "natural result of an uninterrupted contact of half-breeds with one another is a class of men in which pure type fades away as completely as do all the good qualities, physical and moral, of the primitive races, engendering a mongrel crowd as repulsive as mongrel dogs." See Professor and Mrs. Louis Agassiz, *A Journey in Brazil* (Boston: Houghton, Osgood, and Company, 1879), 298, 296–98; Painter, *A History of White People*, 198–202.
9. *PT*, Feb. 23, 1887.
10. *EB*, Feb. 23, 24, 1887; *Philadelphia Public Ledger* (*PL*), Feb. 24, 1887; *PI*, Feb. 24, 1887; *Baltimore Sun* (*BS*), Feb. 24, 1887.
11. The original news story listed Mr. Mathews instead of Mr. Mattheas. See *EB*, Feb. 25, 1887; *PI*, Feb. 26, 1887; *PL*, Feb. 26, 1887; and *Doylestown Intelligencer* (*DI*), Feb. 26, 1887.
12. *EB*, Feb. 24, 1887; *PT*, Feb. 24, 1887.
13. *EB*, Feb. 24, 1887.
14. *PT*, Feb. 24, 26, 1887; *PL*, Feb. 25, 1887.
15. Howard O. Sprogle, *Philadelphia Police: Past and Present* (Philadelphia: Howard O. Sprogle, 1887), 288–89; *EB*, Feb. 24, 1887.
16. *PT*, Feb. 24, 1887.
17. During the trial, witnesses claimed that the detectives showed Wilson Tabbs's confession in the newspaper, but also that they permitted reporters to question him. *EB*, Feb. 24, 1887. These sentiments, however, are contradicted in *PL*, Feb. 25, 1887. Wilson claims he never said these things, and during the trial his attorneys suggested that he was given alcohol by the detectives so he would further incriminate himself.
18. The officers listed were John Nash, William Wilson, Robert McKelvey, and Samuel Seybert. See *EB*, Feb. 24, 1887. *PL*, Feb. 25, 1887.

19. *PL*, Feb. 25, 1887.
20. *EB*, Feb. 24, 1887; *PI*, Feb. 24, 1887.
21. *EB*, Feb. 25, 1887. See also *1880 US Federal Census*.
22. See Joseph C. Mattheas, in *1880 US Federal Census*; *EB*, Feb. 25, 1887.
23. *EB*, Feb. 25, 1887; *PL*, Feb. 25, 1887.
24. *EB*, Feb. 25, 1887.
25. *EB*, Feb. 25, 1887; *EB*, Feb. 26, 1887. For information that another witness, Herbert A. Galloway, corroborated Mattheas's and Lee's statements, see *PT*, Feb. 27, 1887. City directories list Galloway as a driver living in a house at 1216 Federal Street, see *Gopsill's Philadelphia City Directory* (Philadelphia: James Gopsill's Sons, 1886).
26. *EB*, Feb. 25, 1887.
27. *EB*, Feb. 25, 1887; *EB*, Feb. 23, 25, 1887. For a description of Wilson as semi-idiotic, see *Baltimore Der Deutsche Correspondent (DC)*, Feb. 25, 1887.
28. *EB*, Feb. 25, 1887.
29. *PL*, Feb. 24, 1887.
30. *EB*, Feb. 26, 1887; *PI*, Feb. 26, 1887. A number of plaintiffs described similar experiences with interrogations by the Philadelphia police. See *Commonwealth v. Bessie Elizabeth Minor Banks*, January 6, 1911, testimony notes, pp. 77–78, 79–81, 145–47, case no. 307, August 1910 Sessions files, Quarter Sessions Court records, RG 21.5: Notes of Testimony 1877–1915 (PCA); and *Commonwealth v. Henrietta Cook*, n.d., testimony notes, pp. 124–29, 136, 144; case no. 625, November 1906 Sessions files, Quarter Sessions Court records, RG 21.5: Notes of Testimony 1877–1915 (PCA); and Kali Nicole Gross, "Exploring Crime and Violence in Early-Twentieth Century Black Women's History," in *Contesting Archives: Finding Women in the Sources*, ed. Nupur Chaudhuri, Sherry J. Katz, and Mary Elizabeth Perry (Urbana: University of Illinois Press, 2010), 59–61.
31. *EB*, Feb. 26, 1887.
32. *EB*, Feb. 26, 1887. On William F. Church, assistant superintendent, House of Refuge, h, 2417 N. College Ave, see the 1886 edition of *Gospill's Philadelphia City Directory*.
33. Negley K. Teeters, "Institutional Treatment of Juvenile Delinquents," *Nebraska Law Review* 29, no. 4 (May 1950): 580–82. For more on Philadelphia's institution, see Cecile P. Remick, "The House of Refuge of Philadelphia, 1786–1859" (Ph diss., University of Pennsylvania, 1975).
34. "House of Refuge for Coloured Children," *The Friend: A Religious and Literary Journal* (January 26, 1850): 19–23.
35. On gradual emancipation, see Erica Armstrong Dunbar, *A Fragile Freedom: African American Women and Emancipation in the Antebellum City* (New Haven: Yale University Press, 2008), 3, 9–10, 23–24, 29–31. For early racial turmoil and the role of prisons and policy, see W. E. B. Du Bois, *The Philadelphia Negro: A Social Study* (1896; repr., Philadelphia: University of Pennsylvania Press, 1996), 15–25;

Leslie Patrick, "Numbers That Are Not New: African Americans in the Country's First Prison, 1790–1853," *Pennsylvania Magazine of History and Biography* 119 (January–April 1995): 100–102; Sprogle, *Philadelphia Police*, 76–88; Robert Purvis, *Appeal of Forty Thousand Citizens Threatened with Disfranchisement, to the People of Pennsylvania* (Philadelphia: Merrihew and Gunn, 1837); Bruce Laurie, "Fire Companies and Gangs in Southwark: The 1840s," in *The Peoples of Philadelphia: A History of Ethnic Groups and Lower-Class Life, 1790–1950*, ed. Allen F. Davis and Mark H. Haller (Philadelphia: University of Pennsylvania Press, 1998), 71–88; Sprogle, *Philadelphia Police*. Also see Jasmine Nichole Cobb, *Picture Freedom: Remaking Black Visuality in the Early Nineteenth Century* (New York: New York University Press, 2015), 112–17, 123–26.

36. Cecile P. Frey, "The House of Refuge for Colored Children," *Journal of Negro History* 66, no. 1 (Spring 1989): 10. Anthony Platt, *The Child Savers: The Invention of Delinquency* (New Brunswick: Rutgers University Press, 2009), 3–4, 46–55.

37. Frey, "House of Refuge for Colored Children," 11.

38. Frey, "House of Refuge for Colored Children," 13–15, 18. Geoff K. Ward, *The Black-Child Savers: Racial Democracy and Juvenile Justice* (Urbana: University of Illinois Press, 2012), 53–58. Also see Alexander W. Pisciotta, "Race, Sex, and Rehabilitation: A Study of Differential Treatment in the Juvenile Reformatory, 1825–1900," *Crime and Delinquency* 29, no. 2 (April 1983): 260–62.

39. Frey, "House of Refuge for Colored Children," 17; Ward, *Black-Child Savers*, 53–55. *House of Refuge, Colored Department, History of Boys*, p. 1234 (HSP). Though poverty plays a seminal role in placement facilities such as the House of Refuge, gender also factored, as many working-class parents committed daughters when they breached social mores such as chastity and obedience. See Sherrie Broder, *Tramps, Unfit Mothers, and Neglected Children: Negotiating the Family in Late Nineteenth-Century Philadelphia* (Philadelphia: University of Pennsylvania Press, 2002), 1–6, 115–23.

40. *House of Refuge, Colored Department, History of Boys*, p. 1234 (HSP). Wilson reportedly told the doctor who treated him for the seizure in custody that his mother died from the same kind of "fit." *EB*, Feb. 23, 1887.

41. *House of Refuge, Colored Department, History of Boys*, p. 1234 (HSP). Around this time Wilson's aunt lists her name as Martha Wallace. I believe she wed either James Wallace or Nathaniel Wallace, and, for a time, they lived around the corner from Richard Street at 1640 Helmuth Street. See the 1886 edition of *Gopsill's Philadelphia City Directory*.

42. *House of Refuge Monthly School Report, Colored Department, April 24, 1885*, see "Education on Admission" and "Education on Discharge" (HSP).

43. *House of Refuge Medical Reports* (HSP).

44. *PL*, Feb. 24, 1887.

45. Frey, "House of Refuge for Colored Children," 17.

46. House of Refuge, Monthly School Report, 1879 (HSP).

47. *Report of the Special Committee to Investigate the Alleged Cruelties and Abuses at the House of Refuge in Philadelphia* (Harrisburg, Pa.: B.F. Meyers, State Printer, 1875), 9–12, 19–25.

48. Kali Nicole Gross, *Colored Amazons: Crime, Violence, and Black Women in the City of Brotherly Love, 1880–1910* (Durham: Duke University Press, 2006), appendix, table I. See also letter from A. Sydney Biddle, Nov. 1883, *Minutes of the Pennsylvania Prison Society, Sept. 9, 1883–Jan. 24, 1889, vol. 7*, 8–9 (HSP).

49. *EB*, Feb. 26, 1887.

50. *EB*, Feb. 28, 1887.

51. *EB*, Feb. 28, 1887. *BS*, Feb. 26, 1887; *PT*, Feb. 20, 1887.

52. *PT*, May 17, 1887. On Wilson being "almost white in color," see *PL*, Jun. 1, 1887. Gross, *Colored Amazons*, 111–15.

53. *EB*, Feb. 23, 1887.

54. *EB*, Feb. 23, 1887. Another account noted that Wilson "looks more like a Cuban or Spaniard than a negro," see *EB*, May 31, 1887.

55. *EB*, Feb. 25, 1887.

56. Washington, *Medical Apartheid*, 144–45; Lempel, "Mulatto in United States Race Relations," 248–49, 253; Williamson, *New People*, 95, 109. Passing proved especially worrisome because it threatened to destabilize white racial authority. See Gayle Wald, *Crossing the Line: Racial Passing in Twentieth-Century U.S. Literature and Culture* (Durham: Duke University Press, 2000), 3–5. Michael Omi and Howard Winant also discuss the slippery nature of racial identification and ways that individuals have and can switch racial performance. See Omi and Winant, *Racial Formation in the United States*, 3rd ed. (New York: Routledge, 2015), 2–3, 23–27.

57. *EB*, Feb. 28, 1887.

58. Mary Bailey had also been a resident of Helmuth Street, Wilson's former neighborhood. See *PI*, Feb. 24, 1887; and *1880 US Federal Census*.

59. *EB*, Feb. 28, 1887.

60. *EB*, Feb. 21, 1887.

61. *EB*, Feb. 28, 1887; *PI*, Mar. 1, 1887.

62. *EB*, Feb. 28, 1887.

63. *EB*, Feb. 28, 1887; *PI*, Mar. 1, 1887; *PT*, Mar. 1, 1887.

64. *EB*, Feb. 28, 1887.

65. *PI*, Mar. 1, 1887.

66. *EB*, Feb. 28, 1887.

67. Over the course of the investigation and trial, descriptions of Tabbs went from her being light-skinned, to mulatto-colored, to her being characterized as black and ugly. In her mug shot, she looks to be brown-skinned. The songs, poems, and stories circulated contained romantic images of slavery days that contrasted chaotic, pathological depictions of free African Americans and black life in the urban North. See Gross, *Colored Amazons*, 112, 108–10.

68. *EB*, Feb. 28, 1887; *PI*, Mar. 1, 1887.
69. *EB*, Feb. 28, 1887.
70. *EB*, Feb. 28, 1887.
71. *EB*, Feb. 28, 1887.

Chapter 5

1. *The Philadelphia Times Almanac for the Years 1887–1890* (Philadelphia, 1891), 52. Roger Lane, *Violent Death in the City: Suicide, Accident, and Murder in Nineteenth-Century Philadelphia* (Columbus: Ohio State University Press, 1999), appendix A, 147–49.
2. Lane, *Violent Death in the City*, 16.
3. Lane, *Violent Death in the City*, 58–59.
4. *Official Hand Book, City Hall, Philadelphia* (2 vols., Philadelphia: City Publishing Co., 1901), 14.
5. Lane, *Violent Death in the City*, 148. Also see Lincoln Steffens, *The Shame of the Cities* (New York: Farrar, Straus and Giroux, 1904), 150–53.
6. James Poupard, *A History of Microbiology in Philadelphia: 1880–2010* (Xlibris, 2010), 18–19; *University of Pennsylvania Medical Magazine* 4 (October 1891–September 1892) (Philadelphia: University of Pennsylvania Press, 1892), 736.
7. *University of Pennsylvania Medical Magazine*, 736.
8. Henry Formad, *Comparative Studies of Mammalian Blood, with Special Reference to the Microscopical Diagnosis of Blood Stains in Criminal Cases* (Philadelphia: A. L. Hummel, 1888), 31–46.
9. Allen Steinberg, *The Transformation of Criminal Justice, Philadelphia, 1800–1880* (Chapel Hill: University of North Carolina Press, 1989), 20–21; Lawrence Friedman, *Crime and Punishment in American History* (New York: Basic, 1993), 244, 252–53.
10. Friedman, *Crime and Punishment in American History*, 242–43.
11. I am building on ideas explored in A. Cheree Carlson's research on gender in nineteenth-century courtrooms and Kidada E. Williams's work on how African Americans deployed testimonies to recover from trauma and contest racial violence. Carlson, *The Crimes of Womanhood: Defining Femininity in a Court of Law* (Urbana: University of Illinois Press, 2008), 1–11; Williams, *They Left Great Marks on Me: African American Testimonies of Racial Violence from Emancipation to World War I* (New York: New York University Press, 2012), 2–6.
12. For notions of inherent criminality and bias, see Kali Nicole Gross, "African American Women, Mass Incarceration, and the Politics of Protection," *Journal of American History* 102, no. 1 (June 2015): 26–28; Kali Nicole Gross, *Colored Amazons: Crime, Violence, and Black Women in the City of Brotherly Love, 1880–1910* (Durham: Duke University Press, 2006), 8–11, 34; Nicole Hahn Rafter,

Creating Born Criminals (Urbana: University of Illinois Press, 1998), 6–8, 118–22. For African Americans' and black women's history in Philadelphia's justice system, see Leslie Patrick, "Numbers That Are Not New: African Americans in the Country's First Prison, 1790–1853," *Pennsylvania Magazine of History and Biography* 119 (January–April 1995): 99–102; and Jack D. Marietta and G. S. Rowe, *Troubled Experiment: Crime and Justice in Pennsylvania, 1682–1800* (Philadelphia: University of Pennsylvania Press, 2006), 248–63.

13. Borrowing the phrase from Nell Irvin Painter, *A History of White People* (New York: W. W. Norton, 2010), 129. Harryette Mullen explains that "racism reifies whiteness to the extent that it is known or presumed to be unmixed with blackness. 'Pure' whiteness is imagined as something that is both external and internal. While the white complexion of the mulatto or octoroon is imagined as something superficial, only-skin deep, the black blood passing onto the body an inherited impurity." Harryette Mullen quoted in Jennifer DeVere Brody, *Impossible Purities: Blackness, Femininity, and Victorian Culture* (Durham: Duke University Press, 1998), 12.

14. *The Philadelphia Evening Bulletin (EB)*, Mar. 2, 1887. Also see *Prisoners for Trial Docket of Philadelphia County*, Mar. 2, 1887: Wilson, charged on oath of F. R. Kelly "with Murder of Wakefield Gains"; Tabbs charged "with being an accessory to the death of Wakefield Gaines"; *Prison Commitment Docket, Female* (1840–1956), RG 38.56, Mar. 2, 1887 (PCA).

15. *The Philadelphia Inquirer (PI)*, Mar. 3, 1887; *EB*, Mar. 2, 1887; *PI*, Mar. 3, 1887; Gross, *Colored Amazons*, 110–15.

16. *EB*, Mar. 2, 1887. See George S. Graham in the *1880 US Federal Census*.

17. *PI*, Mar. 3, 1887.

18. On black women's virtuosity, meaning being morally upright and in a manner that also helped rehabilitate the image of the race, see Paula Giddings, *When and Where I Enter: The Impact of Black Women on Race and Sex in America* (New York: Perennial, Harper Collins, 2001), 87–88; and Laurie Wilkie, *The Archaeology of Mothering: An African-American Midwife's Tale* (New York: Routledge, 2003), 79–80. *PI*, Mar. 3, 1887; *EB*, Mar. 2, 1887.

19. *EB*, Mar. 2, 1887.

20. *EB*, Mar. 2, 1887.

21. *EB*, Mar. 2, 1887; *PI*, Mar. 3, 1887.

22. Gross, *Colored Amazons*, 105–7. *EB*, Mar. 2, 1887.

23. *EB*, Mar. 2, 1887.

24. *EB*, Mar. 2, 1887; *Philadelphia Public Ledger (PL)*, Mar. 1, 1887.

25. *EB*, Mar. 2, 1887.

26. *EB*, Mar. 2, 1887.

27. *EB*, Mar. 2, 1887.

28. *EB*, Mar. 2, 1887; *Philadelphia Times (PT)*, Mar. 3, 1887.

29. *EB*, Mar. 2, 1887.

30. *EB*, Mar. 2, 1887.

31. Quoted in *EB*, Mar. 2, 1887. Also see *PI*, Mar. 3, 1887; *PL*, Mar. 3, 1887; *PT*, Mar. 3, 1887.

32. James R. Grossman, "A Chance to Make Good: 1900–1929," in *To Make Our World Anew: A History of African Americans since 1800*, vol. 2, ed. Robin D. G. Kelly and Earl Lewis (New York: Oxford University Press, 2005), 117–18; Jennifer Lynn Ritterhouse, *Growing Up Jim Crow: How Black and White Southern Children Learned Race* (Chapel Hill: University of North Carolina Press, 2006), 30; Bertram Wilbur Doyle, *The Etiquette of Race Relations in the South: A Study in Social Control* (Urbana: University of Illinois Press, 1937), 14. Thomas J. Sugrue also references these "southern 'customs' " as black soldiers in the 1940s aimed to defy them. See Sugrue, *Sweet Land of Liberty: The Forgotten Struggle for Civil Rights in the North* (New York: Random House, 2008), 65.

33. Quoted in *PT*, Mar. 3, 1887. Also see *PI*, Mar. 3, 1887; *EB*, Mar. 2, 1887; *PL*, Mar. 3, 1887.

34. Quoted in *PT*, Mar. 3, 1887.

35. *EB*, Mar. 3, 1887; *EB*, Feb. 28, 1887.

36. *EB*, Mar. 2, 1887.

37. *EB*, Mar. 2, 1887.

38. *EB*, Mar. 2, 1887; *PI*, Mar. 3, 1887; *PL*, Mar. 3, 1887.

39. *EB*, Mar. 3, 1887; *PT*, Mar. 3, 1887.

40. *PT*, Mar. 3, 1887; *PI*, Mar. 3, 1887; *PL*, Mar. 3, 1887.

41. *EB*, Mar. 3, 1887; *PT*, Mar. 3, 1887.

42. For examples, see "Mary Tabbs's Confession," *New York Times*, Feb. 23, 1887; *Richmond (VA) Daily Times*, Mar. 1, 1887; "Gaines Murderers," *Wichita (KS) Eagle*, Feb. 24, 1887; *Indianapolis Indiana State Sentinel*, Mar. 2, 1887; "The Gaines Murder Case," *Washington (DC) National Republican*, Jun. 1, 1887; "Will Hang," *Sedalia (MO) Weekly*, Jun. 7, 1887.

43. Lawrence Friedman, *A History of American Law* (New York: Simon and Schuster, 1985), 576.

44. William W. Conway, lawyer, had a number of addresses—presumably for his home and practices, see *Gopsill's Philadelphia City Directory for 1886. PT*, Mar. 5, 1887; *EB*, Mar. 1, 1887. Gray v. Commonwealth, 101 Pa. St. 380, 47 Am. Rep. 733.

45. Many infanticide cases involved fairly extreme acts of brutality. Katie Chizawska, for example, dismembered her newborn and stuffed the body parts in a drainpipe. See Kali Nicole Gross, "Exploring Crime and Violence in Early-Twentieth-Century Black Women's History," in *Contesting Archives: Finding Women in the Sources*, ed. Nupur Chaudhuri, Sherry J. Katz, and Mary Elizabeth Perry (Urbana: University of Illinois Press, 2010), 65–67; *EB*, Mar. 12, 1887.

46. *EB*, Mar. 12, 1887.

47. *EB*, Mar. 12, 1887.

48. *EB*, May 16, 1887; *PI*, May 17, 1887; *PT*, May 17, 1887. Bills of Indictment, RG 21.46, No. 237, May Sessions, 1887, *Commonwealth v. Hannah Mary Tabbs*.

MURDER. True Bill. May 16, 1887; No. 238, May Sessions, 1887, *Commonwealth v. George H. Wilson*. MURDER. True Bill. May 16, 1887 (PCA). See Robert Ralston, Lawyer, 402 Walnut Street, h 233 S 13, in *Gopsill's Philadelphia City Directory for 1888* (Philadelphia: James Gopsill's Sons, 1888); and *Prominent and Progressive Pennsylvanians of the Nineteenth Century* (2 vols., Philadelphia: Record Publishing Company, 1898), 2:415. See Alfred Guillo, in *1880 US Federal Census*.

49. *EB*, May 31, 1887; *PT*, Jun. 1, 1887. See *Quarter Sessions Court Record (1874–1888)*, RG 38. 46, May 31, 1887: Geo. H. Wilson, Mary H. Tabbs (PCA).

50. *EB*, May 31, 1887.

51. *EB*, May 31, 1887.

52. *EB*, May 31, 1887; *PI*, Jun. 1, 1887; *PT*, Jun. 1, 1887. Although few could be verified in census data, most of the jurors appeared in Philadelphia City directories: George Gibbons, appears as a "Horseshoer" at this address. See *Gopsill's Philadelphia City Directory for 1885*; and *Gopsill's Philadelphia City Directory for 1888*. For W, Irish immigrant, see *1880 US Federal Census*; John A. Graham is listed as a "printer" at this address, see *Gopsill's Philadelphia City Directory for 1887*; Charles Harper, "porter," works at this address, see *Gopsill's Philadelphia City Directory for 1887*, Harry S. Huhn, "salesman," see *Gopsill's Philadelphia City Directory for 1887*; and *Philadelphia City Directory for 1889*; Anthony Loftus "carpenter" lived at 925 Carpenter, however, Anthony Loftus Jr. worked as a "finisher" and lived at 926 Carpenter, see *Gopsill's Philadelphia City Directory for 1887*; Robert McLaughlin, "painter," at 172 Church, see *Gopsill's Philadelphia City Directory for 1887*; William Paullin, "real estate," at this address, see *Gopsill's Philadelphia City Directory for 1888*; James Robinson, "finisher," is listed as living at 1024 Adams, *Gopsill's Philadelphia City Directory for 1886*; and for Henry Bearne, see *Gopsill's Philadelphia City Directory for 1887*.

53. First quote from *PL*, Jun. 1, 1887, the second quote from *EB*, May 31, 1887.

54. *EB*, May 31, 1887.

55. *EB*, May 31, 1887; *PT*, Jun. 1, 1887; *PL*, Jun. 1, 1887.

56. *PT*, Jun. 1, 1887.

57. *PR*, Jun. 1, 1887; *PT*, Jun. 1, 1887.

58. *PT*, Mar. 6, 1887. Mrs. Nicholson was a member of the Philadelphia Society for Alleviating the Miseries of Public Prisons and routinely visited prisoners. See *Minutes of the Pennsylvania Prison Society (Sept. 20, 1883–Jan. 24, 1889, vol. 7)*, 22, 115 (HSP). However, the visiting list at the county prison does not show Mrs. Nicholson visiting Tabbs or any of the female prisoners in March 1887, though it shows that Mrs. Robinson, Mrs. Reilly, and Mrs. Hutchinson all visited in the early part of the month. See *Philadelphia County Prison, Prison Diary, Female Department, 1850–1935*, RG 38.68, March 1887 (PCA).

59. I am building on Joseph Laythe's argument that female criminals were viewed through gendered, cultural tropes that made their crimes and behaviors legible.

See Joseph Laythe, *Engendered Death: Pennsylvania Women Who Kill* (Langham: Lehigh University Press, 2011), 37–54. For more on the perils of "playing the lady," see Dorothy Sterling, *We Are Your Sisters: Black Women in the Nineteenth Century* (New York: Norton Paperback, 1971), xv; and Leon Litwack, *Been in the Storm So Long: The Aftermath of Slavery* (New York: First Vintage Books, 1980), 245; Elsa Barkley Brown and Gregg D. Kimball, "Mapping the Terrain of Black Richmond," *Journal of Urban History* 21, no. 3 (March 1995): 332–33. Still, black women found ways to embrace being ladies. See Noliwe Rooks, *Ladies' Pages: African American Women's Magazines and the Culture That Made Them* (New Brunswick: Rutgers University Press, 2005).

60. *EB*, Jun. 1, 1887; *PI*, Jun. 2, 1887; *PT*, Jun. 2, 1887. At this point, Chief Kelly had been replaced as chief of detectives, though press accounts varied between noting him as chief or former chief. The new mayor, the Hon. Edwin H. Fitler, wrote to the Select Council requesting a number of changes to the Department of Public Safety and among his requests are as follows: "Chas. W. Wood, Chief of Detectives, *vice* Francis R. Kelly, removed." See *Journal of the Select Council of the City of Philadelphia (From April 4, 1887, to September 27, 1887. Vol. 1. With an Appendix)* (Philadelphia: Dunlap & Clarke, Printers and Binders, 1887), appendix to journal, 24. I have continued referring to him as Chief Kelly, however, to avoid confusion.

61. *EB*, Jun. 1, 1887; *PI*, Jun. 2, 1887; *PT*, Jun. 2, 1887. On Carrie Kilgore, see Rebecca Mae Salokar and Mary L. Volcansek, *Women in Law: A Bio-Bibliographical Sourcebook* (Westport, Conn.: Greenwood, 1996), 125–27; and Virginia G. Drachman, *Sisters in Law: Women Lawyers in Modern American History* (Cambridge, Mass.: Harvard University Press, 2001), 52.

62. *EB*, Jun. 1, 1887; *PI*, Jun. 2, 1887; *PT*, Jun. 2, 1887.

63. *EB*, Jun. 1, 1887; *PI*, Jun. 2, 1887; *PT*, Jun. 2, 1887.

64. *EB*, Jun. 1, 1887; *PI*, Jun. 2, 1887; *PT*, Jun. 2, 1887.

65. *PT*, Jun. 2, 1887.

66. *EB*, Jun. 1, 1887.

67. *PL*, Jun. 2, 1887.

68. *PL*, Jun. 2, 1887.

69. *PL*, Jun. 2, 1887.

70. *PL*, Jun. 2, 1887.

71. *PL*, Jun. 2, 1887.

72. *EB*, Feb. 23, 1887; *PI*, Feb. 23, 1887; *PT*, Feb. 23, 1887.

73. *PL*, Jun. 2, 1887.

74. *PL*, Jun. 2, 1887.

75. John Loughran, listed as a "Pawnbroker," lived at 1704 South Street. See *Gopsill's Philadelphia City Directory for 1887*. *PL*, Jun. 2, 1887.

76. *PL*, Jun. 2, 1887.

77. *PL*, Jun. 2, 1887.

78. *PL*, Jun. 2, 1887.
79. *PL*, Jun. 2, 1887.
80. *PL*, Jun. 2, 1887; *PT*, Jun. 2, 1887.
81. *PL*, Jun. 2, 1887; *PT*, Jun. 2, 1887.
82. *EB*, Jun. 2, 1887; *PT*, Jun. 3, 1887; *PI*, Jun. 3, 1887.
83. *EB*, Jun. 2, 1887; *PT*, Jun. 3, 1887; *PI*, Jun. 3, 1887.
84. *EB*, Jun. 2, 1887; *PT*, Jun. 3, 1887; *PI*, Jun. 3, 1887.
85. *EB*, Jun. 2, 1887; *PT*, Jun. 3, 1887; *PI*, Jun. 3, 1887.
86. *EB*, Jun. 2, 1887.
87. *EB*, Jun. 2, 1887.
88. *EB*, Jun. 2, 1887.

Chapter 6

1. *Philadelphia Public Ledger* (*PL*), Jun. 3, 1887; *Philadelphia Evening Bulletin* (*EB*), Jun. 2, 1887.
2. William Draper Lewis, "John Innes Clark Hare," *American Law Register* 54, no. 12; vol. 45, New Series (December 1906): 711–17, esp. 711.
3. Robert Davison Coxe, *Legal Philadelphia: Comments and Memories* (Philadelphia: William J. Campbell, 1908), 72–73.
4. Coxe, *Legal Philadelphia*, 74.
5. Legal historians have noted the tensions between the power of judges and the juries. See Lawrence Friedman, *A History of American Law*, rev. ed. (New York: Simon and Schuster, 1985), 435–36; Lawrence Friedman, *Crime and Punishment in American History* (New York: Basic, 1993), 244–48; James D. Rice, "The Criminal Trial before and after the Lawyers: Authority, Law, and Culture in Maryland Jury Trials, 1681–1837," *Journal of American Legal History* 40, no. 4 (October 1996): 473–74.
6. *EB*, Jun. 2, 1887; *Philadelphia Inquirer* (*PI*), Jun. 3, 1887.
7. *EB*, Jun. 3, 1887; *Philadelphia Times* (*PT*), Jun. 4, 1887; *PI*, Jun. 4, 1887; *PL*, Jun. 4, 1887.
8. *EB*, Jun. 3, 1887; *PT*, Jun. 4, 1887; *PL*, Jun. 4, 1887. One account notes that I. Newton Brown explained, "I now propose to ask the witness…whether he inquired as a letter carrier whether George H. Wilson lived there and whether he was there at the time." District Attorney Graham reportedly objected to this question, but again the reason why he objected is omitted. *PI*, Jun. 4, 1887.
9. *EB*, Jun. 3, 1887.
10. Rice, "The Criminal Trial," 472–73; Kali Nicole Gross, *Colored Amazons: Crime, Violence, and Black Women in the City of Brotherly Love, 1880–1910* (Durham: Duke University Press, 2006), 98–99, 115–16; Nicole Hahn Rafter, *Partial Justice: Women, Prisons, and Social Control*, 2nd ed. (New Brunswick: Transaction

Publishers, 2004), 134, 155; Rhonda Frederick, "Creole Performance in *Wonderful Adventures of Mrs. Seacole in Many Lands*," *Gender and History* 15, no. 3 (November 2003): 494. Also see *Quarter Sessions Court Record 1850–1935*, RG 38.68, Jun. 1, 1887, Jun. 2, 1887, Jun. 3, 1887, Jun. 4, 1887: Geo. H. Wilson, Mary H. Tabbs (PCA). Accounts also noted that she seemed more like a "demure" wife or widow than a cold-bolded killer. See *PT*, May 17, 1887.

11. *EB*, Jun. 3, 1887.
12. *EB*, Jun. 3, 1887.
13. *EB*, Jun. 3, 1887.
14. *EB*, Jun. 3, 1887.
15. *EB*, Jun. 3, 1887.
16. *EB*, Jun. 3, 1887.
17. *EB*, Jun. 3, 1887. Also see *Commonwealth v. Henrietta Cook*, testimony notes, pp. 124–29, 136, 144, case no. 625, November 1906 Sessions files, Quarter Sessions Court records, RG 21.5: Notes of Testimony 1877–1915 (PCA).
18. *PL*, Jun. 4, 1887.
19. *PL*, Jun. 4, 1887.
20. *PL*, Jun. 4, 1887.
21. *PL*, Jun. 4, 1887.
22. *PL*, Jun. 4, 1887.
23. *PL*, Jun. 4, 1887.
24. *PL*, Jun. 4, 1887.
25. *PL*, Jun. 4, 1887; *PI*, Feb. 24, 1887. For Graham's quotes, see Bills of Indictment, RG 21.56, No. 238, May Sessions 1887: *Commonwealth v. George H. Wilson*, Motion for a new trial, page 3 (PCA).
26. *PL*, Jun. 6, 1887. For Graham's quotes, see No. 238, May Sessions 1887: *Commonwealth v. George H. Wilson*, Motion for a new trial, pages 6–7 (PCA).
27. Gross, *Colored Amazons*, 162, tables 9, 10; Patrick, "Numbers That Are Not New," 98, 100–101, 111, table 5. Steinberg, *The Transformation of Criminal Justice: Philadelphia, 1800–1880* (Chapel Hill: University of North Carolina Press, 1989), 43; Roger Lane, *Roots of Violence in Black Philadelphia, 1860–1900* (Cambridge, Mass.: Harvard University Press, 1986), 88; Rafter, *Partial Justice*, 134, 144–49, 155.
28. *PL*, Jun. 6, 1887; No. 238, May Sessions 1887: *Commonwealth v. George H. Wilson*, Motion for a new trial, pages 6–8 (PCA).
29. *PL*, Jun. 6, 1887; No. 238, May Sessions 1887: *Commonwealth v. George H. Wilson*, Motion for a new trial, page 9 (PCA).
30. *PL*, Jun. 6, 1887.
31. *PL*, Jun. 6, 1887; No. 238, May Sessions 1887: *Commonwealth v. George H. Wilson*, Motion for a new trial, pages 10–11 (PCA).
32. *PL*, Jun. 6, 1887; No. 238, May Sessions 1887: *Commonwealth v. George H. Wilson*, Motion for a new trial, pages 11–12 (PCA).

33. For Hare's quotes, see No. 238, May Sessions 1887: *Commonwealth v. George H. Wilson*, Motion for a new trial, pages 11–12 (PCA).

34. Rice, "The Criminal Trial before and after the Lawyers," 463–64.

35. *PI*, Jun. 6, 1887.

36. *PI*, Jun. 6, 1887.

37. *PI*, Jun. 6, 1887; *PI*, Jun. 6, 1887.

38. No. 238, May Sessions 1887: *Commonwealth v. Geo. H. Wilson*, Motion in arrest of judgment and reasons, filed June 8, 1887, Costa, Brown (PCA).

39. No. 238, page 1 (PCA).

40. No. 238, page 2 (PCA).

41. The second motion was filed with the first and contained in the same folder. See No. 238, pages 1–2 (PCA).

42. No. 238, May Sessions 1887: *Commonwealth v. George H. Wilson*, Motion for a new trial, pages 6–12 (PCA).

43. *PT*, Jul. 2, 1887; *PI*, Jul. 2, 1887. Also according to *Quarter Sessions Court Records* Tabbs and Wilson returned to court on June 24, 1887 and June 25, 1887, respectively (PCA).

44. *PT*, Jul. 2, 1887; *PI*, Jul. 2, 1887; *Quarter Sessions Court Records*, Jul. 1, 1887: Geo. H. Wilson (PCA).

45. *PI*, Jul. 2, 1887; *PT*, Jul. 2, 1887.

46. Mark H. Haller, "Plea Bargaining: The Nineteenth Century Context," *Law and Society Review* 13, no. 2 (January 1979): 273; Friedman, *Crime and Punishment*, 251–52; Friedman, *History of American Law*, 212.

47. *PI*, Sept. 29, 1887; *EB*, Sept. 28, 1887; *PI*, Sept. 29, 1887; *PT*, Sept. 29, 1887. Also see *Quarter Sessions Court Record*, Sept. 28, 1887: Mary H. Tabbs (PCA).

48. *PI*, Sept. 29, 1887; *EB*, Sept. 28, 1887; *PI*, Sept. 29, 1887; *PT*, Sept. 29, 1887.

49. *PT*, Sept. 29, 1887.

50. *PI*, Sept. 29, 1887.

51. *EB*, Sept. 28, 1887; *PI*, Sept. 29, 1887; *PT*, Sept. 29, 1887.

52. *PT*, Sept. 29, 1887.

53. *PI*, Sept. 29, 1887.

54. *PI*, Sept. 29, 1887.

55. *PI*, Sept. 29, 1887.

56. *PI*, Oct. 4, 1887; *PT*, Oct. 4, 1887.

57. *PI*, Oct. 28, 1887; *PL*, Oct. 28, 1887; *PT*, Oct. 28, 1887.

58. *PI*, Jun. 6, 1887.

59. *Eastern State Penitentiary, Discharge Descriptive Dockets (1873–1934)*, RG 15, Department of Justice, No. 3826 (PSA).

60. *The Eastern State Penitentiary of Pennsylvania: An Investigation by Authority of the Legislature* (1897); also see Gross, *Colored Amazons*, 141.

61. Although the name was fairly common for both blacks and whites in Philadelphia, few black Philadelphians tracing their births to the late nineteenth

century were born in Connecticut. See George Wilson, *1920 US Federal Census* and *1930 US Federal Census*. I have found death records for black men named George Wilson, but most are earlier and lack conclusive data, for an example, see George Wilson, 1898, Death Record, FHL No. 1870500 (PCA). Marriage license records have been more promising, though the dates are a little off, see Applicant for Marriage, George Wilson and Mary Jones, License No. 112807, 1899.

62. *Eastern State Penitentiary, Discharge Descriptive Dockets (1873–1934)*, RG 15, Department of Justice, No. 3928 (PSA).

63. Hannah A. Tabbs, Feb. 9, 1891, file no. 310974, United States Civil War Widows and Other Dependents Pension Files (NA).

64. Handwritten letter, dated July 2, 1916, ibid.; Hannah Mary Tabbs to disbursing clerk, July 3, 1816, typed letter, ibid. The special examiner's note has two names, what appears to be F. E. McLaughlin, with E. M. Taber stamped over it and on the front. The letter also has Tabbs's signature, and she had moved to 654 Josephine.

65. See James H. Anderson, *1910 US Federal Census*. The record indicates that Tabbs had three living children by that point, though only Lucy is listed; if we count Annie Richardson that still leaves one unaccounted for. See James H. Anderson, Baltimore Marriage Index, 1908, MSA; also see Baltimore City, Health Department Bureau of Vital Statistics, 1875–1972 (Death Record, Index), MSA; Baltimore City, Health Dept. Bureau of Vital Stats (Death Record) 1875–1972, CM1132, MSA. For examples, see Mary E. Anderson, US National Cemetery Interment Control Forms, 1928–1962, available at Ancestry.com; and Mary E. Anderson, U.S. Find A Grave Index, 1600s–Current, available at Ancestry.com.

66. Tabbs's conduct similarly parallels that of Mrs. Seacole in Rhonda Frederick's discussion of Seacole's creolized performance of race and gender. See Rhonda Frederick, "Creole Performance," 494.

Epilogue

1. See Emory Gaines, *1870 US Federal Census*; also see Silas Wakefield Gaines, Return of Marriage, Seaford of Delaware, Sussex County, December 7, 1882 (DPA).

2. Silas Wakefield Gaines, Return of Marriage, Seaford of Delaware, Sussex County, December 7, 1882 (DPA). "Emory Chandler Gaines," pp. 39–40, *Sussex County Deed Book*, vol. 94: *1881–1882*, Office of the Recorder of Deeds (Sussex County Administrative Office, Georgetown, Del.) (DPA); "Emory Chandler Gaines," pp. 523–24, *Sussex County Deed Book*, vol. 106: *1894*, ibid. Patience Essah, *A House Divided: Slavery and Emancipation in Delaware, 1638–1865* (Charlottesville: University of Virginia Press, 1996), 76–80; William H. Williams, *Slavery and*

Freedom in Delaware, 1639–1865 (Wilmington: A Scholarly Resources Book Inc., 1996), xii–xiii, 90.

3. Silas Wakefield Gaines, Return of Marriage (1882).

4. *PT*, Feb. 26, 1887; *PI*, Mar. 4, 1887; *PR*, Mar. 3, 1887; *EB*, Feb. 25, 1887; *EB*, Feb. 28, 1887.

5. Emory C. Gaines, Certificate of Death, State of Delaware, 1904; Will of Chandler Gaines, Recorded Book, R #7; Will of Charlotte Gaines, Recorded Book, 1913–1919, X #23, 109.

6. Saidiya Hartman, "Venus in Two Acts," *Small Axe* 12, no. 12 (June 2010): 12.

7. *EB*, Mar. 16, 1887; *PI*, Jun. 6, 1887.

8. I am building on what Saidiya Hartman refers to as *founding violence*. She uses it to describe the legacies of slavery and colonialism that structured the archive and sources in a way to permit certain voices and foment the silencing of others. She explains, "The archive of slavery rests on a founding violence. This violence determines, regulates and organizes the kinds of statements that can be made about slavery and as well it creates subjects and objects of power." See Hartman, "Venus in Two Acts," 11. On trauma and how it takes hold or possesses those who experience it, see Cathy Caruth, *Trauma: Explorations in Memory* (Baltimore: Johns Hopkins University Press, 1995), 4, and see Cathy Caruth, *Unclaimed Experience: Trauma, Narrative, and History* (Baltimore: Johns Hopkins University Press, 1996), 58–63. I am also building on Kai Erikson's contention that trauma "can surely be called pathological in the sense that it induces discomfort and pain, but the imageries that accompany the pain have a sense all their own." See Kai Erikson, "Notes on Trauma and Community," in *Trauma*, ed. Caruth, 198. I am interested in the implications this has for black women's history of trauma—imagery but also the imaginaries.

9. I am borrowing the term "rightlessness" from Lisa Marie Cacho's important work, which argues that certain groups are permanently criminalized and rendered ineligible for personhood. She explains that these "populations are subjected to laws but refused legal means to contest those laws as well as denied both the political legitimacy and moral credibility necessary to question them. These populations are excluded from the ostensibly democratic processes that legitimate US law, yet they are expected to unambiguously accept and unequivocally uphold a legal and political system that depends on the unquestioned permanency of their rightlessness." See Lisa Marie Cacho, *Social Death: Racialized Rightlessness and the Criminalization of the Unprotected* (New York: New York University Press, 2012), 6–8.

10. This isn't meant to deny the nihilism imbedded in her conduct within the black community. In this sense Cornel West's writing is especially helpful here. See Cornel West, *Race Matters* (New York: Beacon, 1993), 14–15. See also Kali Nicole Gross, *Colored Amazons: Crime, Violence, and Black Women in the City of Brotherly Love, 1880–1910* (Durham: Duke University Press, 2006), 88–89. In

some ways, her behavior might mark a misguided bid for sovereignty—though, I am not using "sovereign" in quite the ways that John Locke, Thomas Hobbes, and Max Weber define this term. Rather, my thinking has been more readily influenced by Achille Mbembe's discussion of the idea that sovereignty has multiple meanings and concepts but also the notion that the "ultimate expression of sovereignty resides, to a large degree, in the power and the capacity to dictate who may live and who must die." See Achille Mbembe, "Necropolitics," *Public Culture* 15 (Winter 2003): 11–13.

11. *EB*, Mar. 1, 1887; *PT*, Mar. 2, 1887.

BIBLIOGRAPHY

Institutions and Record Collections

DPA   DELAWARE PUBLIC ARCHIVES, NORTH DOVER, DEL.

Delaware Marriage Record Index, 1855–1934
Delaware Marriage Records, 1806–1933
Sussex County, Probate Index, 1683–1925
Sussex County, Register of Wills, Probate Files, 1683–1960
Sussex County Deed Book, Office of the Recorder of Deeds, 1881–1882

HSP   HISTORICAL SOCIETY OF PENNSYLVANIA, PHILADELPHIA, PA.

Minutes of the Pennsylvania Prison Society, 1883–1889
House of Refuge, Colored Department:
   Female Department, 1883–89
   History of Boys, c. 1879
   Medical Report (Boys), c. 1879
   Monthly School Report (Boys), 1879

MSA   MARYLAND STATE ARCHIVES, ANNAPOLIS, MD.

Anne Arundel County Commissioner of Slave Statistics, 1864
Anne Arundel County Justice of the Peace (Docket), 1833–1939
Baltimore City Police Department (Criminal Docket, Eastern District), 1863–1959

Baltimore City Police Department (Criminal Docket, Southern District), 1867–1960
Baltimore City Court of Common Pleas, Marriage Record, 1886–1919
Baltimore County Court of Common Pleas, Marriage Index, Male, 1851–85
Baltimore County Court of Common Pleas, Marriage Index, Male, 1886–1914
Baltimore City, Health Department Bureau of Vital Statistics, Death Record, Index, 1875–1972
Baltimore City, Health Department Bureau of Vital Statistics, Death Record, 1875–1972

NA   NATIONAL ARCHIVES, WASHINGTON, D.C.

Compiled Military Service Records of Volunteer Union Soldiers Who Served with the United States Colored Troops: 1st through 5th United States Colored Cavalry, 5th Massachusetts Cavalry (Colored), 6th United States Colored Cavalry, publication M1817 (microfilm, 107 reels, National Archives and Records Administration)
United States Civil War Widows and Other Dependents Pension Files (National Archives and Records Administration, Washington, D.C.)

PCA   PHILADELPHIA CITY ARCHIVES, PHILADELPHIA, PA.

Philadelphia County Prison
Prison Diary, Female Department, 1850–1935
Prisoners for Trial Docket, 1790–1948
Bills of Indictment, December 1838–October 1915
Quarter Sessions Court
Notes of Testimony, 1877–1915
Court Record, 1874–88
Death Register, 1803–1915
Prison Commitment Docket, Female, 1840–1956
Marriage License Bureau, October 1, 1885–December 30, 1915

PSA   PENNSYLVANIA STATE ARCHIVES, HARRISBURG, PA.

Discharge Descriptive Dockets, 1873–1935
Eastern State Penitentiary
Convict Description Register, 1829–1903
The Eastern State Penitentiary of Pennsylvania: An Investigation by Authority of the Legislature, 1897
Warden's Journals, 1829–1961

BIBLIOGRAPHY

SP SPRUANCE LIBRARY, DOYLESTOWN, PA.

Coroners Papers, 1700–1900, Bucks County Archives

CH CHEYNEY UNIVERSITY OF PENNSYLVANIA ARCHIVES, CHEYNEY, PA

The William H. Dorsey Scrapbook Collection

Newspapers

BS *Baltimore (Md.) Sun*
DC *Baltimore (Md.) Der Deutsche Correspondent*
DI *Doylestown (Pa.) Intelligencer*
EB *Philadelphia (Pa.) Evening Bulletin*
NE *Newtown (Pa.) Enterprise*
PI *Philadelphia (Pa.) Inquirer*
PL *Philadelphia (Pa.) Public Ledger*
PR *Philadelphia (Pa.) Record*
PT *Philadelphia (Pa.) Times*

ADDITIONAL NEWSPAPERS SOURCES

Cleveland (Ohio) Gazette
Emporia (Ky.) Weekly News
Indianapolis (Ind.) State Sentinel
New York Times
Richmond (Va.) Daily Times
Richmond (Va.) Dispatch
Saint Paul (Minn.) Daily Globe
Sedalia (Mo.) Weekly
Washington (D.C.) National Republican
Wichita (Kans.) Eagle

Record Collections from *Ancestry.com*
Gopsill's Philadelphia City Directory: 1884–92
U.S. Find A Grave Index, 1600s–Current
Wood's Baltimore City Directory: 1865–76
U.S. National Cemetery Interment Control Forms, 1928–62
United States Federal Census Data: *1850 Slave Schedules; 1860 Slave Schedules; 1860 Census; 1870 Census; 1880 Census; 1900 Census; 1910 Census; 1920 Census; 1930 Census, 1940 Census*

ADDITIONAL ONLINE SOURCES

"Civil War Battle Summaries by State," *The American Battlefield Protection Program*, http://www.nps.gov/abpp/battles/bystate.htm.

"To the Honorable Judges of the Orphans Court for Anne Arundel County," April 3, 1860, PAR number 20986043, the *Race and Slavery Petitions Project*, http://libraryuncg.edu/slavery/petitions/details.aspx?pid=18103.

Published Primary Sources

Agassiz, Professor, and Mrs. Louis. *A Journey in Brazil*. Boston: Houghton, Osgood, and Company, 1879.

Bedford, Sarah. *Harriet Tubman: The Moses of Her People*. 1886; repr., Bedford, Mass.: Applewood Books, 1993.

Boies, Henry. *Prisoners and Paupers: A Study of the Abnormal Increase of Criminals, and the Public Burden of Pauperism in the United States*. New York: Putnam, 1893.

"Caroline Hammond." In *Slave Narratives: A Folk History of Slavery in the United States from Interviews with Former Slaves*, vol. 8: *Maryland Narratives*, comp. Federal Writers' Project. Washington, D.C.: Library of Congress Printing Office, 1941.

Coxe, Robert Davison. *Legal Philadelphia: Comments and Memories*. Philadelphia: William J. Campbell, 1908.

The District Reports of Cases Decided in All the Judicial Districts of the State of Pennsylvania, During the Year 1910, vol. 19. Philadelphia: Howard W. Page, 700 West End Trust Building, 1910.

Douglass, Frederick. *Narrative of the Life of Frederick Douglass, An American Slave*. Boston: Anti-slavery Office, 1845.

Darwin, Charles. *The Origin of the Species by Means of Natural Selection*. London: John Murray, 1859.

Davis, William W. H. *The History of Bucks County, Pennsylvania from the Discovery of the Delaware to the Present Time*. New York: The Lewis Publishing Company, 1905.

Du Bois, W. E. B. *The Philadelphia Negro: A Social Study*. 1896; repr., Philadelphia: University of Pennsylvania Press, 1996.

Formad, Henry. *Comparative Studies of Mammalian Blood, with Special Reference to the Microscopical Diagnosis of Blood Stains in Criminal Cases*. Philadelphia: A. L. Hummel, 1888.

Fredic, Francis. *The Autobiography of Rev. Francis Fredic*. Baltimore: J. J. Woods Printer, 1869.

Geyer, Frank P. *The Holmes-Pitezel Case: A History of the Greatest Crime of the Century and of the Search for the Missing Children*. Philadelphia: Publisher's Union, 1896.

Gilliam, E. W. "The African Problem," *North American Review* 139, no. 336 (November 1884): 417–30.

Hoffman, Frederick L. *Race Traits and Tendencies of the American Negro*. New York: Macmillan, 1896.

"House of Refuge for Coloured Children." *The Friend: A Religious and Literary Journal* (January 26, 1850): 19–23.

Ingram, J. S. *The Centennial Exposition, Described and Illustrated*. Philadelphia: Hubbard Bros., 1876.

Jacobs, Harriet. *Incidents in the Life of a Slave Girl*. Boston: Harriet Jacobs, 1861.

Jefferson, Thomas. *Notes on the State of Virginia*. Paris: n.p., 1783.

Jordan, H. E. "A Comparative Microscopic Study of the Melanin Content of Pigmented Skins with Special Reference to the Question of Color Inheritance among Mulattos." *American Naturalist* 45, no. 536 (August 1911): 451–70.

Laws of the General Assembly of the State of Pennsylvania. Harrisburg, PA, 1881–1909.

Lewis, William Draper. "John Innes Clark Hare," *The American Law Register* 54, no. 12, n.s. (December 1906): 711–17.

Lossing, Benson J. *Pictorial History of the Civil War in the United States of America*, vol. 3. Hartford, Conn.: T. Belknap, 1868. Repr. by Applewood.

"Mrs. Nancy Howard." In *The Refugee: Or the Narratives of Fugitive Slaves in Canada. Related by Themselves, with an Account of the History and Condition of the Colored Population of Upper Canada*, by Benjamin Drew. Boston: John P. Jewett and Company, 1856.

Nott, Josiah C. "The Mulatto a Hybrid—Probable Extermination of Two Races if the Whites and Blacks Are Allowed to Intermarry." *The American Journal of the Medical Sciences* 66 (July 1843): 252–56.

Nott, Josiah C., *Two Lectures on the Natural History of the Caucasian and Negro Race*. Mobile, AL: Dade and Thompson, 1844.

Nott, Josiah C., and Geo. R. Gliddon. *Types of Mankind: Or, Based upon the Ancient Monuments, Paintings, Sculptures, and Crania of Races, and upon Their Natural, Geographical, Philological and Biblical History*. Philadelphia: Lippincott, Grambo & Co., 1854.

Official Hand Book, City Hall, Philadelphia. 2 vols. Philadelphia: City Publishing Co., 1901.

Patrolman's Manual: Bureau of Police of the City of Philadelphia. Philadelphia: Department of Public Safety, 1913, repr. in *Metropolitan Police Manuals, 1817, 1913*, ed. Richard C. Wade. New York: Arno, 1974.

Pennsylvania State Reports, vol. 174, *Containing Cases Adjudged in the Supreme Court of Pennsylvania, January Term, 1896*. New York: Banks & Brothers.

The Philadelphia Times Almanac for the Years 1887–1890. Philadelphia, 1891.

Purvis, Robert. *Appeal of Forty Thousand Citizens Threatened with Disfranchisement, to the People of Pennsylvania*. Philadelphia: Merrihew and Gunn, 1837.

Report of the Special Committee to Investigate the Alleged Cruelties and Abuses at the House of Refuge in Philadelphia. Harrisburg, Pa.: B. F. Meyers, State Printer, 1875.

Sprogle, Howard O. *The Philadelphia Police: Past and Present*. Philadelphia: Howard O. Sprogle, 1887.

Steffens, Lincoln. *The Shame of the Cities*. New York: Farrar, Straus and Giroux, 1904.

Thomas, A. R. *A Practical Guide for Making Postmortem Examinations, and for the Study of Morbid Anatomy, with Directions for Embalming the Dead, and for the*

Preservation of Specimens of Morbid Anatomy, 1873; repr., Lansing: University of Michigan Press, 2005.

University of Pennsylvania Medical Magazine 4 (October 1891–September 1892). Philadelphia: University of Pennsylvania Press (1892), 736.

Secondary Sources

Adler, Jeffrey. "'Bessie Done Cut Her Old Man': Race, Common-Law Marriage, and Homicide in New Orleans, 1925–1945." *Journal of Social History* 44 (Fall 2010): 123–43.

Adler, Jeffrey. "'I Loved Joe, but I Had to Shoot Him': Homicide by Women in Turn-of-the-Century Chicago." *Journal of Criminal Law and Criminology* 92, no. 3 (Spring–Summer 2002): 867–98.

Ardizzone, Heidi, and Earl Lewis. *Love on Trial: An American Scandal in Black and White*. New York: W. W. Norton, 2002.

Ayers, Edward L. *Vengeance and Justice: Crime and Punishment in the Nineteenth-Century South*. New York: Oxford University Press, 1995.

Baptist, Edward. *The Half Has Never Been Told: Slavery and the Making of American Capitalism*. New York: Basic, 2014.

Baptist, Edward. "'My Mind Is to Drown You and Leave You Behind': 'Omie Wise,' Intimate Violence, and Masculinity." In *Over the Threshold: Intimate Violence in Early America*, ed. Christine Daniels and Michael V. Kennedy. New York: Routledge, 1999.

Barra Foundation. *Philadelphia: A 300-Year History*. New York: W. W. Norton, 1982.

Barton, Keith. "'Good Cooks and Washers': Slave Hiring, Domestic Labor, and the Market in Bourbon County, Kentucky." *Journal of American History* 84, no. 2 (September 1997): 436–60.

Bay, Mia. *To Tell the Truth Freely: The Life of Ida B. Wells*. New York: Hill and Wang, 2010.

Beers, Dorothy Gondos. "The Centennial City, 1865–1876." In *Philadelphia: A 300-Year History*, ed. Russell F. Weigley. New York: W. W. Norton, 1982.

Berry, Daina Ramey, and Deleso A. Alford. *Enslaved Women in America: An Encyclopedia*. Santa Barbara, CA: Greenwood, 2011.

Berry, Daina Ramey, and Deleso A. Alford. *"Swing the Sickle for the Harvest Is Ripe": Gender and Slavery in Antebellum Georgia*. Urbana: University of Illinois Press, 2010.

Berry, Mary Frances. *Black Resistance, White Law: A History of Constitutional Racism in America*. New York: Penguin, 1994.

Berry, Mary Frances. *My Face Is Black Is True: Callie House and the Struggle for Ex-Slave Reparations*. New York: Vintage, 2006.

Blackmon, Douglas A. *Slavery by Another Name: The Re-Enslavement of Black Americans from the Civil War to World War II*. New York: Anchor, 2009.

Blair, Cynthia M. *I've Got to Make My Livin': Black Women's Sex Work in Turn-of-the-Century Chicago*. Chicago: University of Chicago Press, 2010.

Blakely, Robert L., and Judith M. Harrington, eds. *Bones in the Basement: Postmortem Racism in Nineteenth-Century Medical Training*. Washington, D.C.: Smithsonian Institution Press, 1997.

Broder, Sherrie. *Tramps, Unfit Mothers, and Neglected Children: Negotiating the Family in Late Nineteenth-Century Philadelphia*. Philadelphia: University of Pennsylvania Press, 2002.

Brody, Jennifer DeVere. *Impossible Purities: Blackness, Femininity, and Victorian Culture*. Durham: Duke University Press, 1998.

Brown, Elaine. *A Taste of Power: A Black Woman's Story*. New York: Anchor, 1993.

Brown, Elsa Barkley, and Gregg D. Kimball. "Mapping the Terrain of Black Richmond." *Journal of Urban History* 21, no. 3 (March 1995): 296–346.

Brown, Elsa Barkley, and Gregg D. Kimball. "Negotiating and Transforming the Public Sphere: African American Political Life in the Transition from Slavery to Freedom." *Public Culture* 7 (Fall 1994): 107–46.

Buick, Kirsten Kai. *Child of the Fire: Mary Edmonia Lewis and the Problem of Art History's Black and Indian Subject*. Durham: Duke University Press, 2010.

Cacho, Lisa Marie. *Social Death: Racialized Rightlessness and the Criminalization of the Unprotected*. New York: New York University Press, 2012.

Camp, Stephanie M. H. *Closer to Freedom: Enslaved Women and Everyday Resistance in the Plantation South*. Chapel Hill: University of North Carolina Press, 2004.

Carby, Hazel V. "Policing the Black Women's Body." *Critical Inquiry* 18, no. 4 (Summer 1992): 738–55.

Carby, Hazel V. *Reconstructing Womanhood: The Emergence of the Afro-American Woman Novelist*. New York: Oxford University Press, 1987.

Carlson, A. Cheree. *The Crimes of Womanhood: Defining Femininity in a Court of Law*. Urbana: University of Illinois Press, 2008.

Caruth, Cathy, ed. *Trauma: Explorations in Memory*. Baltimore: Johns Hopkins University Press, 1995.

Caruth, Cathy. *Unclaimed Experience: Trauma, Narrative, and History*. Baltimore: Johns Hopkins University Press, 1996.

Chaff, Sandra L. "Images of Female Medical Students at the Turn of the Century." *Signs: Journal of Women in Culture and Society* 4, no. 1 (1978): 203–7.

Chateauvert, Melinda. *Marching Together: Women of the Brotherhood of Sleeping Car Porters*. Urbana: University of Illinois Press, 1998.

Christian, Barbara. "The Race for Theory." *Cultural Critique* 6 (Spring 1987): 51–63.

Clinton, Catherine. "Reconstructing Freedwomen." In *Divided Houses: Gender and the Civil War*, ed. Catherine Clinton and Nina Silber. New York: Oxford University Press, 1992.

Cobb, Jasmine Nichole. *Picture Freedom: Remaking Black Visuality in the Early Nineteenth Century*. New York: New York University Press, 2015.

Cohen, Patricia Cline. *The Murder of Helen Jewett*. New York: Vintage, 1999.

Cole, Simone. *Suspect Identities: A History of Fingerprinting and Criminal Identification.* Cambridge, Mass.: Harvard University Press, 2001.

Collier-Thomas, Bettye. *Jesus, Jobs, and Justice: African American Women and Religion.* New York: Alfred A. Knopf, 2010.

Collier-Thomas, Bettye, and V. P. Franklin. *Sisters in the Struggle: African-American Women in the Civil Rights–Black Power Movement.* New York: New York University Press, 2001.

Davis, Allen F., and Mark Haller, eds. *The Peoples of Philadelphia: A History of Ethnic Groups and Lower-Class Life, 1790–1940.* Philadelphia: Temple University Press, 1998.

Davis, Angela Y. *Blues Legacies and Black Feminism: Gertrude "Ma" Rainey, Bessie Smith, and Billie Holiday.* New York: Vintage, 1999.

Doyle, Bertram Wilbur. *The Etiquette of Race Relations in the South: A Study in Social Control.* Urbana: University of Illinois Press, 1937.

Drachman, Virginia G. *Sisters in Law: Women Lawyers in Modern American History.* Cambridge, Mass.: Harvard University Press, 2001.

Dunbar, Erica Armstrong. *A Fragile Freedom: African American Women and Emancipation in the Antebellum City.* New Haven: Yale University Press, 2011.

Erikson, Kai. "Notes on Trauma and Community." In *Trauma: Explorations in Memory,* ed. Cathy Caruth. Baltimore: Johns Hopkins University Press, 1995.

Essah, Patience. *A House Divided: Slavery and Emancipation in Delaware, 1638–1865.* Charlottesville: University of Virginia Press, 1996.

Ezratty, Harry A. *Baltimore in the Civil War: The Pratt Street Riot and a City Occupied.* Charleston, S.C.: The History Press, 2010.

Fanon, Franz. *The Wretched of the Earth.* 1961; repr., New York: Grove Press, 2005.

Faust, Drew Gilpin. *James Henry Hammond and the Old South: A Design for Mastery.* Baton Rouge: Louisiana State University Press, 1982.

Faust, Drew Gilpin. *This Republic of Suffering: Death and the American Civil War.* New York: Vintage, 2009.

Fields, Barbara Jeanne. *Slavery and Freedom on the Middle Ground: Maryland during the Nineteenth Century.* New Haven: Yale University Press, 1985.

Floyd, Claudia. *Maryland Women in the Civil War: Unionists, Rebels, Slaves and Spies.* Charleston, S.C.: The History Press, 2013.

Flowe, Douglass. "'Dem niggas wuzn' skeered of nothing': Saloons, Dives, and Male-Centered Criminal Economy in Manhattan's Negro Bohemia, 1890–1910." Paper delivered at the annual meeting of the Association of the Study of African American Life and History, Jacksonville, Florida, October 2013, p. 29.

Foster, Thomas A. "The Sexual Abuse of Black Men under American Slavery." *Journal of the History of Sexuality* 20, no. 3 (September 2011): 445–64.

Frederick, Rhonda. "Creole Performance in *Wonderful Adventures of Mrs. Seacole in Many Lands.*" *Gender and History* 15, no. 3 (November 2003): 487–506.

Frey, Cecile P. "The House of Refuge for Colored Children." *Journal of Negro History* 66, no. 1 (Spring 1989): 10–25.

Friedman, Lawrence. *Crime and Punishment in American History*. New York: Basic, 1993.

Friedman, Lawrence. *A History of American Law*, rev. ed. New York: Simon and Schuster, 1985.

Gaines, Kevin K. *Uplifting the Race: Black Leadership, Politics, and Culture in the Twentieth Century*. Chapel Hill: University of North Carolina Press, 1996.

Giddings, Paula. *Ida: A Sword among Lions: Ida B. Wells and the Campaign against Lynching*. New York: Harper Paperbacks, 2009.

Giddings, Paula. *When and Where I Enter: The Impact of Black Women on Race and Sex in America*. New York: Perennial, Harper Collins, 2001.

Gilfoyle, Timothy. *A Pickpocket's Tale: The Underworld of Nineteenth-Century New York*. New York: W. W. Norton, 2007.

Gill, Tiffany M. *Beauty Shop Politics: African American Women's Activism in the Beauty Industry*. Urbana: University of Illinois Press, 2010.

Glymph, Thavolia. *Out of the House of Bondage: The Transformation of the Plantation Household*. Cambridge: Cambridge University Press, 2008.

Gore, Dayo F. *Radicalism at the Crossroads: African American Women Activists in the Cold War*. New York: New York University Press, 2012.

Gould, Stephen J. "American Polygeny and Craniometry before Darwin: Blacks and Indians as Separate, Inferior Species." In *The "Racial" Economy of Science: Toward a Democratic Future*, ed. Sandra Harding. Bloomington: Indiana University Press, 1993.

Griffin, Farah Jasmine. *"Who Set You Flowin'?": The African-American Migration Narrative*. New York: Oxford University Press, 1996.

Gross, Ariela. *Double Character: Slavery and Mastery in the Antebellum Southern Courtroom*. Athens: University of Georgia Press, 2000.

Gross, Kali Nicole. "African American Women, Mass Incarceration, and the Politics of Protection." *Journal of American History* 102, no. 1 (June 2015): 25–33.

Gross, Kali Nicole. *Colored Amazons: Crime, Violence, and Black Women in the City of Brotherly Love, 1880–1910*. Durham: Duke University Press, 2006.

Gross, Kali Nicole. "Exploring Crime and Violence in Early-Twentieth Century Black Women's History." In *Contesting Archives: Finding Women in the Sources*, ed. Nupur Chaudhuri, Sherry J. Katz, and Mary Elizabeth Perry. Urbana: University of Illinois Press, 2010.

Grossman, James R. "A Chance to Make Good: 1900–1929." In *To Make Our World Anew: A History of African Americans since 1800*, vol. 2, ed. Robin D. G. Kelly and Earl Lewis. New York: Oxford University Press, 2005.

Hale, Grace Elizabeth. *Making Whiteness: The Culture of Segregation in the South, 1890–1940*. New York: Vintage, 1999.

Haley, Sarah. "'Like I Was a Man': Chain Gangs, Gender, and the Domestic Carceral Sphere in Jim Crow Georgia." *Signs* 39, no. 1 (Autumn 2013): 53–77.

Haller, Mark H. "Plea Bargaining: The Nineteenth-Century Context." *Law and Society Review* 13, no. 2 (January 1979): 273–79.

Hammonds, Evelynn M. "Toward a Genealogy of Black Female Sexuality: The Problematic of Silence." In *Feminist Genealogies, Colonial Legacies, Democratic Futures*, ed. M. Jacqui Alexander and Chandra Talpade Mohanty. New York: Routledge, 1997.

Harley, Sharon, ed. *Sister Circle: Black Women and Work*. New Brunswick: Rutgers University Press, 2002.

Hartman, Saidiya. *Scenes of Subjection: Terror, Slavery, and Self-Making in Nineteenth-Century America*. New York: Oxford University Press, 1997.

Hartman, Saidiya. "Venus in Two Acts," *Small Axe* 12, no. 2 (June 2008): 1–14.

Hazzard-Gordon, Katrina. *Jookin': The Rise of Social Dance Formations in African-American Culture*. Philadelphia: Temple University Press, 1992.

Heap, Chad. *Slumming: Sexual and Racial Encounters in American Nightlife, 1885–1940*. Chicago: University of Chicago Press, 2010.

Hershberg, Theodore. "Mulattoes and Blacks: Intra-Group Differences and Social Stratifications in Nineteenth-Century Philadelphia." In *Philadelphia: Work, Space, Family, and Group Experience in the Nineteenth Century: Essays Toward an Interdisciplinary History of the City*, ed. Theodore Hershberg. New York: Oxford University Press, 1981.

Hicks, Cheryl D. *Talk with You Like a Woman: African American Women, Justice, and Reform in New York, 1890–1935*. Chapel Hill: University of North Carolina Press, 2010.

Higginbotham, A. Leon. *In the Matter of Color: Race and the American Legal Process: The Colonial Period*. New York: Oxford University Press, 1980.

Higginbotham, Evelyn Brooks. "African-American Women's History and the Metalanguage of Race." *Signs* 17, no. 2 (Winter 1992): 251–74.

Higginbotham, Evelyn Brooks. "Beyond the Sound of Silence: Afro-American Women in History." *Gender and History* 1, no. 1 (1989): 50–67.

Higginbotham, Evelyn Brooks. *Righteous Discontent: The Women's Movement in the Black Baptist Church, 1880–1920*. Cambridge, Mass.: Harvard University Press, 1994.

Hine, Darlene Clark. "Rape in the Inner Lives of Black Women in the Middle West: Preliminary Thoughts on the Culture of Dissemblance." In *Signs* 14, no. 4 (Summer 1989): 912–20.

Hine, Darlene Clark, and Kathleen Thompson. *A Shining Thread of Hope: The History of Black Women in America*. New York: Broadway, 1999.

Hobbs, Allyson. *A Chosen Exile: A History of Racial Passing in American Life*. Cambridge, Mass.; Harvard University Press, 2014.

Hunter, Tera W. "'The Brotherly Love' for Which This City Is Proverbial Should Extend to All: The Everyday Lives of Working-Class Women in Philadelphia and Atlanta in the 1890s." In *W. E. B. Du Bois, Race, and the City: The Philadelphia Negro and Its Legacy*, ed. Michael Katz and Thomas Sugrue. Philadelphia: University of Pennsylvania Press, 1998.

Hunter, Tera W. *To 'Joy My Freedom: Southern Black Women's Lives and Labors after the Civil War*. Cambridge, Mass.: Harvard University Press, 1998.

Ignatiev, Noel. *How the Irish Became White*. New York: Routledge, 1995.

Jacobson, Matthew Frye. *Whiteness of a Different Color: European Immigrants and the Alchemy of Race*. Cambridge, Mass.: Harvard University Press, 1998.

Jones, Jacqueline. *A Dreadful Deceit: The Myth of Race from the Colonial Era to Obama's America*. New York: Basic, 2013.

Jones, Jacqueline. *Labor of Love, Labor of Sorrow: Black Women, Work, and the Family from Slavery to the Present*. New York: Basic, 2009.

Johnson, David R. *Policing the Urban Underworld: The Impact of Crime on the Development of the American Police, 1800–1887*. Philadelphia: Temple University Press, 1979.

Johnson, Paula C. *Inner Lives: Voices of African American Women in Prison*. New York: New York University Press, 2003.

Kilbride, Daniel. "Southern Medical Students in Philadelphia, 1800–1861: Science and Sociability in the 'Republic of Medicine,'" *Journal of Southern History* 65, no. 4 (November 1999): 697–732.

King, Wilma. *Stolen Childhood: Slave Youth in Nineteenth-Century America*, 2nd ed. Bloomington: Indiana University Press, 2011.

Klaus, Sydney. "A History of the Science of Pigmentation." In *The Pigmentary System: Physiology and Pathophysiology*, ed. James J. Nordlund et al. New York: Oxford University Press, 1998.

Lane, Roger. *Murder in America: A History*. Columbus: Ohio State University Press, 1997.

Lane, Roger. *Roots of Violence in Black Philadelphia, 1860–1900*. Cambridge, Mass.: Harvard University Press, 1986.

Lane, Roger. *Violent Death in the City: Suicide, Accident, and Murder in Nineteenth-Century Philadelphia*. Columbus: Ohio State University Press, 1999.

Lane, Roger. *William Dorsey's Philadelphia and Ours: On the Past and Future of the Black City in America*. New York: Oxford University Press, 1991.

Larson, Edward J. *Sex, Race, and Science: Eugenics in the Deep South*. Baltimore: Johns Hopkins University Press, 1995.

Laurie, Bruce. "Fire Companies and Gangs in Southwark: The 1840s." In *The Peoples of Philadelphia: A History of Ethnic Groups and Lower-Class Life, 1790–1950*, ed. Allen F. Davis and Mark H. Haller. Philadelphia: University of Pennsylvania Press, 1998.

Laythe, Joseph. *Engendered Death: Pennsylvania Women Who Kill*. Langham: Lehigh University Press, 2011.

Lebsock, Suzanne. *A Murder in Virginia: Southern Justice on Trial*. New York: W. W. Norton, 2003.

Lee, Chana Kai. *For Freedom's Sake: The Life of Fannie Lou Hamer*. Urbana: University of Illinois Press, 2005.

LeFlouria, Talitha. *Chained in Silence: Black Women and Convict Labor in the New South*. Chapel Hill: University of North Carolina Press, 2015.

Lempel, Leonard Richard. "The Mulatto in United States Race Relations: Changing Status and Attitudes, 1800–1940." Ph diss., Syracuse University, 1979.

Lerner, Gerda, ed. *Black Women in White America: A Documentary History*. New York: Vintage, 1992.

Little, Craig B. "The Criminal Courts in 'Young America': Bucks County, Pennsylvania, 1820–1860, with Some Comparisons to Massachusetts and South Carolina." *Social Science History* 15, no. 4 (Winter 1991): 457–78.

Little, Craig B. "Horse Thief Pursuing Companies of Nineteenth-Century Bucks County, Pennsylvania." *Mercer Mosiac* 3 (1986): 5–18.

Little, Craig B., and Christopher P. Sheffield. "Frontiers and Criminal Justice: English Private Prosecution Societies and American Vigilantism in the Eighteenth and Nineteenth Centuries." *American Sociological Review* 48 (1983): 796–808.

Litwack, Leon. *Been in the Storm So Long: The Aftermath of Slavery*. New York: First Vintage, 1980.

MacDonald, Helen. *Human Remains: Dissection and Its Histories*. New Haven: Yale University Press, 2005.

Marietta, Jack D., and G. S. Rowe. *Troubled Experiment: Crime and Justice in Pennsylvania, 1682–1800*. Philadelphia: University of Pennsylvania Press, 2006.

Martin, Charles D. *The White African American Body: A Cultural and Literary Exploration*. New Brunswick: Rutgers University Press, 2002.

Mbembe, Achille. "Necropolitics." *Public Culture* 15 (Winter 2003): 11–40.

McCaffery, Peter. *When Bosses Ruled Philadelphia: The Emergence of the Republican Machine, 1867–1933*. University Park: Pennsylvania State University Press, 1993.

McGuire, Danielle L. *At the Dark End of the Street: Black Women, Rape, and Resistance—A New History of the Civil Rights Movement from Rosa Parks to the Rise of Black Power*. New York: Vintage, 2011.

McLaurin, Melton A. *Celia, A Slave*. New York: Avon, 1999.

Millward, Jessica. *Finding Charity's Folk: Enslaved and Free Black Women in Maryland*. Athens: University of Georgia Press, 2015.

Mitchell, Michele. *Righteous Propagation: African Americans and the Politics of Racial Destiny after Reconstruction*. Chapel Hill: University of North Carolina Press, 2004.

Mitchell, Michele. "Silences Broken, Silences Kept: Gender and Sexuality in African American Women's History." *Gender and History* 11, no. 3 (November 1999): 433–44.

Monkkonen, Eric H. *Police in Urban America, 1860–1920*. Cambridge: Cambridge University Press, 1981.

Morgan, Jennifer. *Laboring Women: Reproduction and Gender in New World Slavery*. Philadelphia: University of Pennsylvania Press, 2004.

Morley, David, and Kuan-Hsing Chen, eds. *Stuart Hall: Critical Dialogues in Cultural Studies*. New York: Routledge, 1996.

Muhammad, Khalil Gibran. *The Condemnation of Blackness: Race, Crime, and the Making of Modern Urban America*. Cambridge, Mass.: Harvard University Press, 2010.

Myers, Amrita Chakrabarti. *Forging Freedom: Black Women and the Pursuit of Liberty in Antebellum Charleston*. Chapel Hill: University of North Carolina Press, 2011.

Noll, E. P. *Combined Atlases of Bucks County, Pennsylvania, 1876–1891: Indexed*. Mt. Vernon, Ind.: Windmill, 1992.

O'Flaherty, Brendan, and Rajiv Sethi. "Homicide in Black and White." *Journal of Urban Economics* 68, no. 3 (November 2010): 215–30.

Omi, Michael, and Howard Winant. *Racial Formation in the United States*, 3rd ed. New York: Routledge, 2015.

Oshinsky, David M. *"Worse Than Slavery": Parchman Farm and the Ordeal of Jim Crow Justice*. New York: Free, 1997.

Painter, Nell Irvin. *A History of White People*. New York: W. W. Norton, 2010.

Painter, Nell Irvin. *Sojourner Truth: A Life, A Symbol*. New York: W. W. Norton, 1997.

Painter, Nell Irvin. *Southern History across the Color Line*. Chapel Hill: University of North Carolina Press, 2002.

Pascoe, Peggy. *What Comes Naturally: Miscegenation Law and the Making of Race in America*. Oxford: Oxford University Press, 2009.

Patrick, Leslie. "Numbers That Are Not New: African Americans in the Country's First Prison, 1790–1853." *The Pennsylvania Magazine of History and Biography* 119 (January–April 1995): 95–128.

Pinzer, Maimie. *The Maimie Papers: Letters from an Ex-Prostitute*. Edited by Ruth Rosen and Susan Davidson. New York: Feminist, 1996.

Pisciotta, Alexander W. "Race, Sex, and Rehabilitation: A Study of Differential Treatment in the Juvenile Reformatory, 1825–1900." *Crime and Delinquency* 29, no. 2 (April 1983): 254–69.

Platt, Anthony. *The Child Savers: The Invention of Delinquency*. New Brunswick: Rutgers University Press, 2009.

Poupard, James. *A History of Microbiology in Philadelphia: 1880–2010*. Xlibris, 2010.

Rafter, Nicole Hahn. *Creating Born Criminals*. Urbana: University of Illinois Press, 1998.

Rafter, Nicole Hahn. *Partial Justice: Women, Prisons, and Social Control*, 2nd ed. New Brunswick: Transaction, 2004.

Ransby, Barbara. *Ella Baker and the Black Freedom Movement: A Radical Democratic Vision*. Chapel Hill: University of North Carolina Press, 2005.

Remick, Cecile P. "The House of Refuge of Philadelphia, 1786–1859." Ph diss., University of Pennsylvania, 1975.

Rice, James D. "The Criminal Trial before and after the Lawyers: Authority, Law, and Culture in Maryland Jury Trials, 1681–1837." *Journal of American Legal History* 40, no. 4 (October 1996): 455–75.

Ritterhouse, Jennifer Lynn. *Growing Up Jim Crow: How Black and White Southern Children Learned Race*. Chapel Hill: University of North Carolina Press, 2006.

Robinson, Jo Ann. *Montgomery Bus Boycott and the Women Who Started It: The Memoir of Jo Ann Gibson Robinson*. Knoxville: University of Tennessee Press, 1987.

Rockman, Seth. *Scraping By: Wage Labor, Slavery, and Survival in Early Baltimore.* Baltimore: Johns Hopkins University Press, 2009.

Roediger, David. *Toward the Abolition of Whiteness: Essays on Race, Politics, and Working-Class History.* New York: Verso, 1994.

Roediger, David. *The Wages of Whiteness: Race and the Making of the American Working Class.* New York: Verso, 1994.

Rooks, Noliwe. *Ladies' Pages: African American Women's Magazines and the Culture That Made Them.* New Brunswick: Rutgers University Press, 2004.

Rosen, Hannah. *Terror in the Heart of Freedom: Citizenship, Sexual Violence, and the Meaning of Race in the Postemancipation South.* Chapel Hill: University of North Carolina Press, 2008.

Roth, Randolph. *American Homicide.* New York: Belknap, 2012.

Salokar, Rebecca Mae, and Mary L. Volcansek. *Women in Law: A Bio-Bibliographical Sourcebook.* Westport, Conn.: Greenwood, 1996.

Sappol, Michael. *A Traffic of Dead Bodies: Anatomy and Embodied Social Identity in Nineteenth-Century America.* Princeton: Princeton University Press, 2002.

Sernett, Milton C. *Harriet Tubman: Myth, Memory, and History.* Durham: Duke University Press, 2007.

Sollors, Werner. *Neither Black nor White, yet Both: Thematic Explorations of Interracial Literature.* Cambridge, Mass.: Harvard University Press, 1997.

Spillers, Hortense. "Interstices: A Small Drama of Words." In *Pleasure and Danger: Exploring Female Sexuality,* ed. Carole S. Vance. New York: Routledge, 1984.

Spillers, Hortense J. *Black, White, and in Color: Essays on American Literature and Culture.* Chicago: University of Chicago Press, 2003.

Steinberg, Allen. *The Transformation of Criminal Justice: Philadelphia, 1800–1880.* Chapel Hill: University of North Carolina Press, 1989.

Stephan, Nancy Leys, and Sander Gilman. "Appropriating the Idioms of Science: The Rejection of Scientific Racism." In *The "Racial" Economy of Science: Toward a Democratic Future,* ed. Sandra Harding. Bloomington: Indiana University Press, 1993.

Sterling, Dorothy. *We Are Your Sisters: Black Women in the Nineteenth Century.* New York: Norton Paperback, 1971.

Sugrue, Thomas J. *Sweet Land of Liberty: The Forgotten Struggle for Civil Rights in the North.* New York: Random House, 2008.

Sutherland, John F. "Housing the Poor in the City of Homes." In *The Peoples of Philadelphia: A History of Ethnic Groups and Lower-Class Life, 1790–1950,* ed. Allen F. Davis and Mark H. Haller. Philadelphia: University of Pennsylvania Press, 1998.

Teeters, Negley K. "Institutional Treatment of Juvenile Delinquents." *Nebraska Law Review* 29, no. 4 (May 1950): 577–605.

Terborg-Penn, Rosalyn. *African American Women in the Struggle for the Vote, 1850–1920.* Bloomington: Indiana University Press, 1998.

Theoharis, Jeanne. *The Rebellious Life of Mrs. Rosa Parks.* Boston: Beacon, 2013.

Thompson, Debra. "Racial Ideas and Gendered Intimacies: The Regulation of Interracial Relationships in North America," *Social and Legal Studies* 18, no. 3 (September 2009): 353–71.

Trouillot, Michel-Rolph. *Silencing the Past: Power and the Production of History.* Boston: Beacon, 1995.

Tye, Larry. *Rising from the Rails: Pullman Porters and the Making of the Black Middle Class.* New York: Owl Books, Henry Holt, 2005.

Wald, Gayle. *Crossing the Line: Racial Passing in Twentieth-Century U.S. Literature and Culture.* Durham: Duke University Press, 2000.

Ward, Geoff K. *The Black-Child Savers: Racial Democracy and Juvenile Justice.* Urbana: University of Illinois Press, 2012.

Washington, Harriet A. *Medical Apartheid: The Dark History of Medical Experimentation on Black Americans from Colonial Times to the Present.* New York: Doubleday, 2006.

Washington, Margaret. *Sojourner Truth's America.* Urbana: University of Illinois Press, 2011.

Wells, Ida B. *Crusade for Justice: The Autobiography of Ida B. Wells.* Edited by Alfreda M. Duster. Chicago: University of Chicago Press, 1991.

West, Cornel. *Race Matters.* New York: Beacon, 1993.

White, Deborah Gray. *Ar'n't I a Woman?: Female Slaves in the Plantation South.* New York: W. W. Norton, 1999.

White, E. Frances. *Dark Continent of Our Bodies: Black Feminism and the Politics of Respectability.* Philadelphia: Temple University Press, 2001.

Wilderson III, Frank B. "The Prison Slave as Hegemony's (Silent) Scandal." *Social Justice* 30, no. 2 (2003): 18–27.

Wilf, Steven. *Law's Imagined Republic: Popular Politics and Criminal Justice in Revolutionary America.* Cambridge: Cambridge University Press, 2010.

Wilkie, Laurie. *The Archaeology of Mothering: An African-American Midwife's Tale.* New York: Routledge, 2003.

Williams, Kidada E. *They Left Great Marks on Me: African American Testimonies of Racial Violence from Emancipation to World War I.* New York: New York University Press, 2012.

Williamson, Joel. *New People: Miscegenation and Mulattoes in the United States.* Baton Rouge: Louisiana State University Press, 1995.

Wilson, Francille Rusan. *Segregated Scholars: Black Social Scientists and the Creation of Black Labor Studies, 1890–1950.* Charlottesville: University of Virginia Press, 2006.

Wolcott, Victoria. *Remaking Respectability: African American Women in Interwar Detroit.* Chapel Hill: University of North Carolina Press, 2000.

INDEX

Figures and notes are indicated by f and n following the page number.
HMT indicates Hannah Mary Tabbs.

INDEX

CPSIA information can be obtained
at www.ICGtesting.com
Printed in the USA
BVHW042356070722
641000BV00007B/5